FORT SNELLING.

TAH́-KOO WAH-KAŃ;

OR,

THE GOSPEL AMONG THE DAKOTAS.

BY

STEPHEN R. RIGGS, A. M.

MISSIONARY OF THE A. B. C. F. M., AND AUTHOR OF THE DAKOTA GRAMMAR AND DICTIONARY.

With an Introduction,

BY

S. B. TREAT,

SECRETARY OF THE A. B. C. F. M.

Written for the Congregational Sabbath-School and Publishing Society, and approved by the Committee of Publication.

BOSTON:

CONG. SABBATH-SCHOOL AND PUBLISHING SOCIETY.

DEPOSITORY, 13 CORNHILL.

TO ALL

WHO LOVE THE LORD JESUS,

AND WITH FAITH AND PATIENCE PRAY, AND WAIT, AND WORK

FOR THE COMING OF HIS KINGDOM,

THIS BOOK

IS AFFECTIONATELY INSCRIBED,

BY THE AUTHOR.

THE PREFACE.

TÁH-KOO WAH-KÁN is the marvellous, the mysterious, the incomprehensible, of the Dakótas. It covers the whole of the spirit-world and the god-manifestation to men. Hence it very properly represents, not only the heathen superstitions of the Da-kó-ta people, but also the marvellous workings of the Spirit, in leading them into the Christian faith.

This book is the child of necessity. For several years past, friends of the mission have been asking for some account of the strange work of the Lord among the Dakotas. In 1867, the Synod of Minnesota, by a resolution, requested the missionaries to prepare and publish a history of this work. At the next meeting of the Synod, a portion of the manuscript and a synopsis of the whole were submitted for examination. The committee, to which these papers were referred, said in their report: "After a careful examination of the manuscript of a work entitled, 'The Gospel among the Dakotas,' we hereby cordially recommend it to the Synod as a work full of interesting and instructive narrative, facts, and incidents, and as eminently fitted to illustrate the power of the gospel among the Indians."

It was hoped, at first, that this narrative would bear the more popular impress of a younger mind; but circumstances determined otherwise, and the work drifted into the hands of the author.

The first six chapters are mainly taken up with giving some account of Dakota Life and Religion, without the gospel. Chapters five and six, on the "Dakota Takoo Wakan" and "Dakota Worship," are a carefully-prepared statement of their polytheistic notions and their forms of worship, by Rev. A. L. Riggs.

The history of the mission work is arranged topically, grouping related facts and incidents. Although this plan has its disadvantages, it is resorted to, in this instance, in order to give more life to the narrative.

The ten chapters, from the seventh to the sixteenth inclusive, present, in the form above indicated, the mission work from its commencement in

1835, down to the time of the Indian outbreak in 1862. While the nine chapters that follow give some account, from a mission stand-point, of that uprising and its results, — the most important of which is the wonderful spread of the gospel among the Dakotas, — and closing with facts and arguments bearing on the civilization, education, and evangelization of this people.

In the Appendix will be found an interesting chapter on "Dakota Medicine," by Rev. T. S. Williamson, M. D.; one by Rev. A. L. Riggs on "Dakota Songs and Music;" and also brief notices of the work of other missionary societies in the Dakota field.

To those already mentioned, who have contributed to the interest and value of this work; to Rev. S. W. Pond and Rev. G. H. Pond, for materials furnished; and, indeed, to all the present and former members of the Dakota mission, — the author gives thanks; in the language of the Dakotas, he says, "*Pidamayayapi.*" He is grateful, moreover, for the interest which the Senior Secretary of the American Board, Rev. S. B. Treat, has taken in this undertaking, and for the various suggestions which he has kindly made.

The work of foreign missions is the author's first love, never lost; and now, when gray hairs are coming thickly upon him, he looks back upon it as having furnished him the privilege of walking upon the high places of the earth.

That this book may find a home at many Christian firesides, and be a plea for the civilization, education, and evangelization of the Indians and other heathen nations, is the desire of the

AUTHOR.

BELOIT, WIS., Mar. 4, 1869.

CONTENTS.

CHAPTER I.

THE LAND AND THE PEOPLE.

CHAPTER II.

THE DAKOTA LANGUAGE.

CHAPTER III.

DAKOTA EVERY-DAY LIFE.

APPENDIX.

DAKOTA MEDICINE.

DAKOTA SONGS AND MUSIC.

LABORS OF OTHER MISSIONARY SOCIETIES.

INTRODUCTION.

A SIGNIFICANT feature of the recent Exposition at Paris was the Mission House, in which different Protestant societies submitted the proofs of their success in heathen lands. The American Board sent thither specimens of the Christian literature which it had developed in twenty-five different languages, as also sundry articles illustrating the great change which had been wrought at the Sandwich Islands. The Queen of Holland was pleased to honor this collection with her notice; and it occurred to her to say to the gentleman having it in charge, "What have you done for the Indians?" He replied by pointing to a map which exhibited the stations which the Board had commenced among the various tribes, and by saying, "Madam, here are the missions of one of the several American societies, a glance at which may convince you that, if the Government of the United States has at times been guilty in its conduct toward the Indians, the Christian church has at least endeavored to do her duty." The Queen appeared to be satisfied with the answer.

Long before the Paris Exposition, it was objected to American missionary societies, that they were strangely neglectful of our own aboriginal population; and the same charge is still preferred against them. But it has been reserved for the Indian Peace Commissioners to give the indictment an official sanction. In their Report of January 7, 1868, published to the world as Executive Document No. 97, they make the following extraordinary statement: "While our missionary societies and benevolent associations have annually collected thousands of dollars from the charitable, to be sent to Asia and Africa for the purposes of civilization, scarcely a dollar is expended, or a thought bestowed, on the civilization of Indians at our very doors." The distinguished names appended to this paper preclude the idea of intentional error. It is much to be regretted, however, that men who have described with such fidelity the wrongs inflicted upon the red man, have seen fit to reflect with such severity upon our American Christianity. But the answer to this unexpected allegation is easy.

1. *It is not true.* The American Board began its efforts for the amelioration of the Indian race more than fifty years ago; and, though it has encountered obstacles which were wholly unexpected, it has never ceased from its labors. It was in January, 1817, that Rev. Cyrus Kingsbury repaired to Chickamaugah, and laid the foundation of the Cherokee mission. In the following year, he proceeded to Eliot, and laid the foundation of the Choctaw mission. For more than forty years, through all the trials and sorrows of these large and interesting tribes, whether on this side of the Mississippi or in their present home, the Board was faithful to the trust which it had assumed in their behalf. Fourteen other missions, in regions that stretch almost from the Atlantic to the Pacific, it has directed and sustained; and the stations which it has occupied amount to ninety-one. It has sent forth to this self-denying service more than five hundred laborers, male and female, exclusive of the native brethren who, as preachers, catechists, and teachers, have been "fellow-workers unto the kingdom of God;" and it has expended, in aid of their efforts, at least $1,100,000!

Other missionary societies have toiled with zeal

and fidelity in the same "line of things." And it is due to the Presbyterian Board of Foreign Missions, that a special reference should be made to its patient and earnest endeavors, under the guidance of the venerable Walter Lowrie, who has so recently and so honorably finished his course.

If, however, these organizations were under the necessity of making a less favorable exhibit, they might offer an excuse which any commission, created by our national Government, would find it difficult to gainsay. For,

2. *The administration of our Indian Affairs has been a serious obstacle to Indian missions.* This very Report of the Peace Commissioners, if examined carefully, will prove it. With a frankness which deserves the highest commendation, they have published the history of our later troubles with the aborigines west of the Missouri. Beginning with the year 1851, they have traced the course of events down to 1868. The Downing massacre of May, 1864, and the Chivington massacre of November, 1864, they have honestly, though briefly, described, closing the account of the latter with a declaration which must stand as a lasting memorial of our national dishonor: "It is enough to say that

it scarcely has its parallel in the records of Indian barbarity."

But the melancholy record does not end here. "No one will be astonished," they say, "that a war ensued which cost the Government $30,000,000, and carried conflagration and death to the border settlements." "The result of the year's campaign satisfied all reasonable men, that war with Indians was useless and expensive. Fifteen or twenty Indians had been killed, at an expense of more than a million of dollars apiece; while hundreds of our soldiers had lost their lives, many of our border settlers had been butchered, and much property destroyed."

But the Commissioners have not confined their attention to recent occurrences. They have looked through our Indian annals, and they have laid bare some of the causes of the scanty success hitherto achieved in converting the red man into a white man.

Missionary societies have often lamented the injury inflicted upon their work by the transfer of the people under their care to new and distant homes. In reference to this topic, the Commissioners have expressed a decided opinion. "It is useless," they affirm, "to go over the history of Indian removals. If it had been done but once, the record would be less revolting; from the eastern to the middle States; from there to Illinois and Wisconsin; thence to Missouri and Iowa; thence to Kansas, Dakota, and the plains; whither now, we cannot tell. Surely, the policy was not designed to perpetuate barbarism, but such has been its effect." And the difficulty is aggravated by the fact that many are "beyond the region of agriculture, where the chase is a necessity." And it is added, in words that have received the fullest confirmation from the history of Indian missions: "So long as they have to subsist in this way, civilization is almost out of the question."

Another embarrassment which this work has encountered grows out of the bitter memories which the stronger race has implanted in the weaker. The following testimony of the Commissioners, in this regard, has a painful significance: "It is now rather late in the day to think of obliterating from the minds of the present generation the remembrance of wrong. Among civilized men, war usually springs from a sense of injustice. The best possible way, then, to avoid war, is to do no act of injustice." "But, it is said, our wars with them have been almost constant. Have we been uniformly unjust? We answer, unhesitatingly, 'Yes.'"

It has been argued and urged that our Indian affairs are unwisely managed at Washington; and the Commissioners appear to entertain the same opinion. While they admit that "the legislation of Congress has always been conceived in the best intentions," they feel constrained to add, that "it has been erroneous in fact, or perverted in execution." And they have ventured to make another averment, which is sufficiently comprehensive: "Nobody pays any attention to Indian matters." "When the progress of settlement reaches the Indian's home, the only question considered is, 'How best to get his lands.' When they are obtained, the Indian is lost sight of."

Those who are charged with the direction of Indian missions have often complained of the agents and employés connected with this department of our national administration. On this subject, likewise, the Commissioners have expressed themselves with characteristic boldness. "That there are many bad men connected with this service," they say, "cannot be denied. The records are abundant to show that agents have pocketed the funds appropriated by the Government, and driven the Indians to starvation. It cannot be doubted that Indian wars have originated from this cause. The Sioux [Dakota] war in Minnesota is supposed to have been produced in this way. For a long time these officers have been selected from partisan ranks, not so much on account of honesty and qualification, as for devotion to party interests, and their willingness to apply the money of the Indian to promote selfish schemes of local politicians."

Another complaint comes from the opposite quarter. It is sometimes objected to these societies, not that so little, but that so much is done for the red man. The field, it is said, is singularly sterile. Though the tillage is costly, the harvest is very meagre. But,

1. *Missionary organizations in the United States are under peculiar obligations to the Indians.* (1) They are dwelling in the midst of us; and they may become, in due time, — and with their own consent should become, — a part of ourselves, like our colored population. (2) They were the earliest proprietors of this western world; and when our fathers came hither, it was with the avowed pur-

pose of giving them the gospel. (3) They have received countless wrongs from the dominant race; and it would be a grievous reproach to our Christianity, if, after all which they have suffered, nothing had been done to lead them up to a Christian civilization.

2. *The success of Indian missions has been greater than most have supposed.* At the very beginning of the work of the American Board among the Cherokees, a church was formed at Chickamaugah. During the next ten years the number who professed their faith in the Saviour amounted to about two hundred. Hardly any other mission had received richer spiritual blessings. In other respects the progress of the people was highly gratifying. Then, however, a new and disastrous era began. An iron purpose, long cherished and deeply rooted, demanded their removal. And it was not the mere transfer of the Cherokees to their present territory that proved so harmful. A great wrong had been committed, the memory of which they were not slow to cherish. The sense of injustice had been intensified, moreover, by the loss of one fourth of their population. And, worst of all, animosities had been sown broadcast among them, the bitter fruit whereof

long remained. It is not strange, therefore, that the early prosperity of the mission never returned.

Still, its endeavors were not wholly in vain. With diminished strength it continued in the field till 1860, when the Board resolved to withdraw therefrom, assigning, as one reason for the step, the fact that the Cherokees had become a Christian people, and might properly claim the fostering care of our home missionary societies. The church members reported at that time by evangelical missionaries, connected with different denominations, were said to exceed one third of all the adults in the nation!

The ten years which promised the most for the Cherokees (1818–1828), promised the least for the Choctaws. A few only, during this period, sought to become the followers of Christ; and in other respects there was but little progress. In 1828, however, the missionaries reached a new era; and three years later they had reported about four hundred persons as already admitted to their churches. Then came the removal, less disastrous, indeed, than that of the Cherokees, but a grievous hindrance, nevertheless, to the missionary work; so that the whole number of communicants in 1840 was only two hundred and twenty-five. From that time onward, however, the blessing of God was largely vouchsafed; and when the Board discontinued its labors in 1859, there had been received into Christian fellowship two thousand seven hundred persons, who had given substantially the same evidence of piety, according to the testimony of the missionaries, as is furnished by church members elsewhere.

Nor was this all. The missionaries had found the Choctaws a savage people. Ignorance and superstition, polygamy and infanticide, wars and fightings, were a part, and only a part, of their sad heritage. On their native stock, moreover, they had engrafted some of the worst vices of civilization. They were emphatically a drunken people. When Mr. Kingsbury inquired, at an early day, "Is there not a sober man among you?" he was told in reply that there was one! In 1859, however, they had learned to value knowledge; and many of them were well educated. They had given up the chase; and agriculture was duly honored. They had a written constitution, with a "declaration of rights," which embodied nearly all the great principles of civil and religious freedom. They had struggled against the evils of intemperance with singular courage and persistency. Through the efforts of the missionaries, a law was passed in 1823, embracing the principles of what is known as "the Maine law," but which may be called with greater propriety "the Choctaw law." This enactment remained in force till the statutes of Mississippi were extended over the nation; then, of course, it became a dead letter. But when the Indians had reached their present home, their very first act of legislation was to restore their abrogated temperance law; and it is in full vigor to-day.

This volume of Mr. Riggs illustrates the foregoing topics. It attests, especially, the fidelity of the Board to the trust which it early assumed in behalf of the red man. In the autumn of 1849, fourteen years from the commencement of the Dakota mission, the obstacles to the progress of Christianity were so formidable that, had the Prudential Committee decided to withdraw from the field, as the Methodist and Swiss missionaries had already done, their justification would have seemed complete. In 1862, when all their hopes were dashed to the ground in a moment, they might have said, "Now, certainly, our obligations to these Indians are cancelled." It has been the policy of the Committee, however, never to commence a mission, except for strong reasons, and never to discontinue one, except for stronger reasons. They know very well that, in all endeavors to convert the heathen, times of discouragement and anxiety are to be looked for; and they suppose that such things are to be accepted, for the most part, as divinely appointed trials of the faith and patience of the saints.

On the other hand, it is presumed that every Christian who is conversant with the recent triumphs of the gospel among the Dakotas, will concede that the toil and money expended in securing these results have been wisely invested. And those who contend that civilization is the highest achievement of modern evangelism, cannot fail to rejoice that so much has been done, especially within the last six years, for the intellectual and social progress of these Indians.

For more than twenty-one years the writer of these introductory pages has had the official supervision of the Dakota mission. His correspondence with the brethren who compose it has been extensive; his personal interviews with them have been frequent; he may fairly claim, therefore, to have some knowledge of the men and their work. In

1854, he ascended the valley of the Minnesota from Fort Snelling to Lacquiparle; and many of the places referred to in the following chapters are remembered as if they were pictures seen but yesterday.

He takes great pleasure in saying that he regards this book of Mr. Riggs' as one of special and permanent value. The author was admirably qualified to prepare it, as well by his personal acquaintance with the Dakotas, as by his large participation in the missionary work; and he has performed his task with singular fidelity. With the materials accessible to him, he might have constructed a more popular work; indeed, with the materials which he has actually used, he might have made a more thrilling narrative. But he has chosen to be thoroughly honest. He has preferred to understate many things, so that he might be sure not to overstate them. He has sought to give a faithful and instructive account of a form of paganism that is soon to pass away, so that those who may desire in coming years to study the customs, religion, modes of thought, and manner of life, of this large tribe, may have the requisite facilities therefor. He has endeavored to convey a correct idea of the operations of the Board in a field which has proved to be unlike all others. Incidents that might have taken their place as gems in our sensational literature, he has set forth with the utmost simplicity. And that marvellous work of grace in 1862-3, which the God of missions was pleased to inaugurate so unexpectedly and so strangely, and which may almost claim a separate chapter in the annals of the church, he has described as if he were unconscious (though he was by no means unconscious) of the value and significance of his own record.

But the reader should receive a formal introduction to the author. A lineal descendant of Miles Riggs (who came to Plymouth soon after the landing of the Pilgrims), he was born at Steubenville, Ohio, March 23, 1812, and finished his academical studies at Jefferson College in 1834. Having married Mary Ann C. Longley, of Hawley, Massachusetts, a daughter of Gen. Thomas Longley, as also a pupil of Miss Lyon at Buckland and Miss Grant at Ipswich,* he received ordination from

---

* Mrs. Riggs has closed her earthly labors since the Introduction was written. She died at Beloit, Wisconsin, bearing witness to the love and faithfulness of her Saviour, and frequently saying, "He strengthens me."

the presbytery of Chillicothe soon afterwards, and joined the Dakota mission a few weeks later. He resided first at Lacquiparle, then at Traverse des Sioux, then at Lacquiparle a second time, and finally at Hazelwood, whence he was obliged to flee with his family at the epoch of the great Indian outbreak. Since that time he has ceased to dwell among the Dakotas, but he has not ceased to labor in their behalf.

Of the eight children of Mr. Riggs, the oldest is a minister in Wisconsin; and the second, Mrs. Isabella B. Williams, resides at Kalgan, enjoying the confidence and affection of the North China mission.

Mr. Riggs has a familiar acquaintance with the Dakota tongue. As a preacher and as a translator, his services have been exceedingly valuable. As will be stated hereafter, he published a Grammar and Dictionary of the Dakota language in 1852, under the auspices of the Smithsonian Institution, which is regarded as an important contribution to Indian philology.

Other names of frequent occurrence in this volume should receive a passing notice. Dr. Williamson, in some sort the founder of the mission, deserves to be held in honor by all the friends of the American Board. One third of a century has elapsed since he began his self-denying labors. Many a dark hour has he seen; many a formidable hindrance to his efforts has he encountered; but his faith has never wavered, his courage has never failed. And now, in a good old age, he is permitted to see the reward of his patient continuance in well-doing.

It has been his privilege, moreover, to reckon among his fellow-laborers, one of his own sons, inspired with the same steady and serene hopefulness, but possessing yet greater facilities for usefulness; for it was the good fortune of the latter to acquire the language of the Dakotas in childhood, and to grow up as one of themselves. The tribute paid to this young brother in Chapter XXI. of this volume is well bestowed; and he is entitled to the esteem and confidence of all the friends of missions.

The Messrs. Pond, though they have exchanged the foreign service for the home service, for reasons which are entirely satisfactory to the Prudential Committee, are entitled to a special mention. Before the mission of the Board was commenced, they established one of their own, — two young laymen from Connecticut, — without the patronage of any benevolent organization, but fully persuaded that the Lord had a work for them to do among the aborigines of this country. That humble cabin on the banks of Lake Calhoun, erected "in advance of all others," was a noble testimony to their faith, their zeal, their courage. And the youngest of these brothers is now represented on the Missouri by his oldest son, the wife of the latter having been herself a child of the mission.

TAH′-KOO WAH-KAN′.

CHAPTER I.

THE LAND AND THE PEOPLE.

The name of these Indians. — Supposed origin of the name *Sioux*. — DAKOTA their real name. — Divided into many bands. — The Dakota country. — Probable number of the tribe.

" Thou art worthy; for thou wast slain, and hast redeemed us to God by thy blood, out of every kindred, and tongue, and people, and nation."

AMONG the Aborigines of the North-West, none are more numerous, more powerful, or more warlike than the *Dakotas*. In former times they were known to white people as the Sioux, — a name which has a French rather than an Indian look. Rev. E. D. Neill, in his History of Minnesota, states, on the authority of French *voyageurs*, that by the Algonquins they were called *Nad-ouessioux*, which signifies *enemies;* and that the name Sioux was taken from the last part of this word. The language of Charlevoix is: "The name of Sioux, that we give to these Indians, is entirely of our own making, or rather it is the last two syllables of the name Nadouessioux, as many nations call them."

The Ojibwas are said to call the Iroquois Indians *Nadowe*, which signifies a *large serpent.* It is further stated, that the name given by the Ottawas to the Dakotas is *Nadowesé*, which name is also sometimes used by the Ojibwas, though they commonly call them *Bwan.* This latter name appears in *Assinaboine.* It does not appear that either has properly the signification of enemy, except so far as a serpent may be thus regarded.

The name by which they designate themselves is *Dakota*, which signifies *alliance* or *friendship.* This word is now used to denote a family of peoples or languages, which includes, of course, the Dakotas proper, or Sioux, and the Assinaboines, a branch of the same people; and also the Mandans, Rickarees, Poncas, Omahas, Winnebagoes, and others. The Dakota tribe proper is composed of many bands; as *the Leaf-Shooters, the Spirit-Lake Villages, the Leaf Villages, the Swamp Villages, the Cut-Heads, the End Villages, and the Prairie Villages;* which last are further divided into *the Hoonkpatees, the Burnt-Legs, the Two Boilings, the No-Bows, the Planters by the Water, the Black-Feet, the Hoonkpapas,* and *the Ogallallas;* but all are Dakotas. These various bands intermarry, and, to a considerable extent, have common traditions and customs. The Indians belonging to the first three bands above named are now commonly called the *Isanyatee*, shortened into *Santees;* which name refers them back to the time when they made their villages on the *Isantamde* or *Knife Lake*, called by the French "Mille Lac."

When the mission was commenced among them, and for many years afterwards, their country extended from the Mississippi River westward to the Black Hills. On the north-east, the line between them and the Ojibwas was often fought over. They then lived on the Mississippi, where Winona and Red Wing have since grown up, and near Saint Paul, and all along up the Saint Peter or Minnesota River. At that time, there was no white settlement above Cassville on the Mississippi;* now, one will find white villages as far up the Minnesota as Lacquiparle, and northward to the sources of the Father of Waters.

* Except military posts and fur-trading establishments. Prairie du Chien had long been occupied in both these ways many years before Dubuque and Galena were known, and had, at the time spoken of here, quite a community of French *voyageurs*.

The eastern part of this land of the Dakotas is too well known to need any description here. It is the State of Minnesota, in the western part of which the prairie land begins greatly to predominate, and wood becomes so scarce as to make its settlement a slow process. But all through to the western border of the State, and even beyond, the land is fertile, and the climate sufficiently moist to insure good returns from tillage. This cannot be said of the country from the James, or Dakota River Valley westward, and the Upper Missouri generally. More than half the summers prove too dry for corn. Consequently the Indians, in that vast extent of prairie country, were then, as now, only "mighty hunters" of buffalo.

If any one asks for the number of the Dakotas, the answer must be, "They have not yet been counted." They were estimated by government agents, a third of a century ago, at thirty thousand. In one of his first letters to the Committee at Boston, Dr. Williamson put them down at twenty-five thousand. And, five years after, when Messrs. Riggs and Huggins made a route of exploration to the Missouri country, after careful inquiry, they agreed with the latter estimate. But, very recently, the Peace Commission have set down the Dakotas occupying the country of the Missouri and its branches westward at twenty-three thousand. And there are, on the Coteau des Prairies and in the region of Devil's Lake, uncounted by them, five or six thousand more. This might lead to the conclusion that the Dakotas have increased during the quarter of a century past. That is not probable. Nor is it probable that they have, as a tribe, greatly diminished.

CHAPTER II.

THE DAKOTA LANGUAGE.

Different bands of the Dakotas speak substantially the same language. — Not heretofore written. — Story of Hennepin. — Reduced to a written form by the missionaries. — Dakota grammar and dictionary. — Language defective in some things. — Names of places and persons; how formed. — Language not unusually difficult of acquisition. — The Dakota tongue enriched and elevated by the Bible.

"*And there was given Him dominion, and glory, and a kingdom, that all people, nations, and languages should serve Him.*"

Do these Dakotas, scattered over such a wide extent of country, speak the same language? If so, what is its character? Is it meagre, or sufficiently full to receive civilized and Christian ideas? Is it difficult or easy of acquisition? A brief answer to these questions will convey some idea of the people, among whom the gospel is to be preached, and of the difficulties of that work.

The Dakota language, as spoken by the

various bands, is the same; but yet there are considerable dialectic differences. The *n* of one dialect becomes *h*, or *k*, or *g*, in others. In the Teeton or "Prairie Village" dialect, *l* is extensively used, which sound is not heard among the eastern branches of the nation. But, with all these differences, it is the general opinion that the same books can be used by all, though perhaps not with equal facility.

When Dr. Williamson and his associates went among the Dakotas, their language was an unwritten one. Travellers among them, like Hennepin, had gathered a few words. When in a Dakota camp, he started and *ran* off a little distance, running back also, and then asked them what that was. By this means he obtained the Dakota verb *in-yan-ka*, to run. Officers of the army, stationed at Fort Snelling, had made English Dakota vocabularies, embracing several hundred words, chiefly the names of things. But there were sounds in the language which these men did not hear, and others which they had no means of representing.

The missionaries had to agree on a system of notation, which would represent all the sounds in the language, or, in other words, become the alphabet. Then, years of labor were required to gather the words and find out their significations; by and by, the principles of the language were slowly evolved. Thus grew up a dictionary and grammar. Sixteen years after the commencement of the mission, a grammar and dictionary were prepared by the writer, the latter containing fifteen thousand words, and published by the Smithsonian Institution, under the patronage of the Historical Society of Minnesota. This work will afford a better idea of the Dakota language than it is proper to give here.

Is it a meagre language? The statement made above will in part answer this question. It is full and rich in some respects, and yet, of course, defective and poor in others. The Dakota verb is quite complex, and capable of expressing shades of meaning and forms of action in much greater variety than the English verb. Two years after Dr. Williamson went to Lacquiparle, he wrote, respecting the language, as follows: "It may be as complete, so far as their present mode of life requires language, as that of any other people; but it has been well observed, that our knowledge of words cannot be more extensive than our knowledge of things. The Dakotas are ignorant of all that pertains to civilized life. Of a king, government, and whatsoever relates to courts of justice, they have no knowledge, and, of course, no words to express such things. They have no nouns corresponding to our words *time*, *space*, *color*, and very few expressive of what we term abstract ideas. They had no names originally for domestic animals, except the dog. A horse is a *great dog*, or *sacred dog*, and a cat is a *dog wildcat.*"

Their names of places are generally descriptive, either geographically or historically. Some physical feature may determine the name of a place, or it may originate in some historical circumstance. Like all primitive peoples, they have no family names; and their proper names, or names given to persons, all have meanings. Sometimes they are only the names of things, as *corn*, *goose*, *house*, *iron*, *elk*. More commonly, they are formed of two nouns, or a noun and adjective, as *Iron-Elk*, *Good-Road*, *Good-House*, *Beautiful-Bird*, *Blue-Eyes*, *Her Scarlet-House*, *Long-Buffalo*, *Sleepy-Eyes*, *Burnished-Metal*, *Iron-Cutter*, etc. Sometimes they consist of a noun and verb or participle, as *Standing-Soldier*, *Walking-Spirit*. Indeed, almost any combination of the language may be used as a proper name. Not unfrequently the name is given to a person because of some peculiarity, defect, or otherwise; as, *Burnt-Legs*, *Big-Eyes*, *Crooked-Feet*, *Bit-Nose*.

Is the language difficult to learn? Who knows? Probably it is, and probably it is not. The clicks and gutturals, which rather abound in the language, were quite difficult, for persons whose vocal organs were already hardened, to make readily. Then the pronouns and prepositions, which almost always push themselves right into the middle of a verb, make it hard for a foreigner to learn to speak grammatically. Dr. Williamson had been working at it two years when he wrote: "I think I am warranted in saying that the Sioux language is uncommonly difficult to learn, not only from the small progress my asssociates and myself have made in learning it, but from the fact that I have met with no person, nor even heard of one, not born of a Dakota mother, who had well learned it: men, who, for the purposes of trade, have lived in the country twenty or thirty years, with Dakota wives, and having little intercourse with any other people, speak Sioux badly." This would represent the language as very difficult of acquisition. But this view is hardly borne out by the after experience of the missionaries, who learned to speak and preach in it quite well.

The language of every heathen people, as ignorant and degraded as the Dakotas were, will present on the surface much that is impure and even vile. The Dakota language was not an exception. But as men become purified and elevated in heart and life, the impurity disappears from their conversation. Thus are the barbarous languages of the world brought up into the Christian household.

CHAPTER III.

DAKOTA EVERY-DAY LIFE.

The teepee or wigwam. — How pitched and furnished. — Wigwam-cooking. — Digging teepsinna. — Division of labor. — Summer houses. — Smoking the pipe. — Trip of Mr. G. H. Pond. — Camp living. — Nothing to eat. — Crossing streams. — How they cook turtles. — How they wipe dishes. — A goose for supper. — Camp on a lake shore. — Sabbath moving. — Mr. Pond stays behind. — Has a musk-rat for breakfast. — Cold weather. — The ducks disappear. — Eating dead fish. — The camp separates. — Three families remain. — The Ojibwas come. — They are feasted by the Dakotas. — The three families killed. — Burying the slaughtered ones. — All start for Lacquiparle. — Two weary weeks. — The great wailing. — Begging in the name of the first-born. — A hard life. — The Indian mother's lament.

"*Rude in speech, or grim in feature,*
Dark in spirit tho' they be;
Show that light to every creature,
Prince or vassal, bond or free."

LIKE the Arabs of the desert, the Dakotas usually live in tents, or *teepees*. These are of a conical form, like the Sibley army-tent, the Dakota teepee being the original pattern. In the late spring and summer, when the skins of the buffalo are worthless for robes, the Dakota women dress them for moccasins or tents. From seven to fifteen buffalo skins, thus dressed, are sewed together for one tent, according to the size of the household, or the ambition of the owners. Instead of being supported by a tripod, as the Sibley tent is, a Dakota teepee is made by setting up any number of poles, from six to a dozen, fastening them together at the top, and spreading out the bottoms, so as to suit in size the covering, which is then drawn around them and fastened with a row of pins in front, leaving a hole at the bottom for entrance, and one at the top for the smoke to pass out. The lower edge of the covering is then fastened down by pins driven into the ground; while the flap, which regulates the smoke-hole, is arranged so as to be accommodated to the wind.

This finished, the industrious Dakota wife gathers a bundle of dried grass, which she spreads on the ground in the inside, and on this she places her skin mats and robes. These form the carpet by day, and the bed by night. In the centre, a space is left for the fire; and the woman takes her axe and cuts and carries home a bundle of dry wood. She is then ready for the return of her husband with his ducks or other game, if he has been so fortunate as to find any. If the man has no powder, or has been unsuccessful in finding game, perhaps he brings in some eggs, or turtles, or fish; or, possibly, there has been a buffalo hunt, and fresh meat is abundant. Or, if that is not so, it may be the time when *teepsinna* are abundant. This is a root with a hard rind, and a sweet, farinaceous bulb within, which grows in the high and dry prairie. The women and children are the *teepsinna* diggers. When the root is tolerably abundant, a woman goes out in the morning, and returns about two o'clock with half a bushel, which makes a peck when hulled.

The kettle is swung over the fire, and whatever there is on hand, or whatever has been obtained by the day's labor, for the day's food, is boiled, and served out in the common wooden dishes, to be eaten with knives or horn spoons. If it is the time for taking furs, the skin of the animal is taken off and stretched for drying, and the flesh is put into the kettle.

The man, perhaps, has gone out in the early morn, without any breakfast, and now it is afternoon. It is only right that the woman should have hominy or boiled corn ready for him on his return. And as she neither goes to war, nor kills ducks, deer, buffaloes, — in fact, because she is only a woman, — it is highly proper, on the principle of a division of labor, that she should plant and hoe the corn. The corn, then, by the common custom, which is common law, is regarded as belonging to the woman; and so are the tent and many other things.

We have spoken of the skin teepee. When the buffalo become scarce, skin tents are difficult to be obtained; and then cotton cloth is procured from the trader, and substituted for the more substantial dressed skins. Then, too, there is the summer-house, which is made at or near the planting place, and constructed of poles tied together and covered with bark. These bark houses are permanent fixtures. They are more roomy, cool, and pleasant for the summer than the common teepee. Usually, they are square or oblong; though, in some portions of the tribe, the circular form is fashionable. In the latter case, the sides of the house are made of split sticks set on end, and the covering is of earth, thrown on poles laid close together. The square or oblong ones are finished within, with a raised platform about two feet high, running along the two sides, and across the farther end. This platform is covered with bark, and on it are spread the mats and robes on which they sit, and lie down, and sleep. The fire is made on the ground, in the centre, and a hole is left on the ridge for the smoke to pass out. But, with the best arrangement and the greatest care, a Dakota summer or winter house is often a very smoky place.

And, as if the smoke of the fire was not enough, there is added the smoke of the pipe. The Dakotas are great smokers. The Red Pipe Stone Quarry, which, according to tradition, is the assembling place of the nations, is in the land of the Dakotas. The tobacco is furnished by the trader; and the Indian finds the *Kinnekenick** growing along the streams. When the Dakotas are without pipe and tobacco, they are not usually

* Kinnekenick is the inner bark of the dogwood, and also of a species of willow, which is scraped off and dried, and then mixed with tobacco to moderate and flavor the smoke.

in a good humor. A boy learns to smoke when quite young, but a girl is not expected to indulge in that way until she becomes a woman. And occasionally you will find a woman who does not smoke.

Smoking takes up much of their time when they are awake. A man, when alone, lights his pipe and smokes frequently. But, when two or three are together, the pipe is kept going around, and seldom or never gets cold. If one Indian meets another on the prairie, they sit down and smoke before they talk. At their feasts, before and after eating, they smoke, but especially before; indeed, the pipe, on many of these occasions, is held up reverently to the god they wish to propitiate, and the prayer is offered, "Have mercy on me." When the camp moves, the women take down the tents, roll them up and pack them on the horses, or on their own backs, and start off, while the men sit down and take a last smoke around the camp fires. Thus smoking and eating make up very much of Dakota life.

In the early years of the mission, Mr. Gideon H. Pond used to wish that he could be an Indian for a little while, that he might know how a Dakota felt and reasoned. It was, perhaps, to realize this wish that he made a trial of camp life, the record of which will well illustrate the subject of this chapter.

He started from Lacquiparle April, 1, 1838, with a blanket on his shoulder, in company with a few Indian families, to spend a few weeks in the camp. The party ascended the Chippewa River towards the forks of the stream, to join others who were hunting in that part of the country. At night, they lay down "empty," as Indians say when they have killed no game during the day, and slumbered on the bank of the river, under the broad blue sky. Mr. Pond, however, had brought a little food, which he shared with the company, as generosity is a necessary virtue in an Indian camp.

The next morning, they reached a streamlet, which ordinarily might be stepped across; but now, swollen by late rains and melting snow, it was a formidable river. The Indians smoked, and contrived, and hesitated, and smoked again, each waiting for the others to lead the way. The water was cold, and came up to the shoulders of a man; and it was not a little amusing to see the younger wife of one of the men cling, with her copper-colored arms, around his savage neck, as he tugged her across, both nearly buried in the water. She was too short to carry herself over. The baggage, carried on the head, and supported by the hands, being all taken over dry, and the water wrung from the clothes, the party resumed their march along the narrow trail.

At the Forks, the Chippewa was full to overflowing; and the afternoon was consumed in crossing over in a little canoe which belonged to Round Wind, whose teepee stood on the farther bank. Round Wind's teepee was circular, about twelve feet in diameter, with a fire in the centre, and contained all the baggage of the family. That night, fifteen persons, besides unnumbered dogs, lodged in it.

At this place, Eagle Help made a little canoe for musk-rat hunting, which detained the party two days. In the evening of the first day, Little Crow, then a young man, and his wife, whom he had recently taken, brought in about half a bushel of little turtles, which they had found sunning themselves along the shores of the river and lakes. Another brought in an otter, and another a crane and two or three ducks. These were to make supper and breakfast for all the party.

It was somewhat painful, to one not accustomed to the operation, to see the turtles cooked alive. They were placed in a large kettle of water and hung over the fire. At first, they seemed to be quite well contented, but as the heated water approached the boiling point, they became restless; and it was sport to the Indians, great and small, to beat them back as they tried to escape over the sides of the kettle. The life was finally boiled out of the poor animals, and they were served up in wooden dishes, with the water in which they had been scalded to death for broth.

Round Wind's wife, who was mistress of the teepee, and exceedingly respectful to her missionary guest, took particular care to wipe out his dish, first with a dry wisp of grass taken from under the mat on which she sat and slept, and afterwards with the corner of her short-gown, which she had worn night and day since autumn; and having thus cleaned the dish, she put into it a turtle and some broth, and set it before him. The pity already excited, and other circumstances, took off the edge of his appetite, however keen it might otherwise have been.

When the canoe was finished, Eagle Help and wife and Mr. Pond started up the left branch of the Chippewa to a place fifteen miles distant, where six familes of Indians were encamped. This was Friday. The three persons above mentioned slept that night on a little hill covered with oaks. They had a goose for supper, the entrails of which, according to Dakota custom, were roasted on the coals, and eaten, while the goose was being boiled. Saturday morning, having breakfasted on what remained from their supper, they continued their march, and reached the camp early. This was the end of *a weary week.*

The teepees stood on the shore of a lake bordered with trees; and the country around was well wooded, and abounded with lakes. Sabbath morning, Iron Heart was sent to the Forks of the Chippewa to borrow Round Wind's horse, to haul a canoe from the lake to the river. As food was scarce, the Indians removed their camp, leaving Mr. Pond behind to rest on the Sabbath and rejoin them the next day. He had a musk-rat for his breakfast. The lakes froze over, and the ducks disappeared; so that from Monday until Thursday, in the teepee of Cloud Man, whose guest Mr. Pond was, they had nothing to eat, except one duck, a few ground nuts, and some dead fish, which the women gathered on the lake shore, and the Indians said were "good!"

Thursday, three of the teepees removed to the river, and Iron Heart came with the horse, accompanied by Round Wind. But what was most to be rejoiced over was, that Red Fisher's son killed a goose. All the men, seven in number, made their supper from that one goose; and it was the best meal Mr. Pond had had since the musk-rat on the Sabbath. Friday morning, there was nothing to eat, and all the Indians started off early on the hunt, except Round Wind, who went back to the lake for a canoe. But he soon returned without it, bringing the sad news that the Ojibwas had, in the night, killed all the inmates of the three teepees which remained behind on Thursday.

Mr. Pond went immediately with Round Wind to the place, where lay scattered the mangled bodies of those who, the day before, had been of his company. They dug a hole in the earth, in which, with feelings

Little Crow.—"Gospel," etc., p. 29.

which can only be imagined, they packed the bodies, limbs, and severed heads of the dead, eleven in number, and hastily covered them with their buffalo-skin teepees. Only two of those who were living there the evening before escaped. It appears that Hole in-the-Day, an Ojibwa chief, with a small party, had visited these tents in the evening, pretending peace. The Dakotas had killed a dog and feasted them. They all lay down to sleep, but the Ojibwas rose up to slay.

When Mr. Pond and Round Wind returned to their camp, at noon, they found the tents all struck, and everything in readiness to start home. A boiled goose-egg had been kindly kept for Mr. Pond. When he had eaten that, Round Wind told him to mount his horse, and he would take him to the Forks of the Chippewa. Safely across the river, he could go in haste, on foot, to the mission station. This, Mr. Pond was now very willing to do. That night he forded the stream over which the Indian carried his wife the week before, and lay down without fire or supper. Dreaming, under such circumstances, was quite out of the question. Saturday at noon he breakfasted at home, after two weary weeks of missionary labor, enriched with a variety of experience of Indian savage life in the wigwam.

One of those who escaped in the above massacre, was a mother. While fleeing, her babe was shot in her arms, and she was slightly wounded. She hastened behind a tree and thus eluded the enemies, from there watching them in their fiendish work. After they departed, she returned to the teepees and watched until the morning. Then, after the Indian manner, fastening two poles to a horse, she placed on them a wounded boy and her own scalped little ones, and started in search of the party that had left them the day before.

These two weeks, spent by Mr. Pond in the Indian teepee, are in some respects an extreme specimen of Dakota camp life. Not always is there so much hunger. Not always is there such danger and death. And yet both are of frequent occurrence.

When the news of this cowardly and treacherous act of the Ojibwas reached Lacquiparle, there was great wailing. Almost every family in the village was, in some way, connected with those who had been slain. Early on one of the mornings after this, there came an old woman to the mission station, with dishevelled hair and haggard looks, wearing a ragged skirt and leggins, and with an old piece of buffalo-skin thrown over her shoulders. She walked around the house wailing, Me-ta′-ko-zha!

Me-ta'-ko-zha! *My grandchild! my grandchild!* And in her estate of sorrow and want, she took occasion to beg *in the name of our first-born.* This was the first time some of us had heard that form of appeal. And coming as it did, under those circumstances, it seemed to be a custom of wonderful power. It was so like asking God for the sake of His Dear Only Begotten. Often afterwards did we hear the same form of request, and it never lost its force.

These are some of the scenes in Dakota life. In such circumstances children are born, and grow up or die. Poorly clad, and often poorly fed, they are usually uncomplaining, and as gleeful as children born and cradled in the lap of plenty. But it cannot be denied that it is a hard life, even for them. And many, unable to endure the excessive hardships necessitated thereby, sink into an early grave. The conjurer, or powwow, is called in to try the power of his song and rattle. But death is already taking possession, and cannot be driven away by such a power. The only thing the conjurer can do, by his song, is to teach the departing soul to walk along "the path of spirits."

A fitting close to this chapter will be the very lifelike "Indian Mother's Lament," written many years ago by Mrs. Riggs.

"Me-choonk-she! Me-choonk-she! *My daughter! my daughter!* Alas! alas! My hope, my comfort has departed, and my heart is very sad. My joy is turned into sorrow, and my song into wailing. Shall I never more behold thy sunny smile? Shall I never more hear the music of thy voice? The Great Spirit has entered my teepee in anger, and taken thee from me, my first-born, my only child! I am comfortless, and must wail out my grief. The pale-faces repress their sorrow, but we, children of nature, must give vent to ours, or die. Me-choonk-she! Me-choonk-she!

"The light of my eyes is extinguished; all, all is dark. I have cast from me all comfortable clothing, and robed myself in skins; for no clothing, no fire, can warm thee, my daughter. Unwashed and uncombed, I will mourn for thee, whose long locks I can never more braid; and whose cheeks I can never again tinge with vermillion. I will cut off my dishevelled hair, for my grief is great: Me-choook-she! Me-choonk-she!

"How can I survive thee? How can I be happy here, and thou a homeless wanderer to the spirit land? How can I eat, if thou art hungry? I will go to the grave with food for your spirit. Your bowl and spoon are placed in your coffin for use on the journey. The feast for your playmates has been made at the place of your burial. Knowest thou of their presence? Me-choonk-she! Me-choonk-she!

"When spring returns, the choicest ducks shall be your portion. Sugar and berries also shall be placed near your grave. Neither grass nor flowers shall be allowed to grow thereon. Affection for thee will keep the little mound desolate, like the heart from which thou art torn.

"My daughter, I come, I come! I bring thee parched corn. Oh! how long wilt thou sleep? The wintry winds wail thy requiem. The cold earth is thy bed, and the colder snow thy covering. I would they were mine. I will lie down by thy side. I will sleep once more with thee. If no one discovers me, I shall soon be as cold as thou art; and together we will sleep that long, long sleep, from which I cannot awake thee: Me-choonk-she! Me-choonk-she!"

CHAPTER IV.

DAKOTA AMUSEMENTS.

Amusements of children in the line of the life-work. — Girls dressing dolls. — Learning to dress skins and carry burdens. —Boys' plays. — The bow and arrow. — Killing the first bird. —Fishing. — Winter sports. — Rude sled. — Shooting-sticks. — Drumming. — Games of chance. — Shooting plum stones. — Hiding in the moccasin. — The ball play. — The tah′-pa and ball-club. — Betting. — Dances. — The sun dance. — The sacred dance. — The circle dance. — The begging dance. — The no-flight dance. — The scalp-dance. — Coming home from the war-path. — Their blankets taken from them. — The scalp; how prepared. — Men and women dance. — The immorality and wrong of the scalp-dance.

"*They send forth their little ones like a flock, and their children dance.*"

Plays and games, and various kinds of amusements, are common among the aborigines of this country, as among other nations. Upon a people low in civilization, time often hangs heavily; and there is, therefore, in them, a greater tendency to engage in various kinds of amusement.

Among the Dakotas, childhood and youth

are emphatically vanity. When food is scarce in a village, the wan and sad faces of children give little indication of glee and sunshine. But when the corn has grown, or the camp has been suddenly supplied with meat, the sadness of want is soon forgotten in the joyfulness of present abundance. Thus, the little girls, who, in the early summer, were engaged much of the time, from daylight until dark, in hunting and digging *teepsinna* on the prairies, have leisure, in the seeming abundance of a small harvest of corn and wild fruits, to gambol and frolic about, or to ornament with beads and paint the doll, which, the world over, is the great plaything of little girls.

It is perhaps fortunate that the amusements of childhood, among every people, should be found mainly on the line of the after-life work. So the great lessons of life are learned partly through life's pleasures.

The little girl, for instance, in choosing the form of her play, is directed by the mother's work. The mother dresses down a skin with her bone or iron tool, and rubs it until she has made it pliable for moccasins or other purposes; and the little girl must "play" dressing skins also. The mother ties up a great bundle of wood and carries it home to make a fire; or, when the camp is to be moved, she takes down the tent and rolls it up with dishes and spoons and mats, and, tying her strap around it, places the great burden on her back, and marches on to the next camping place. The little girl must also have her *packing-strap*, and, in her play, roll up her little bundle and carry it. Thus the girl is mother of the woman. Play is the ABC of life's work.

So also the Dakota boy finds his play running much in the line of a hunter's life. During the long summer days, he amuses himself very much with his bow and arrow. The grandfather, it may be, makes them for him, and teaches him how to place the arrow and to draw the bow. The little fellow takes his weapons and sallies forth to kill his first bird or squirrel. Many an arrow he shoots and gathers up, without any other result than that he is learning to use the hunter's instruments while he is playing. But by and by his first bird is shot, which he brings home with great joy. The father and all the household make it an occasion of rejoicing. A great feast is made, and the men of the village are called to eat; for *Chas-kay*, the eldest born, has killed his first bird! Some old man takes the bird and eats it up without cooking, — bones, flesh, feathers and all, — and the glad father makes the old man a present of a blanket. The boy too must be painted and dressed up in in new clothes; for has he not killed his first bird?

Fishing, too, is an amusement for the Dakota boys in the line of their life-work. Then comes along the learning to use a gun, and the killing of ducks and geese and larger game. In the meantime, they have learned to swim and paddle a canoe, and in each they found amusement.

Winter comes, and the land of the Dakotas is covered with snow. Then comes coasting on the hill-sides. No nicely painted and costly sled is needed by the Dakota boy. If he can get the stave of an old barrel, his wants are satisfied. To the one end of this he attaches a leather string. The bend in the stave is just right for running swiftly. Then, with the string in one hand, and standing upon the board, he guides it as he flies down to the bottom of the hill.

Another form of winter amusement is, playing with the *hoo-te'-na-choo'-tay*. These are sticks shaved out after various patterns, but always with the forward end larger, and either bent up or shaved, so that when projected with force, they glide over the snow or ice to quite a distance. Here perhaps the Dakotas first learn to gamble, the sticks themselves being won and lost by the respective players.

But there are long winter evenings and stormy days, when the smoky wigwam is more comfortable than the "out-doors." Then the flute, but especially the drum, is an unfailing source of amusement. Many long hours are worn away by "drum, drum, drum," and "toot, toot, toot," in the Dakota wigwam.

Games of chance and skill are played by the Dakotas, generation after generation. They are few and simple. The first to be mentioned is the *Kan-soo' koo-tay'-pe*, or *shooting plum-stones.* This game is so called because plum-stones are used in playing it. The stones, or pits, have first been prepared by painting and graving on them figures, which make them, in a sense, *wakan'*, and place them under the mysterious influence of the spirits. The stones are placed in a small wooden bowl or dish, and then thrown up, as one would toss coppers and cry "heads," or "tails." But to bring in the *wakan'* influence, the players *hist*, and *she-e-e*, and wave their hands while the stones are falling.

Very much akin to this, is the game of *Hamp-a'-pay-pe;* literally, *waiting on the moccasin.* Several moccasins are placed before the players, and one puts his hand under each, leaving under one of them, a plum-stone, or some little thing. The others guess which one it is under. And thus the game goes on, and the articles of property staked are won or lost by the skill of the players and the aid which they think they obtain from their gods. By these means, the propensity to gamble is greatly fostered, especially in the Dakota young men, though women also play these games. From playing these simple games, the Dakotas easily and naturally went into playing cards, when they came in contact with the card-playing class of white people.

But the great national game of the Dakotas is *The Ball Play.* The *tah′-pa* is a small, hard, covered ball, about the size used in our base-ball play. It is not thrown with the hand, nor kicked with the foot, but taken up and propelled by means of a ball-club, or *Ta-ke-cha-pse-cha.* This is a stick about thirty-two inches long, with a small hoop at the lower end, about four inches in diameter, which is interlaced so as to take up, hold, and carry the ball in readiness to be thrown. Each player has his ball-club, and comes on the ground stripped to his breech-cloth and moccasins, and his face and body daubed over with paint, according to his own fancy or the teachings of the gods. The company are divided into two parties, with their leaders; or the men of one village are pitted against the men of another village; or band against band. The boundaries are then fixed, towards and over which the two parties are to drive the ball. Then the game commences, after the stakes, or articles put up at hazard, have been arranged, by a public crier making the announcement. The ball being thrown up in the middle of the field, the contestants fight for it with their ball-clubs, as it comes down. When one succeeds in the scramble in getting the ball fairly in the pocket of his club, he waves it aloft and throws it towards the goal to which his party are now working; taking care, if possible, to send it where some one of his own people will take it up. Thus it is thrown, very much as a football is driven, until one side takes it over the bounds. The conflict of ball-clubs very legitimately makes bruised shins, and sometimes causes more serious injuries. The gambling at ball-playing often runs very high. Guns, blankets, coats, knives, hatchets, pipes, moccasins, and trinkets of all kinds are tied to the pole or stake. Not unfrequently horses are staked, and sometimes even women. On these occasions of ball-playing, the old men and women are among the spectators, praising their swift-footed and expert sons; while the young wives and maidens are there to stimulate their husbands and lovers

The Dances of the Dakotas are partly public amusements and partly religious ceremonies. The *Sun Dance* is an example of self-sacrifice. The *Sacred* or *Wakan Dance* is the public exhibition of a secret religious society. Both of these are described in the chapter on "Dakota Worship." Besides being manifestations of their religious life, these are great occasions of public amusement. They are gatherings of the people. But their religious character overshadows their secular.

Next to these, comes the *Circle Dance.* This attracts and engages the multitude, and, in that aspect, is a public amusement, but it is nevertheless the dance of the *War-Prophet.* A war-party is being made up to go on the war-path, but it is needful that the gods should be consulted and propitiated. A tall pole is erected; and in a circle around it, at the distance of twenty-five feet, perhaps, bushes are set in the ground, leaving four gates or places of entrance at the four cardinal points. Near the pole in the centre is a small booth made of tree boughs, into which crawls the war-prophet, who is the high-priest of the occasion. He is naked, except a twist of grass around his loins, and enters the booth with his drum, taking care to pray to the red stone that is placed near the entrance. By fasting and purification previously gone through with, he is prepared to receive a communication from the gods. Four times the dance goes round this war-prophet drumming and singing in his booth; the women dancing in a circle outside of the men: and then the god-image that hangs on the top of the pole is shot down, and the dance is concluded by the announcement of the god-communication.

The Begging Dance includes a variety of fashionable dances, all of which are made for the purpose of begging. It seems to be a dance confined to men alone. Dressed in their best clothes, and painted in the most fashionable styles, with all their eagle's feathers properly arranged in their heads, the men gather around and dance in a ring.

Their bodies are somewhat bent forward, and their knees bent correspondingly; and thus, with a motion up and down, keeping time to the drum and the deer-hoof rattle, they dance and sing their almost monotone song, concluding with a shout and a clapping of the mouth with the hand. Then some warrior steps out into the middle, and, with abundance of gesture, recites some war exploit. This is received with a shout, and the dance again commences. Presently, at one of these intervals, an old man, sitting outside, commences a speech in praise of the man or the people who are expected to make the presents. If the dance is made to a trader, he loses no time in sending out tobacco, or powder and lead, or provisions, or, it may be, all together. If one village is dancing to another village, the women are seen bringing their presents of food or clothing from the different teepees. Another dance of thanks is made, the presents distributed, and the party breaks up or goes to another village.

Sometimes a man takes upon himself the responsibilities of recruiting officer or drill-master, and gets up what is called the *No-flight Dance.* This gathers in the boys and young men who have not yet made their mark on the war-path, and drills them especially for its object, that in concert of action, and by hearing the recital of brave deeds, they may have their hearts made firm for the day of battle. The instructions given on such an occasion are lessons in Indian warfare.

The Scalp-Dance, though treated of last, is not the least in its influence in forming character, and the place it occupies as a public amusement. Under the leadership of some "brave," a party has been on the war-path to the enemy's country, and they are coming home in triumph, bringing scalps with them. Here a curious custom prevails. The warriors have painted themselves black. Their hair is combed out, and hangs around their head. They sit down on some elevation and sing their war dirge. They are met by persons from the village, who strip them of their clothing. And their blankets may afterwards be taken from them on each occasion of painting the scalps red, which ceremony is commonly performed four times. This is a part of the Dakota war honors.

The scalp-dance then commences. It is a dance of *self-glorification*, as their word *E-wa'-ke-che-pe* appears to mean. A hoop two feet in diameter, more or less, with a handle several feet long, is prepared, on which the scalp is stretched. The young men gather together and arrange themselves in a semicircle; those who participated in taking the scalp are painted black, and the others are daubed with red or yellow paint, according to their fancy; and all dance to the beat of the drum. On the other side of the circle stand the young women, arranged in line, one of whom bears the scalp of the enemy. The men sing their war chants and praise the bravery and success of those who have returned from the war-path; and the women, at intervals, join in a species of answering chorus. Night after night is this dance kept up by the young men and women, until the leaves fall, if commenced in the summer; or, if the scalp was brought home in the winter, until the leaves grow again. On each occasion of painting the scalp red, a whole day is spent in dancing around it. And those days are high days — days of giving gifts, feasting, and general rejoicing.

The compliments paid to the successful warriors, in their songs, might seem to a stranger of doubtful character; as, for instance: "Friend, you are a fool; you let the enemy strike you." But the meaning is said to be, on the *Ha-yo'-ka* principle, "Friend, you are a very wise man; you struck the enemy successfully."

The influence of the scalp-dance on the morality of the people is quite apparent. These are occasions for young men to woo maidens; and in so loose a state of society as that of the Dakota, it is not difficult to understand that such frequent and long-continued night meetings must tend to licentiousness. In this respect, however, it would be hard to say that they were more demoralizing than much of the promiscuous dancing practised by white people. But the great wrong of the scalp-dance consists in its being a crime against our common humanity. "If thine enemy hunger, feed him, and if he thirst, give him drink," is a platform of morality too high for a pagan to occupy. But having killed the enemy, to continue to rejoice over and around his scalp, week after week, and month after month, is a crime to be punished by the judges. The government of the United States should at once forbid it, as an offence against humanity. The scalp-dance and the eagle's feather keep up the inter-tribal wars among the Indians.

CHAPER V.

THE DAKOTA TAKOO WAKAN.

Hindrances to the introduction of the gospel. — Evidences of the Takoo Wakan, or supernatural, everywhere. — How this affects the untutored Indian. — The Dakota gods: 1. The Oon-ktay-he. — Their form and origin. — 2. The thunder. — The appearance of the thunder birds. — Their dwelling-place. — 3. The god of motion. — His attributes. — 4. The stone god. — The manner of its worship. — 5. The Ha-yo′-ka or anti-natural god. — Its appearance. — Its nature. — 6. The sun and moon. — 7. The armor god. — Its form and influence. — 8. The spirit of the medicine sack. — Household gods. — 9. Wakan′tanka or the Great Spirit. — His place in the Dakota family of divinities. — Probably the "unknown god" — the god of white men.

"And changed the glory of the uncorruptible God into an image made like to corruptible man, and to birds, and four-footed beasts, and creeping things."

When the gospel of Christ was borne to the Sandwich Islands, it found an open path. The idols were destroyed and the heart of the nation was waiting. Far otherwise was it among the Dakotas. In addition to the common hindrances of grossness, sensuality, and selfishness, dulling the ear, deadening the mind, and fortifying the heart, the gospel here met an active and powerful enemy in their false religion. This will surprise many who have received their ideas from poetical representations of the Indian's worship of the Great Spirit, which would seem to be the beautiful aspiration of simplicity feeling after the true God, and not only harmless, but the very foundation of a more perfect religion, whose clearer light would receive most earnest welcome.

On the other hand, when one comes to learn the characters of their various gods, contradictory, monstrous, and absurd as they all are, and especially as he discovers the prevalent scepticism concerning them among their own worshippers, he will not see how such a religion can have either vitality in itself, or be any obstacle in the way of Christianity.

But the religious faith of the Dakota is

not in his gods as such. It is in an intangible, mysterious something of which they are only the embodiment, and that in such measure and degree as may accord with the individual fancy of the worshipper. Each one will worship some of these divinities, and neglect or despise others; but the great object of all their worship, whatever its chosen medium, is the TA′-KOO WA-KAN′, which is the *supernatural* and *mysterious*. No one term can express the full meaning of the Dakota's *wakan′*. It comprehends all mystery, secret power, and divinity. Awe and reverence are its due. And it is as unlimited in manifestation as it is in idea. All life is *wakan′*. So also is everything which exhibits power, whether in action, as the winds and drifting clouds; or in passive endurance, as the boulder by the wayside. For even the commonest sticks and stones have a spiritual essence which must be reverenced as a manifestation of the all-pervading mysterious power that fills the universe.

The condition of the Indian, as he stands affected, in the midst of the visible universe, by its invisible powers, cannot be better described than it has been in the words of Rev. G. H. Pond. "The Indian," he says, "feels that he is in a world of mysteries, and is oppressed with a consciousness that, while all around him is beyond his control, and he comprehends nothing, he is constantly exposed to all evil. The very earth on which he treads, teems with life incomprehensible. It is *wakan'*, and excites by turns his superstitious hopes and fears; thrilling with such a joy as a savage can feel, or chilling him with tormenting anxiety and dread. The forests, the streams, the lakes, the springs, the hills, the vales, are to him full of awful mystery. He looks up to the sun, the moon, and the stars, and sees so many gods or goddesses, gazing down upon him in silent dreadfulness. A thousand questions concerning these things arise in his mind, but he hears no response, except that a dreadful thrill runs through him, and, with his hand on his mouth, he involuntarily exclaims, *Wakan! A-tay, on'-she-ma-da! Mystery! Father, have mercy upon me!* He extends his propitiatory pipe in every direction, and lifting up his voice, *chay'-ke-yas, prays.*

"When he enters upon the chase, to which stern necessity drives him for subsistence, the beast which he pursues to-day, shuns his approach, apparently, with the ability of an intelligent being, and to-morrow seems to be completely destitute of even brutal instinct, and has no power to escape. Again, he lays his hand on his mouth and wonders, while all the sentiments of his soul respond, *wakan'!* And he promptly pays his religious devotions to the spirit of the beast whose body lies dead at his feet, and on which he and his family will feast that night.

"He sees at one time a strong and active hunter and warrior instantly seized with pain, and in a few moments expire in awful agony, and, at another time, another waste away almost imperceptibly, through long years, without pain, and die in utter stupidity; and again, amazed, he wails out the deep sentiments of his soul, and echo rolls back in wild notes, on the night breeze, *wakan'!* and in sullen silence he resolves to offer the costly sacrifice of the so called 'medicine dance' to the *Oon-ktay'-he*, and to the spirits of the dead.

"Again: pains, often excruciating, in one part of his own body, at the next moment leap to another part, and then perhaps as suddenly vanish altogether; and his superstitious feelings vent themselves in a wild chant to the gods, and in the vapor-bath, it may be, he presents his body to the *Ta'-koo-shkan-shkan', the moving god*, or hangs himself to the elevated pole, in honor of the *Wa-ke'-yan, the thunder god*, or of the Sun, as the so-called medicine-man may direct.

"To them heaven and earth are full of demons rankling with hate, and engaged in eternal strife; but there is no glimpse of the Almighty God of love and grace, to calm their agitated minds and soothe their sorrows. Dread of future evil fills their souls, and 'through fear of death they are all their lifetime subject to bondage.' They are slaves to the *wakan*, 'and they bow down their back always.'" *

* Rev. G. H. Pond: Presbyterian Quarterly Review, Jan., 1861. Article: "Paganism a Demon-Worship."

The Gods of the Dakotas are of course innumerable; but of the superior gods, these are the chief: —

1. The *Oon-ktay′-he; the god of the waters.* This name is supposed to signify extraordinary vital energy; and the gods of this name — for there are many — are the most powerful of all. In their external form, the *Oon-ktay′-he* are said to resemble the ox, only they are of immense proportions. They can extend their horns and tails so as to reach the skies. These are the organs of their power. The dwelling place of the male is in the water, and the spirit of the female animates the earth. Hence, when the Dakota seems to be offering sacrifices to the water or the earth, it is to this family of gods that the worship is rendered. They address the male as grandfather, and the female as grandmother.

The first *Oon-ktay′-he*, created out of a

rib, as some say, by the *Wakan'tanka*, or Great Spirit himself, was a male, and the second was a female. From these two sprang all the numerous *Oon-ktay'-he*, both male and female, that are now scattered through the waters, and upon the face of the earth.*

One of these gods, it is believed, dwells under the Falls of St. Anthony, in a den of awful dimensions, which is constructed of iron.

2. The *Wa-ke'-yan; the thunder god!* This is a being of terrific proportions, in shape somewhat like a bird. As it flies, hid by the thick clouds, the lightnings flash forth, and the thunder is its voice. As are all the Dakota gods, with the exception of *Wa-kan'-tan-ka*, or the Great Spirit, these

* James W. Lynd, one of the keenest observers of Dakota customs, but an unfortunate victim of the Sioux massacre. In this chapter the materials of both Mr. Lynd and Rev. G. H. Pond are freely used.

gods are male and female. There are four varieties. One is black, with a long beak, and has four joints in his wing. Another is yellow, without any beak at all, and with wings like the first, only that he has but six quills in each wing. The third is of a scarlet color, and is remarkable chiefly for having eight joints in each of its enormous wings. The fourth is blue, and globular, and is destitute of both eyes and ears. In the place of the eyebrows are semicircular lines of lightning, from beneath which project downwards two chains of lightning, zigzagging and diverging as they descend. Two plumes of soft down serve it for wings.

At the western extremity of the earth is a high mountain, having on its summit a beautiful mound, whereon stands the palace of this family of gods. The palace opens towards each of the four cardinal points, and at each doorway is stationed a watcher, — a butterfly at the east, a bear at the west, a reindeer at the north, and a beaver at the south. Each of these *wakan* sentries is enveloped, except the head, in scarlet down of the most exquisite softness and beauty. These gods are the gods of war; and they are ever on the war-path. They are ruthless, cruel, and destructive. A deadly enmity exists between them and the *Oonktay'-he.*

3. The *Ta'-koo-shkan-shkan'; the moving god.* This god is too subtle in essence to be perceived by the senses, and is as subtile in disposition. He is everywhere present. He exerts a controlling influence over instinct, intellect, and passion. He can rob a man of the use of his rational faculties, and inspire a beast with intelligence, so that the hunter will wander idiot-like, while the game on which he hoped to feast his

family at night, escapes with perfect ease. Or, if he please, the god can reverse his influence. He is much gratified to see men in trouble, and is particularly glad when they die in battle or otherwise. Passionate and capricious in the highest degree, it is very difficult to retain his favor. His symbol and supposed residence is the *boulder*, as it is also of another god, the *Toon-kan′*. Hence boulders are universally worshipped by the Dakotas. He also lives in the *Four Winds*, and in the consecrated spear and tomahawk. To his retinue belong the buzzard, the raven, the fox, the wolf, and animals of a like nature.

4. The *Toon-kan′*, or *In′-yan;* the *Stone-god*, or *Lingam*. This god dwells in stones and rocks, and is, as the Dakotas say, the oldest god. If asked why it is considered the oldest, they will tell you because it is the hardest, — an Indian's reason. It may

be that they connect with endurance the idea of duration. The usual form of the stone used in worship is round or oval, and about the size of a man's head. The devout Dakota paints this *Toon-kan'* red, puts swan's down upon it, and then prays to the god which is supposed to dwell in or hover near it. This seems to belong to a far simpler worship and less corrupted religion than that which prevails in the present age among the Dakotas.

5. The *Ha-yo'-ka*; *the anti-natural god.* Like the *Wa-ke'-yan*, there are four varieties of this god, all of which assume the human form, and the differences are not important. They are all armed with the bow and arrow and the deer-hoof rattle, which are charged with electricity. One of the varieties carries a drum, and for a drum-stick holds a small *Wake'yan* god by the tail, striking the drum with its beak. This

would seem an unfortunate position for a god to be in, but it must be remembered that it is *wakan'*, and the more absurd a thing is, the more *wakan'*. One of these gods manifests himself at times as the zephyr of the ancients, in the gentle whirlwind, sometimes visible in the delicate waving of the tall grass on the prairie.

The nature of the *Ha-yo'-ka* is the very opposite of nature. He expresses joy by sighs and groans and a most doleful countenance, and sorrow and pain by the opposite sounds and looks. Heat causes his flesh to shiver, and his teeth to chatter, while cold makes him perspire. In the coldest winter weather, when the mercury congeals, these gods seek some prominence on the prairie, where they put up bushes to shield themselves from the rays of the sun, and under which they sit naked, and fan themselves as they swelter with heat. But in the oppressive heat of summer, they wrap around them robe on robe, and lean over a rousing fire, snivelling and shaking with the cold, like one in a fit of the ague. They feel perfect confidence when beset with dangers, and quake with fear when safe. With them, falsehood and truth are reversed. Good is their evil, and evil their good. Their aid is sought especially for the gratification of libidinous passions.*

* Brinton, in his "Myths of the New World," p. 151, gives an idea of *Ha-yo′-ka* which confounds him with the "thunder god," and makes him typify "the paradoxical nature of the storm." This is a mistake In the Dakota theogony they are entirely distinct in character, offices, and symbolic representation. The picture sign of *Ha-yo′-ka* is an old man with a cap on, and bow and arrows in hand, while that of the "thunder god is a bird with extended wings. That lightnings are one of the accompaniments of Ha-yo′-ka, and a young "thunder bird" is his drumstick, may arise from the fact that in the characters of all the gods, there is no attempt at making them consistent with each other, but rather the votaries of each one endeavor to represent him as supreme. It is true that

6. The *Sun* and *Moon*. Although as a divinity, the Sun is not represented as a malignant being, yet the worship given him is the most dreadful which the Dakotas offer. This will be spoken of further along. Aside from the Sun-dance, there is another proof of the divine character ascribed to the Sun in the oath taken by him: "As the Sun hears me, this is so."

The Moon is worshipped rather as the representative of the Sun, than separately. Thus, in the great Sun-dance, which is held in the full of the moon, at night, the dancers turn their eyes on her.

7. The *Armor god*. This is not any one spirit, but the tutelar divinity assigned to each young man as he comes to years of ma-

---

Ha-yo'-ka typifies the paradoxical, but it is the paradoxical in all nature, not merely in a part of it. And it also seems to represent the paradoxical in human nature. There may be reference to the "power of contrary choice;" or it may be what Edgar A. Poe calls the "Imp of the Perouse."

turity, and resides in the consecrated armor then given him, which consists of a spear, an arrow, and a small bundle of paint. It is the spirit of some animal or bird, as the wolf beaver, loon, or eagle. He must not kill or harm this animal, but hold it ever sacred, or at least until he has proved his manhood, by killing an enemy. Frequently the young man forms an image of this sacred animal, and carries it about with him, regarding it as having a direct influence upon his every-day life and ultimate destiny; a thing supernatural, all powerful, and sacred.*

8. The *Spirit of the Medicine Sack.* This is similar to the preceding, in that it is a divinity appropriated by a single individ-

* Parkman says, — in his "Jesuits in N. A." p. lxxi, note, — that the knowledge of this guardian spirit comes through dreams at the initiatory fast. If this is ever true among the Dakotas, it is not the rule. This knowledge is communicated by the "war-prophet."

ual, protecting and aiding him, and receiving his worship. It is conferred at the time of initiation into the Order of the Sacred Dance, and of course is confined to its members.

It may be well to notice in this connection the existence of other gods, more especially household gods. It has been supposed that the Dakotas had no *penates* or household gods; but recently such have come into the possession of the missionaries. One of these images is that of a little man, and is inclosed in a cylindrical wooden case, and enveloped in sacred swan's down.

9. *The Wa-kan'-tan-ka; the Great Wakan*, or "the Great Spirit," as this name has been generally but incorrectly translated. This god is properly named last and least among their divinities. In no sense is he held in that high reverence, which white men have supposed. No worship is offered

to him, nor is he named except in the presence of white men, and then not as often as the interpreters indicate. For their appeal is generally to the *Ta′-koo-wa-kan*, and not to the *Wa-kan′-tan-ka.*

It has been a debated question whether the *Wa-kan′-tan-ka* is the ancient and true God, from whose worship the Dakotas have lapsed, or a recent creation to fill up their list of divinities. The latter appears to be the true idea. The name itself is proof of this. It is not a primitive, but a derived form. A parallel word is their name for the horse, *shoon′-ka-tan′-ka* or *shook-tan′-ka*, which is compounded of shoon′-ka, *dog*, and tan′-ka, *great*. Whether, as has been generally supposed, horses were first introduced to this continent by Europeans, or not, the acquaintance of the Dakotas with them is of late date, and time was when the dog was their only domestic animal.

When therefore the horse came into the same cirle of domestic uses, he was naturally the "great dog." In their wonder, they also named him *shoon'-ka-wa-kan'*, or the *wakan'* dog.

So, also, as the Europeans break in upon savage life with their strange faces, language, and dress; with their wonderful horses, their fire-speaking guns, and their bird-like ships, the Indians, either seeing or hearing from afar, and the marvel growing with each league it travels, called them gods, or *wa-she'-choon*. And, in accordance with their theory that every man and race of men are under the guardianship of their own special divinities, what is more natural than that they should give expression to the corresponding greatness of the white man's god, in comparison with their own *wakan*, by calling him the *Great Wakan?*

Still it must be remembered that his

greatness is all foreign to them, and does not bring him into the range of their worship. He is simply the white man's god, and they find no better way to name him.

In accordance with this view is the fact that the *Wakan'-tanka* has no character ascribed to him by the heathen Dakota, nor do any ancient traditions belong to him. A few traditions, of evidently recent origin, have come in through the influence of Christianity. This would not be strange after three centuries of intercourse with white men. Such is the tradition that *Oon-ktay'-he* was created by *Wa-kan'-tan-ka.*

Well says Mr. Parkman, "The primitive Indian, yielding his untutored homage to one all-pervading and omnipotent Spirit, is a dream of the poets, rhetoricians, and sentimentalists." Still we may believe that some unsatisfied longing souls found, in the new god of the white man, the "Unknown

God" for which they, as the Athenians of old, had been vainly seeking in the multitude of their own divinities. Now, of course, through the gospel, *Wakan'-tanka* has a Christian meaning. And many a Dakota now worships him as the only true God and Jehovah, the God of the whole earth, the God of the Indian as well as of the white man.*

* This enumeration of the *Dakota gods* is not intended to be exhaustive. There are, besides the *E'-ya*, or *god of Gluttony*, and the *Chan-o'-te-dan*, or *Hoh-no'-ge-cha*. This latter is a fabulous creature, dwelling usually in the woods, as the first name of it indicates. The latter name would seem to give it a place by the doors of the tents. Thus they both have a strong claim to being styled "household gods." S. R. R.

CHAPTER VI.

DAKOTA WORSHIP.

Rites of worship. — Sacrifices. — Paint. — The pipe. — The sacred feast. —Wo/-hdoo-za. — Self-immolation. — The sun-dance. — Purification. — The vapor-bath. — Feast of the first fruits. — Feast of raw fish. — The Wa-kan men or sorcerers. — The Dakota religion national. — The order of the sacred dance. — Ceremonies. — Rules of conduct and promises — Initiation into the order. — General characteristics of the Dakota worship. — The worship of demons. — Witchcraft. — Jugglery. — Spirit seeking. — Modern spiritualism much like the older forms. — Phases of the older forms. — Of the soul and a future state. — The number of souls a man has, and what becomes of them after death. — The Dakota religion unsatisfying.

"Double, double toil and trouble;
Fire burn, and cauldron bubble.
Fillet of a fenny snake
In the cauldron boil and bake:
Eye of newt, and toe of frog,
Wool of bat, and tongue of dog,
Adder's fork, and blind-worm's sting,
Lizard's leg, and owlet's wing,
For a charm of powerful trouble,
Like a hell-broth boil and bubble."

RITES OF WORSHIP.

THE radical forms of worship obtaining among the Dakotas are few and simple. The most primitive and ancient is *Sacrifice*. To every divinity which they worship they make sacrifices. Upon recovery from sickness, upon the recurrence of a long-wished for event, on disease appearing in a family or camp, and even on the most trivial occasions, the gods are either thanked, or supplicated by sacrifice. The idea of sacrifice is at the foundation of all their ancient ceremonies, and shows itself even in their everyday life. The sacrifices made upon recovery from sickness are usually a small strip of muslin, or a piece of red cloth, a few skins of some animal, or other things, of no great value. Sometimes a pan or kettle is laid up for sacrifice. But, after a short time, the end for which the sacrifice is made is attained, and it is removed.

Paint occupies an important place in all their worship. Scarlet or red is the religious color for sacrifices, while blue is used in many ceremonies. The use of paints, the Dakotas aver, was taught them by the gods.

Oon-ktay'-he taught the first "medicine men" how to paint themselves when they worshipped him, and what colors to use. *Ta'-koo-shkan-shkan'* whispers to his favorites what colors are most acceptable to him. *Ha-yo'-ka* hovers over them in dreams, and informs them how many streaks to make upon their bodies, and the tinge they must have. No ceremony of worship is complete without the *wakan'*, or sacred application of paint. The down of the female swan, colored scarlet, also forms a necessary part of sacrifices.

Tobacco and tobacco-smoke are often offered. The mouth-piece of the pipe is turned in the direction of the supposed deity or spirit, or smoke is blown upon his image. A dog is considered an offering most acceptable to the gods. In this the Dakota honors his god as he would be honored himself; for dog-meat is his greatest luxury.

Sacrifices are universally made to the spirits of the dead. They are often articles of food brought for the use of the spirit of the deceased. These offerings are now consecrated, and cannot be used by those devoting them, but they may be sold by them; or, if left on the grave, as they often are, they are public property, and he who wishes, takes them.

The *Wakan' feast* is a common form of sacrifice. Guided by their dreams, or directed by their *wakan' men*, they often incur great expense to provide a feast in honor of some of the gods. To such feasts they invite many, but they themselves religiously refrain from partaking. The drumming and rattling and singing that always precede the eating in these gatherings, are acts of worship.

The sacrifices made in the hunt are among the most common. Particular portions of each animal killed are held sacred to the god of the chase or other deities. If a deer is killed, the head, heart, or some other portion of it, is sacrificed by the one who kills it. The part sacrificed differs with different individuals. In a bear, the breast is most commonly used to make a *wakan'* feast. In ducks and other fowls, the most common sacrifice is that of the wing, though many sacrifice the heart, and some the head. The same part is always sacrificed by the same individual. This custom is called *Wo'-hdoo-za*, meaning that an injunction is upon them to hold a certain thing sacred. It is *taboo*. A special *wo'-hdoo-za*, or vow, may be assumed, which expires when the object is attained for which the vow was made. Another form of the *wo'-hdoo-za*, and instituted for a different purpose, is that which is a part of the initiation of every young man to the status of manhood. Here the animal in which his *armor-god* resides is *taboo* to him, as has already been described.

But the highest form of sacrifice is *self-immolation*. It exists in the *Sun Dance*, and in what is called *Vision seeking*. Some, passing a knife under the muscles of the breast and arms, attach cords thereto, which are fastened at the other end to the top of a tall pole, raised for the purpose; and thus they hang suspended only by those cords, without food or drink, for two, three, or four days, gazing upon vacancy; their minds intently fixed upon the object in which they wish to be assisted by the deity, and waiting for a vision from above. Others, making incisions in the back, have attached, by hair ropes, one or more buffalo heads, so that every time the body moves in the dance, a jerk is given to the buffalo heads behind. This rite exists at present among the western bands of the Dakotas in the greatest degree of barbarity. After making the cuttings in the arms, breast, or back, wooden setons — sticks about the size of a lead-pencil — are inserted, and the ropes are attached to them. Then, swinging on the ropes, they pull until the setons are pulled out with the flesh and tendons; or, if hung with the buffalo heads, the pulling out is done in the dance, by jerk, jerk, jerk, keeping time with the music, while the head and body, in an attitude of supplication, face the sun, and the eye is unflinchingly fixed upon it. Catlin, in his "Okeepa," has illustrated such scenes, as he witnessed them among the Mandans.

Another prominent idea in Dakota worship is *purification.* It is the preparation for the highest forms of sacrifice. If a Dakota wishes to be particularly successful in any important undertaking, he first purifies himself by the *E'-nee-pee*, or vapor-bath, and by fasting for a term of three days. During the whole of this time he avoids women and society, is secluded in his habits, and endeavors in every way to etherealize himself, preparatory to the performance of his religious rites, in order that he may be pure enough to receive a revelation from the deity he invokes.

The purificatory rite of the vapor-bath is performed in this way: A number of poles, the size of hoop poles or less, are taken, and their larger ends being set in the ground in a circle, the flexible tops are bent over and tied in the centre. This framework is then covered with robes and blankets, a small hole being left on one side for entrance. Before the door a fire is built, and round stones, about the size of a man's head, are heated in it. When hot, they are rolled within, and, the door being closed, steam is made by pouring water upon them. The devotee, stripped to the skin, sits within this steam-tight dome, sweating profusely at every pore, until he is nearly suffocated. Sometimes a number engage in it together, and unite their prayers and their songs. Then the hut is larger, and more ceremony is observed.

Connected with this idea of purification is the making of *new fire* in all sacred ceremonies where it is required, and also the religious care with which the sacred armor of the man is kept pure from contact with an adult woman. A virgin only can touch it. For this reason, in their travelling companies, one will often see the scarlet-wrapped bundle containing the sacred armor borne on the back of a little girl.

Dances and feasts are the chief public ceremonials of their religion. These are not occasions of mere amusement, though they have such. The *Wakan* feast, or feast of the *first fruits*, is the most common, and is made in thanks for the increase of the earth and the fruits of the hunt. It is also made to propitiate favor.

In the feast to *Ha-yo'-ka*, the worshippers assemble in a lodge, tricked out in tall, conical hats, and nearly naked. They sing and dance frantically around a huge kettle hung over the fire and full of boiling meat, now and then plunging their hands into the seething mass and seizing large pieces of the hot meat, which they devour at once. Then the scalding fluid is thrown over their backs and legs, at which they never wince, only complaining that it is *cold*.

In the *raw fish feast* the dancers are likewise naked, except breech-cloth and moccasins; but they are painted all over in various colors, and ornamented with white and red swan's down. The fish, just as they were taken from the water, lie on some boughs in the centre, and near them stand dishes of sweetened water. After dancing and chanting a while, the inspiration comes. Then, in a rage, like starving beasts, they attack the fish, and, without using their hands, tear off piece after piece — scales, bones, entrails, and all — and swallow them, drinking the while out of the dishes of sweetened water. It is not hard to believe that, as they assert, their inspiration is by the spirit of the cormorant. Such are the appropriate rites of a religion whose gods are beasts, unearthly monsters, and spirits of the pit.

The Dakota religion has no temples and no proper priesthood. It is, consequently, deficient in the organization and ceremonial which give unity and power. This is, however, compensated for in part by an inner power. Each individual is a priest, and may receive revelations from the gods, and can offer his own sacrifices. Even their great dances, such as the sun-dance, may be performed by only one or two, the company being made up by the crowd of idle gazers. Still, there is a special class of men who have intercourse with divinity in far greater degree than ordinary men, and are generally employed as priests in these great ceremonies, as diviners to prognosticate the future, and as conjurers and sorcerers to drive out evil spirits and heal the sick. These are

THE WAKAN MEN, OR SORCERERS,

generally and wrongly called by white men "medicine men." According to their own story, they are not members of the human family, though in human form; they are incarnations of the gods. The original essence of these men and women — for they appear in both forms — first wakes into existence floating in ether. Gently wafted by the "four winds" through space, in due time they find themselves in some one of the families of the superior gods, by whom they are received into intimate fellowship. There they remain until they become essentially assimilated to them, and perfectly acquainted with their characters, abilities, desires, caprices, and employments, and also with all the chants, feasts, fasts, dances, and sacrificial rites which it is deemed necessary to impose on men. When one of them dies, he returns to the abode of the gods to receive a new inspiration and incarnation. After four incarnations they pass into nothingness. To establish their claims to this inspiration, they lay hold of all that is strange and mysterious, and, if possible, turn it to their advantage. And, by great shrewdness, untiring industry, and more or less of actual demoniacal possession, they convince great numbers of their fellows, and in the process are convinced themselves, of their sacred character and office. With all their honest imposture, there is, of course, large measure of conscious cheat used to bewilder and entrap the populace. But, honestly or dishonestly, they are the champions of their pagan religion, the teachers of its traditions and rites, and, by nature, education, and position, are the inevitable foes of another faith. Such they have proved themselves against Christianity.

The Dakota religion is national, or, more properly, universal; for no such thing as nationality exists among them. It, of necessity, takes in every male Dakota; for his very manhood depends upon a rite of religious initiation. But, aside from this, there is no organization, which, if we may so say, takes into eclesiastical membership the mass of Dakota religionists. Among the eastern bands of the Dakotas,

THE ORDER OF THE SACRED DANCE

has, to a considerable extent, the place of a pagan church. This is a secret society of comparatively late introduction, but has largely supplanted the old forms of religion where it has taken root. It is said to have been instituted by the great *Oon-ktay'-he*, the god of the waters, immediately after the production of the earth and men, to promote his own worship among them. The badge and charm of the order is "the medicine sack," or, literally, the *wakan'* sack. He ordained that it should consist of the skin of either the otter, the raccoon, the weasel, the squirrel, the loon, or one variety of fish and of serpents. It should also contain four species of medicine, of *wakan'* qualities, which should represent fowls, medicinal herbs, medicinal trees, and quadrupeds. These are represented by the down of the female swan, grass roots, bark from the roots of trees, and hair from the buffalo; all of which are carefully preserved in the sack. From this combination proceeds a *wakan'* influence so powerful that no human being can, unassisted, resist it.

The rules of conduct are, that they shall honor and revere the "*wakan'* sack;" honor all who belong to the dance; make frequent sacred feasts; refrain from theft; not listen to birds — slander; and that the female members shall not have a plurality of husbands. The reward of the faithful is honor from the members of the order, frequent invitations to the feast, abundance of fowl and other food, with supernatural assistance to consume it, and long life here, with a red dish and spoon in the life to come.

The ceremonies of initiation, include purification in the vapor-bath for four successive days, instruction in the mysteries, vigils, fasting, and, on the great day of the feast, the being shot by the "*wakan'* sack," with feigned death, from which the candidate recovers by having the spittle from the chewed bone of the god, spirted over him, and by the power of the magic shell supposed to have been fired into his body. He now receives his "sack," and is a member in possession of the awful mysteries. Between these mysteries and the simple truth of the gospel, there could be only deadly enmity; and it is to be remembered that it was enmity organized and aroused to fight for its own existence.

GENERAL CHARACTERISTICS.

In carefully studying the religion of the Dakotas, some general characteristics are noticeable. The sum and substance of it all is *demon-worship*. The gods they worship are destitute of all the attributes of the true God. Even the best of them, or the Great Spirit, has but a negative char-

Buffalo, a Dakotah Chief.—"Gospel," etc.

acter. So far as forms and names are concerned, they are the creation of their own deluded and foul imaginations. They are self-projected monstrosities. But underneath their uncouth forms there are substantial spiritual powers. For the worship of the Dakota does not fall on vacancy, but is consciously paid to spiritual beings, which can be none other than the spirits of darkness. And the perpetuation of their worship is largely owing to manifestations of demoniacal presence and power. The Dakota, having his eyes shut to the presence and character of the true God, misinterprets the kindly discipline of life, and credits the chastisements of a loving father to the spite of these vengeful demons, whose special delight it is to make man more miserable, or to destroy him. Demons wander through the earth, causing sickness and death. Spirits of evil are ever ready to pounce upon the unwary. The thunder-bird scatters his fire here and there, striking down whom he lists. Spirits of the darkness, spirits of the light, spirits of earth, air, fire, and water, surround him on every side, with but one great object in view, — the misery and destruction of the human race.

But have they no longings after the true God? Do they feel no stirring of his spirit in their hearts? They must. For God leaves no soul without a witness of himself and of the better life; and they show this in their consciousness of sin and their efforts for purification and atonement.

Sorcery is another noticeable characteristic. The very basis of their worship is converse with evil spirits. And beside the great host of evil deities which all may invoke, every one has one or more "familiar spirit." Those who are endowed, by their intercourse with the spirits, with more than the usual degree of *wakan′* power, profess, and are generally believed, to be able to work spells upon a distant enemy, causing misfortune, sickness, and death. By this supposed power, the so-called "medicine men" hold their communities in awe and subjection.

Jugglery is the necessary and natural accompaniment of a religion based on ignorance and superstition. It is not otherwise with the Dakotas. Although those who devote themselves to the higher mysteries of their religion may be honestly deluded into a full belief and unswerving discipleship, yet they find it necessary to employ craft and artifice to attach to their leadership the populace, who cannot or will not follow them into these higher mysteries. Thus the whole ceremony of initiation into the Order of the "sacred dance" is a piece of jugglery.

The candidate, after his recovery from a sham death, caused by a pretended shot, goes through a most distressing performance to vomit up the magic shell, supposed by the gaping crowd to have been shot into his body by the god, but really placed on his tongue by his attendant. So also is the notable endurance of the worshippers of *Ha-yo'-ka*, who plunge their hands into boiling water and cast it over their naked bodies. The skin has previously been deadened by rubbing it with sheep sorrel.

Another of their sacred performances is a noted juggler's trick, the world over. A lodge is cleared of every thing in it, and one of these *faquirs* produces ropes and thongs, desiring some of the stronger men to tie him tightly. The tying is usually done by those not connected with the performance, and some of these affirm that they have tied the arms, elbows, and feet so tightly as to break

the skin, and then tied the feet and hands together, and enveloped the whole body in knots and twists that it would seem impossible to undo. The person thus tied is placed in the empty lodge by himself, and the door made fast from without. No one is allowed to touch, or go near the lodge; and the Indian, thus bound, remains alone, singing a few minutes; when he cries out, the door is opened, and he comes forth free from bonds. This is looked upon as in the highest degree *wakan'*.

Throughout the study of the Dakota religion, one is struck with the likeness of many phenomena, to some which have made great stir in our so-called Christian land, and which many believe to be a higher development of Christianity itself. If here they are found to belong to a pagan religion, it only discloses their true character, and also the fact that a great substratum of paganism underlies our vaunted civilization. Thus *spiritualism* is found to be an element in the religion of the Dakotas, which, in its phenomena, practices, and pretensions, is much the same as that which sets itself up for a new religion in our Christian land. Except, perhaps that the pagan form has less of pretension and more of reality, and does not disguise, but confesses the fact, that its true character is a combination of demon-worship, sorcery, divination, and jugglery. Altogether, the pagan form is the more venerable, honest, and, if we may use the word in this connection, respectable, of the two.

They believe that some have power to call up and converse with the spirits of the dead, and they frequently make feasts to these spirits, and elicit information from them of distant relatives and friends. Assembling at night in a lodge, they smoke, put out the fire, and then, drawing their blankets over their heads, remain singing in unison in a low key, until the spirit gives them a picture; and many a hair-erecting tale is told of spirits' power to reveal, and the after confirmation.

Another phase of spiritualism will be seen in the following: — A sick man, whom all his conjurers and doctors had failed to cure, was, on consultation, committed to the care of Red Bird, a conjurer and *wakan'* man who had in his service many of the gods called *Ta'-koo-shkan-shkan'*. A tent having been prepared, Red Bird was bound with ropes, as in the juggler's trick already mentioned, and then wrapped in a buffalo-robe and tied again. He had in his bosom a little boulder, a symbol of the gods. In this condition he was rolled into the tent, and the sick man placed by his side. Over him was hung a drum and also a deer-hoof rattle. The lights were extinguished, and in an instant the tent was struck by a strong wind, and the conjurer cried out, as if in great fear: "Boys, come carefully; your father is very weak; be careful." The gods did not seem to regard the admonition, but beat the drum, shook the rattle, and heaved the tent furiously. The tent seemed to be full of them, and they were very talkative and rude, but their voices were so fine and so soft that their meaning could not be comprehended by those outside. While they performed the cermony of exorcising the sick man, the gods called for a pipe and smoked many pipes'-full, indicating that there were a large number of them. Suddenly the gods all departed, and the conjurer ordered the torches to be lighted. All expected to see him still bound, as he was when thrust into the tent; but, to their surprise, he was out of the robe; had slipped out of all his fastenings, though not a single knot had been untied. The sick man began from that time to recover, though they admit that all treated in this way do not recover.

OF THE SOUL AND A FUTURE STATE

a few words will tell all that there is to be told. To the human body the Dakotas give four spirits. The first is supposed to be the spirit of the body, and dies with the body. The second is a spirit which always remains with or near the body. The third is the soul which accounts for the deeds done in the body, and is supposed by some to go to the south, by others to go to the west, after the death of the body. The "milky way" in the heavens is called the *wa-na'-ge ta-chan'-koo*, the *path of spirits*. The fourth always lingers with the small bundle of the hair of the deceased, kept by the relatives until they have a chance to throw it into the country of their enemies, when it becomes a roving, restless spirit, bringing death and disease to the enemy in whose country it wanders. Some aver that there is a fifth spirit, which enters the body of some animal or child at death.

It is difficult to ascertain the real belief of the Dakotas about the resurrection of the body. They place their dead on scaffolds, and have a hereditary and universal opposition to burying them under ground, until decay makes it necessary to do so.

With regard to the place of abode of the four souls of men, though they appear to believe that the true soul which goes *south* or *west* is immortal, they have no idea, nor do they appear to have any particular concern, as to what may become of them after death. Many of them say they would quite as lief live in the house of the Bad Spirit as in the house of the Good Spirit.

Thus it is seen that the Dakota's religion, though so intangible and contradictory, is a powerful system, which permeates and enwraps his whole life. Indeed it may be said to be his life. It gives the law to all social customs and domestic industries. It regulates the hunt, the journey, and the camp. And a fearful life it leads him. His worst passions and darkest fears are ever developed by it. He must be a *savage* as long as he is a *pagan*. And, above all, his fear of his gods, which darkens his whole life, makes the forsaking of their worship the sure presage of innumerable woes, and often of death.

CHAPTER VII.

1835–1838.

THE DAKOTA MISSION.

Exploring visit of Dr. Williamson. — Dr. Williamson, Mr. Stevens, and others, reach Fort Snelling. — The Messrs. Pond had preceded them. — The cabin at Lake Calhoun. — Personal notices of the laborers. — Formation of a church at Fort Snelling. — Selection of mission stations. — Mr. Stevens builds at Lake Harriet. — Description of places. — Fort Snelling. — Falls of St. Anthony. — Minnehaha. — The group of lakes. — Dr. Williamson goes to Lacquiparle. — Up the Minnesota. — Across the prairies. — Mda-e-ya′-dan or Lacquiparle. — Welcomed by Mr. Renville. — Mr. Riggs joins the mission. — Mr. G. H. Pond married. — Native church at Lacquiparle.

"*Go ye into all the world, and preach the Gospel to every creature.*"

THE work of Christian missions should ever be aggressive. The command is, "Go, teach all nations." Its onward movements are conflicts, and its successes are victories. It will be the purpose of this work, to delineate truthfully the progress of the gospel among the Dakotas.

The mission of the American Board to the

Dakotas was commenced in the summer of 1835. In the previous year, Dr. Williamson, under the direction of the Prudential Committee, made a visit of exploration up the Mississippi as far as Fort Snelling, at the mouth of the Saint Peter or Minnesota River. His report was favorable to the commencement of a mission among the Sioux, or Dakotas; and, accordingly, that same year, Thomas S. Williamson, M.D., and Jedediah D. Stevens, *missionaries*, and Alex. G. Huggins, *farmer*, with their wives, and Miss Sarah Poage and Miss Lucy C. Stevens, *teachers*, were placed under appointment. It was expected that they would reach the land of the Dakotas in the autumn; but low water in the Mississippi, and other causes, made it impracticable.

In the meantime they were preceded by other laborers. As early as 1833, Mr. Samuel W. Pond, a young man from Washington,

Connecticut, came westward and stopped at Galena. While there, he became acquainted with Rev. Aratus Kent, who had exerted a very great formative religious influence in the West. Mr. Kent would fain have kept him to labor in the white settlements; but Mr. Pond was unwilling to stop there. Making himself acquainted, as far as might be, with the circumstances and wants of the Dakota field, he sent for a younger brother, Gideon H. Pond, to join him at Galena. Together they went up to Fort Snelling, and, with the approbation of the commandant of the garrison and the Indian Agent, Major Taliaffero, they attached themselves to the Indian village at Lake Calhoun.

This was in the early summer of 1834. Being unmarried men, they built for themselves a little log-cabin on the margin of the lake, assisted the Indians in cultivating the land, and were useful to them in various ways, while they applied themselves chiefly to the work of learning the Dakota language. This was all undertaken at their own expense. Some time afterwards they both became preachers of the gospel, and missionaries of the American Board.

"Dr. Williamson and Mr. Stevens, with their associates, arrived at Fort Snelling in May, 1835; the former having ascended the Mississippi River from the mouth of the Ohio, and the latter having proceeded through Lake Michigan, Green Bay, and the Fox and Wisconsin Rivers to Prairie du Chien."

Thomas Smith Williamson, a native of South Carolina, was educated in a free state, graduated at Jefferson College, and for some years was a practising physician in Ripley, Ohio. When he decided that it was his duty to go to the heathen, he spent some time at Lane Theological Seminary, and was licensed to preach, and ordained as an evangelist by the Presbytery of Chillicothe. *Mrs. Margaret Williamson* and *Miss Sarah Poage* were sisters, born in Mason county, Kentucky; but their father, at an early day, removed to Ohio, and became one of the proprietors of the town of Ripley. *Alexander Gililland Huggins* was a native of North Carolina; but when he was a lad, his father and other relatives removed to Brown county, Ohio. *Mrs. Lydia Huggins*, whose maiden name was Pettijohn, was a native of southern Ohio. These five constituted the missionary band that carried the gospel and education to Lacquiparle, two hundred miles west of Fort Snelling.

Jedediah Dwight Stevens was a native of New York State, studied theology at Peterboro', and was licensed and ordained by the Courtland Presbytery. *Mrs. Julia Stevens* was the daughter of Judge Eggleston of

Stafford, N. Y. In the year 1827, Mr. and Mrs. Stevens commenced missionary labors on the Island of Mackinaw, and afterwards were removed to the Stockbridges on Fox River, near Green Bay. *Miss Lucy Cornelia Stevens* was a niece of Mr. Stevens, and afterwards married to Rev. Daniel Gavan, one of the Swiss missionaries to the Dakotas, sent out by the Lausanne Missionary Society. *Miss Cordelia Eggleston*, a sister of Mrs. Stevens, afterwards joined them and became the wife of Mr. S. W. Pond.

"Upon the arrival of the mission families at Fort Snelling, they were hospitably received by Majors Bliss and Loomis, and by the Indian Agent, Maj. Taliaffero. During their stay there, which was about a month, they organized a Christian church, to which eight persons connected with the garrison, who had been hopefully born again, during the preceding winter and spring, were admitted on profession, together with six others, who had been members of other churches; and on the second Sabbath of June, they, with the members of the mission families, amounting to twenty-two in all, sat down in the wilderness to commemorate the dying love of Jesus the Saviour of sinners, hundreds of miles in advance of where a like scene had been witnessed or enjoyed." *

After due consultation, two places were selected as mission stations: *Lake Harriet*, about eight miles a little north of west from Fort Snelling, six miles south-west from the Falls of Saint Anthony, and one mile from the Indian village on the margin of Lake Calhoun, where the Messrs. Pond had erected their log-cabin; and *Lacquiparle*, which is a widening of the Saint Peter or Minnesota River, about two hundred miles

* Missionary Herald.

by land, as commonly travelled, west from the same place.

Fort Snelling, built on the commanding point of land formed by the intersection of the Minnesota with the Mississippi, was commenced in the year 1820, and carried forward under the superintendence of Lieut. Col. Leavenworth. It was named for Col. Snelling, who assumed command of the garrison in the following year.

When the mission houses were erected on the western shore of Lake Harriet, and occupied by Mr. Stevens' family, the Falls of Saint Anthony were in their native wildness. Only a government saw-mill stood there, on the Minneapolis side. These falls were called *Haha* by the Dakotas, as indeed are all waterfalls, and named *Saint Anthony* by Hennepin, the Franciscan, in honor of Saint Anthony of Padua.

About two and a half miles from Fort

Snelling, on the road up to the Falls of Saint Anthony, then, as now, a bridge spanned a small stream known as Little Falls creek. Immediately below this bridge, there is a very beautiful cascade, now extensively known and admired. At Minnehaha, Longfellow found a name for the wife of Hiawatha. It has not inappropriately been translated *Laughing Water*, though literally it means *Curling Water*. "Niagara," says Mr. Neill, "symbolizes the sublime; Saint Anthony the picturesque; Minnehaha, the beautiful. The fall is about sixty feet, presenting a parabolic curve, which drops, without the least deviation, until it has reached its lower level, when the stream goes on its way rejoicing, curling along in laughing, childish glee, at the graceful feat it has performed in bounding over the precipice."

Following up this stream to the westward,

one comes to a group of beautiful lakes, with pebbly shores, and well stocked with fine fish. Lake Calhoun and Lake Harriet are of this group, and still farther to the west, Lake *Minnetan'ka*, the largest of them all, as its name imports, *Lake Great Water.*

The party of Dr. Williamson started up the Minnesota River from Fort Snelling, in a Mackinaw boat, on the 22d of June, and reached Traverse des Sioux eight days after. At this point they exchanged their mode of conveyance, going from there to Lacquiparle in wagons, a distance of one hundred and twenty-five miles across the broad prairies. They reached the end of their journey on the ninth of July.

Prairie travelling is at once pleasant and fatiguing. Properly equipped, with a good tent and bedding, and necessary provisions, and favored with pleasant weather, one heartily enjoys a week or so, on the great green meadows of the West. But with all its green and blue and gold, the prairie gets to be an old story. The little elevations and depressions are just such as you have seen a hundred times before, and you begin to wish for something different from simple beauty. Then, too, the sun shines out with unwonted force. It blazes and scratches and blisters, and you begin to long for "the shadow of a great rock in a weary land." But the evening comes with its busy camping scenes; and when supper and the evening song and prayer are over, you lie down and wrap your robe around you, saying, "Blessed be night!"

Lacquiparle is the *Lake that speaks.* It was supposed to be the translation into French of the Dakota name, *Mdaeyadan.* But no *echo* is discovered there, and tradition tells of no *Indian talk* which should have given a name to the lake. The French were probably mistaken in the meaning of the Dakota name. It is the *Lake that connects* the Minnesota above and below, being in fact only a spreading out of the stream, about nine miles long and less than one wide.

"Mr. Joseph Renville, the gentleman engaged in the fur trade at Lacquiparle, very kindly furnished a comfortable temporary shelter for the mission families, and a small school of seven or eight scholars was commenced immediately."

In the summer of 1837, Mr. and Mrs. Riggs joined the mission.

They were married in February, and, proceeding westward in the opening spring, reached Fort Snelling about the first of June. Not being able to proceed farther at that time, they remained three months at Lake Harriet, and reached Lacquiparle about the middle of September.

Shortly after their arrival, the marriage of Mr. Gideon H. Pond and Miss Sarah Poage took place. Some time previous to this, the Messrs. Pond had abandoned their cabin on Lake Calhoun, Samuel making his home at Lake Harriet, and Gideon at Lacquiparle. On the occasion of his marriage, Mr. Pond endeavored to carry out the injunction of Christ, "When thou makest a dinner or a supper, call not thy friends, nor thy brethren, neither thy kinsman, nor rich neighbors: But when thou makest a feast, call the poor, the maimed, the lame, the blind." It was a gathering of poorly-clad, gray-headed, limping Dakotas, many of them almost blind. "Thou shalt be blessed; for they cannot recompense thee."

A Christian church had been organized at Lacquiparle, early in the year 1836, which, at the time Mr. and Mrs. Riggs joined the station, numbered seven persons. During the winter following, nine others were received on examination; so that under date of May, 1838, Dr. Williamson wrote: "The whole number of native communicants now at this station, is sixteen; of these one half are full Dakota women, and in the others the Dakota blood greatly preponderates."

CHAPTER VIII.

1836–1844.

PERILS BY THE HEATHEN.

Winter Journey of Mr. S. W. Pond to Lacquiparle. — Travels on foot. — Deep snows. — Indian camps. — Reaches Traverse des Sioux. — Stops with LeBlanc. — The old man's accounts. — Comes to Little Rock with Canadians. — Travels without food. — Scarcity at Mr. Moer's. — Ma'-ma his guide to Lacquiparle. — Provisions eaten up. — More snow-storms. — Ma'-ma's eyes become sore. — He refuses to go on. — Mr. Pond's eyes sore. — He puts snow on them. — Deeper snows. — Blowing snow. — They wander. — Five days without food. — Mr. Pond sick. — Suffering for water. — Ma'-ma ugly. — Mr. Pond apprehensive. — He leaves his guide. — He finds a horse and reaches the mission. — Another experience. — Mission party. — Signs of enemies. — Hastening to the river. — A war-party seen. — Two men killed. — Great excitement. — A horse shot. — Hard walk. — Sleepy Eyes' horse. — His nephew shoots it. — The whizzing arrow. — The guard-house. — Young man released. — Nice venison hams.

"*In perils by the heathen; in weariness and painfulness; in hunger and thirst.*"

In the winter of 1835–6, while the brothers Pond still resided at Lake Harriet, near Fort Snelling, it was thought necessary that the elder brother, Rev. S. W. Pond, should make a journey to Lacquiparle. The distance was about two hundred miles. Between the stations there were trading posts at three places on the Minnesota, — Little Rapids, Traverse des Sioux, and Little Rock.

As the snow was quite deep, the journey must be made on foot. Mr. Pond knew nothing of the country except what he had learned from Indians. The summer road was a well-beaten track; but it crossed wide prairies, and was now covered with snow. It was on a Friday, in the latter part of February, that he strapped his buffalo-robe and blanket on his back, with a loaf of bread for provisions, and started for Lake Harriet with a company of Indians, who were going a short distance up the country to hunt.

The weather was intensely cold. The first night they camped a few miles "below where Shakopee now stands; but it was too cold to sleep much." The next morning,

Mr. Pond started in advance, with an Indian man, to kindle a fire for the party at a point of wood. When they came up, "the women were wailing, and the children crying" on account of the cold. That night Mr. Pond found he had frozen his face somewhat. They reached the Little Rapids, a trading post occupied by Mr. Ferribault, where they all stopped over the Sabbath.

On Monday, they reached the Big Woods, between Belle Plaine and Le Seuer, when Mr. Pond left the party and went on to Traverse des Sioux. He was kindly received and entertained by Mr. Philander Prescott, one of the traders at that place. On the other side of the Minnesota, was the post of Mr. Provencalle, who was generally called Le Blanc.

This man, Le Blanc, was a Canadian Frenchman, "who had spent the most of his life among the Dakota Indians, but was as polite as if he had always lived in Paris. He could neither read nor write, and yet kept his accounts in black and white." With him Mr. Pond spent a day; and when the old gentleman learned that he could write the Dakota language, he desired him to write the names of his Indian debtors in his account-book. He had kept his accounts altogether by signs, "some of which were easily understood. A cluster of dots represented powder, and the straight marks in the margin showed the number of pounds or cups of powder the hunter had received. For an axe, gun, trap, or knife, he made a picture of the article. The pictures were a little rude, but easily recognized. But the old man, with all his ingenuity, could not overcome the difficulty he met with in attempting to write many of the names of his customers. Some gave him no trouble. For 'Eagle Head' he could make the picture of a man with the head of an eagle. But how could he make a picture of *Whistling-Wind*, *Iron-Lightning*, *Spirit-Walker*, *Thunder-Face*, and other such fancy names common among the Dakotas?" Mr. Pond was "much amused at some of the strange figures he had contrived, in his attempt to make the likeness of things that are neither in the heaven above, nor in the earth beneath, nor in the waters under the earth."

The distance to Little Rock was fifty miles. Two Canadians had come down from there for corn. "They had a horse and *train*, which is a long, wide board, bent up at the forward end, so that when the snow is hard it slides beautifully. The load is lashed on with cords." Mr. Pond proposed to accompany them on their return. So, on Friday, they started, Mrs. Prescott having furnished him with a loaf of bread, which would have been quite sufficient for himself alone; but at noon he found that his companions in the voyage had nothing with them but raw corn. Sharing his bread with them, he trusted to sharing with them afterwards, but was disappointed.

At night, he went to sleep before the corn was boiled, and it was hard frozen the next morning; so they started on without eating. About noon, the horse gave out, and the men prepared to camp. But the next day was the sabbath, and Mr. Pond hurried on to Mr. Moer's, at Little Rock. The trader's family he found entirely without food, expecting the corn from below. He could, however, obtain a few quarts of very choice seed-corn from a Frenchman, which, under other circumstances, could not be eaten. But a hungry white man coming, the corn must be ground in a hand-mill and baked into a cake. Mr. Pond says: "This by no means satisfied us. I saw hickory chips which had been boiled to get nourishment from them."

Towards evening of the sabbath, the Frenchmen arrived with the corn, and some Indians came in with musk-rats, so they had "corn and musk-rats" for supper. In the evening, a young man came and danced the *bear dance.* "His dancing did not please me," Mr. Pond wrote, "as well as the dancing of Herodias pleased Herod; but I mention it because he became my companion to Lacquiparle. His name was *Ma'-ma.* He wanted to go to Lacquiparle; was well acquainted with the country, he said, and would be my guide."

So Mr. Pond agreed to give him a blanket when they reached Lacquiparle, if he would carry his buffalo-robe for him, and make the camp-fires. It was eighty or ninety miles to Lacquiparle. Mrs. Moer furnished each of them with a small corn cake; and the Indian had a gun, with which it was supposed he might kill some game. Monday morning they started; and although the snow was deep, they reached Beaver Creek, where they camped that night. Ma′-ma ate up his corn cake that evening; and Mr. Pond, knowing that if he should reserve a part of his he would be expected to share it, profited by the example, and ate his up also, which, he says, "was not difficult."

The next day, about noon, Ma′-ma was suddenly attacked with inflammation of the eyes, caused by the light reflected from the snow. It was with difficulty that Mr. Pond induced him to proceed farther; but, finally, they did reach Hawk River, which the Indian said was the Chippewa. As the mouth of the Chippewa is not more than ten miles from the mission station at Lacquiparle, Mr. Pond began to suspect, what he afterwards found out certainly, that his guide knew nothing about the country. Soon after encamping, Mr. Pond was attacked with severe pain in his eyes; but, following the advice of Mr. Moer, he lay down on his back and applied snow to them until the pain ceased, and he was troubled no more with snow-blindness. Ma'-ma had before refused to do this, but when he saw its good effects on Mr. Pond's eyes, he was willing to adopt the same remedy.

That night, it snowed, and put out their camp-fire. In the morning, it was still snowing; but as they had no food, they started on, the guide going before. But, before long, they came to the same stream which they had left in the morning. The Indian acknowledged that he did not know where they were, nor which way to go. So they concluded to stop until the storm was over, rather than weary themselves out in travelling around in the deep snow. The

Minnesota River was not far from them, but they did not know it; and the Indian insisted that it was a great ways off. There they made a fire and sat down by it, having wrapped their blankets around them, and hoped for the abatement of the storm. That night the falling snow ceased, but the wind arose, and the next day the snow was blowing so furiously that travelling was impossible.

"Under such circumstances," Mr. Pond writes, "we could do nothing better than to keep wrapped up in our blankets, sit still, and meditate. And the meditations of Ma′-ma were not very sweet. He had none of that sagacity and fortitude so common to the Indians, and, indeed, none of their good qualities, but bad ones in abundance. He was bewildered and stupefied most of the time; was sure we should die; and laid all the blame on me, because I had ventured on such a hazardous journey. I tried to encourage him, and, sometimes, he would be comforted, and say he was glad I kept up such good spirits."

During the storm, Mr. Pond took a cold, and, on Thursday, "felt very weak," which he attributed to sickness rather than being without food. Their fire burnt low, and their stock of fuel was exhausted. The Indian refused to make any effort to get wood; but a little while before dark, Mr. Pond took his hatchet, and threw the robe off of his guide, and told him to start. Thus, they obtained fuel for the night.

Friday morning was clear and pleasant, and they proposed to start; but Ma′-ma declared he would go back, and only consented to go forward on condition that Mr. Pond would walk before and break a path. The Indian, however, soon passed Mr. Pond, who was obliged, from weakness, to sit down frequently and rest. He supposed his guide had gone on and left him, but about noon he overtook him. They were now in sight of the Minnesota River, but Ma′-ma declared it was not the Minnesota at all, and he would follow it no longer.

There they built a fire and remained over night. Mr. Pond says: "During that day and night I suffered more from thirst than from hunger. I tried to cut a hole in the ice of the river, but it was very thick; and, after working some time, I desisted, for I thought I might need my strength more for something else. That night each of us slept, if we slept at all, with one eye open. I knew that my companion was very much afraid he should starve to death, and could save his life by taking mine. I knew, too, that he was not too good to do it, and could with perfect safety; for the wolves would soon have finished what he left, leaving no trace that I had been murdered. He had a gun, and I only a hatchet, so that I seemed to be in his power; but his gun was not in very good order, and I suppose he was afraid it might miss fire. I do not think he discovered that I was afraid of him; and I think he had some superstitious fear of me and my Bible.

"Saturday morning, he was very cross, and began to reload his gun as soon as it was daylight. He said he should go no farther. I said nothing. I did not expect to need a buffalo-robe, or a fire, any more on that journey. I had made up my mind to use what strength I had left; and thought if I did not reach Lacquiparle before dark, it would make little difference how or where I passed the night, for my journey would be at an end. I took only my blanket, and parted with my companion without regret. When I started, the river was straight for a hundred rods or more, and so far the Indian could see me. While in sight, I walked very slowly, for I wished to have him think he could overtake me when he pleased; but when I had passed the bend of the river, I quickened my pace. I had recovered from my indisposition, and felt better than I had done for two or three days before. Indeed, I was surprised to find I could walk so fast; for Thursday and Friday, I had supposed my strength was nearly exhausted. I had not gone far before I saw where a wolf had crossed the river and gone to the shore to drink. There I found a spring, and was much refreshed and strengthened by my draught of water. I drank again that day where I found snow melted by the sun in the hollow of a rock.

"That was the fifth day I had been without eating; yet my sufferings from hunger were not at all severe. I remember thinking that I had often suffered much more with the toothache. Neither were my mental sufferings very acute. I thought I should soon find Lacquiparle or Heaven.

"A little after noon, I found a good sized stream coming in from the north, which I thought must be Ma′-ya-wa-kan′, or Chippewa. Mr. Moer had told me that it was only three miles from that river to Lacquiparle. I ascended the bluff, expecting to see the lake before me; but, though I could see more than three miles, no lake was in sight. Now I felt more discouraged than I had done at any time before. I had walked that forenoon, through the deep snow, much of the way following the bends of the river, from near the mouth of the Yellow Medicine to the mouth of the Ma′-ya-wa-kan′, and my strength was nearly exhausted.

"While I stood undetermined what to do next, I espied two horses on the river bottom below me. At first I was undecided whether to try to catch them. It was much easier walking on the bluff than by the river. It had cost me great labor to climb the hill; and if I attempted to catch the horses and failed, I should not only lose precious time, but waste my strength, of which I had none to spare. However, I decided to try the horses. One was a large horse, with a rope around his neck; the other, a colt a year or two old. When I approached them, they made off at first; but when I gathered a handful of the tall dead grass which was sticking up through the snow, and held it out to them, they stopped, and I soon caught the large one. I threw my blanket on him, and jumped on myself.

"The change in my circumstances was very great and very sudden. I had a powerful horse under me, and another that I determined to kill, if I did not find other food before night. I contrived a way to kill him; but there was no need of it. My horse was strong and fleet, and carried me up the river at a good round gallop. Six or seven miles from where I caught him, I found food and shelter, and some of the best friends I ever knew, at the house of Alexander G. Huggins, who has since gone to a better country. Mrs. Huggins dealt with me wisely and kindly; so that I experienced no ill effects from overeating, after my long fast."

Several years later, there was another experience of danger, which may fitly be brought into this connection.

It was a very warm day in the month of June, 1843, when a party of missionaries approached the Ma′-ya-wa-kan′, or Chippewa River, a stream which the old cart trail crossed about five miles from the Lacqui-parle mission. This party consisted of Mr.

and Mrs. Hopkins, who were on their way to reside at that station for a season, and Mrs. Riggs, who was going up to bring down her little Bella, who had been left with mission friends a year before. There were with them, also, the three Dakota young men, who had spent a year in Ohio, and were now returning to their friends. These were Lorenzo Lawrence, Henok, and Simon Big Frenchman. The party had camped at Hawk River, one day's journey from Lacquiparle, on Saturday evening, and spent the sabbath. Very early Monday morning, Lorenzo and Henok started on in advance of the party, and, reaching Lacquiparle early in the day, made known the approach of the others. Upon hearing this, two men, — one of them a brother and the other a near relative of Simon, — together with the wife of one of them, went to meet him.

During the morning, some of the party observed a strange appearance on the top of a small hill some distance off. It was like Indians lying flat on the ground, covered with blankets. But it soon disappeared. No one thought of an enemy watching for scalps. When they were approaching the Chippewa, they were suddenly startled by the report of guns down in the valley. Two Dakota boys, who were of the party, and were hastening to the river for water, came running back, pale with fright, and said, "We have seen Ojibwas!" The sun was blazing down on that broad prairie; the oxen were panting slowly along, lolling their tongues; and all were suffering with thirst; but all that was forgotten, when suddenly there came in sight a party of eighteen or twenty Indians, passing up the river to their right. It was a war-party of Ojibwas. Simon, who was on horseback, and some distance in the advance, met them as they emerged from the wood of the stream, and, being dressed as a white man, he rode immediately up and shook hands with them: whereupon they showed him *two fresh scalps*, one of which was *his own brother's!*

The mission party had no sooner crossed the stream, than they came upon the bodies of the recently murdered men; and not seeing what else they could do then, they threw a wagon-cover over them, and went on. They had gone but a little distance, when they saw the hill before them thronged with Indians, some on horseback and some on foot, armed with guns and bows, — the men whooping and yelling, the women screeching and wailing, and all greatly infuriated.*

* A party of Indians on the war-path is like a bear robbed of her whelps. Commonly, they regard neither property nor life. But in the early years of the mission, Mr. G. H. Pond had a different experience. He and a single Frenchman were taking up to Lacqui-

The Dakota woman, who was a little behind her husband and his friend when they were killed, escaped, and carried back the word to the Indian village. And now, in the estimation of these excited men, the mission party were to be blamed for these murders. Had not the missionaries taken these young men to Ohio? And were not these men killed as they were coming out

---

parle two carts loaded with the winter supplies for the mission. He had camped on the prairie, not far from the present site of Fort Ridgley, where he was overtaken by a war-party of forty or more Dakotas. They filed in and encamped near by. They had nothing to eat, and asked Mr. Pond for provisions. He had already made up his mind that he could not furnish such a company. They said they would dance to him; but he persisted in his refusal. He was afraid of them, and expected they would seize what they wanted; but he took care not to show his fear.

Thus they lay down hungry, and slept; and Mr Pond left camp before daylight the next morning. When they waked, they took the same road he had gone, and all passed him before noon, but did not molest him. He regarded their conduct as very extraordinary.

to meet them? Satisfied with this reasoning, one man drew up his gun and shot one of the horses in the wagon. He would have killed an ox also, but was prevented by his sister.

Mrs. Riggs, carrying her baby daughter of seventeen months, and Mrs. Hopkins, walked the remaining four miles to the mission under a burning sun. Their fears were quelled by recalling and repeating, as they walked, the precious injunction, "Fear not, little flock; for it is your Father's good pleasure to give you the kingdom." But the intense heat and excitement made the walk very exhausting. "It seemed," said Mrs. Riggs, "as though we had spent the strength of years in one half day."

It was about midwinter of 1845, when Sleepy Eyes came in from Swan Lake to the Traverse, and placed his horse for the night at the mission haystack, while he himself went to sleep at the trader's. In the evening, before we had retired to rest, several persons were heard going in haste past the door towards the stable. The writer went out to see what was going on, and found there a woman and two men; one of the latter was shooting arrows into Sleepy Eyes' horse. I asked why they were doing that, and begged them to stop. The young man said he was only shooting his uncle's horse!

The mischief was done, and the party started to go home; but just as I stepped into the porch an arrow came whizzing by. It did no damage, whether so meant or not. The next morning that young fellow started down to Saint Paul to obtain "spirit water;" but the report of what he had done went before him, and when he reached the neighborhood of Fort Snelling, he was met by a file of soldiers, who conducted him to the guard-house. After some weeks, I went down with *Big-Walker*, who was a relative of the young man, to obtain his release. Before the agent and officers of the garrison, he promised to keep the peace, and signed a pledge to drink no more spirit water, and was then permitted to accompany us home. The fellow was grateful for his release. He went immediately up to the region of the Blue Earth to hunt deer, and soon brought two nice venison hams to the mission.

Thus made a mark for the Indian arrow, and sometimes chased by the scalping-knife in the hands of a drunken man, we have realized the gracious fulfilment of the promise, "Thou shalt not be afraid for the terror by night, nor for the arrow that flieth by day."

CHAPTER IX.

1838–1849.

EARLY LABORS.

Success of the first years. — Lacquiparle church to 1843. — The Spirit's witness. — The reaction. — Spirit water. — New stations. — Kapo′-sia and Prairieville. — Indians more reasonable. — Encouragements. — More laborers. — Mr. Adams, Mr. Aiton, Mr. Hancock, and Mr. Potter.

"*Lo! I am with you alway, even unto the end of the world.*"

"*With us when we toil in sadness,*
Sowing much and reaping none;
Telling us that in the future,
Golden harvests shall be won."

"THE Lord has opened to us a wide and effectual door among this heathen people. In the early part of the winter, the prospect was very encouraging. There was a greater anxiety to receive instruction than we had before seen. In one woman we were particularly interested. She came often to our room, wishing to know more about the Great Spirit. She wanted to know how to pray. I said to her once, 'When you want any thing from us, you know how to ask for it. So, if you wish God to give you any thing, ask him in the same way. God knows the Dakota language much better than we do, and he will hear and answer you.' She seemed surprised to know that this was prayer." "At our last communion, in February, ten Dakota women united with the church by profession. I baptized them," says Mr. Riggs, "together with eighteen of their children, at the same time."

This record was made at Lacquiparle in March, 1839. And, passing on two years, we find Dr. Williamson saying, "You will rejoice to know that the manifestations of the Lord's loving kindness and tender mercies are not diminished towards us." And then follows a summary of the results of the mission work, in establishing a church at Lacquiparle: "In the year ending May

1836, three persons were received to the church on examination; in the following year, four; and in the next year, nine; ten in the year ending May, 1839; in the next year, five; and in that ending in the spring of 1841, nine: making forty in all." Of these, two had been suspended, one had died, and three had been dismissed to join other churches; leaving, at the end of six years, a church at Lacquiparle of thirty-four members. It is safe to say, that, up to this time, few missions of the heathen had been more prosperous than the Dakota mission. And the seventh year was not less successful than the first six. In May, 1842, it was recorded: "Within a year, nine full-blooded Dakotas have been received to the church — three men and six women." And as an evidence of the Spirit's teachings in these dark minds, one writes: "We hear our native members using, in prayer, many expressions of religious experience found in the Prophets and the Psalms, not yet translated into their language."

Before this, even those who had learned to read had access to only a very small portion of God's Word. So that those who had professed faith in Christ were far from being grounded and built up in the knowledge of the Truth. They were still babes. And although during the years 1842 and 1843, a large part of the New Testament and some portions of the Old were printed in the Dakota language, the Word, thus made somewhat accessible to them, must wait until after years to do its work upon, and in them.

The time had come, in the providence of God, when the faith of the missionaries was to be tried, and the religious character of the converts tested. During the first years of the mission, there was comparatively little opposition manifested to the new religion. The people did not understand it. The so-called medicine men and the war-prophets were not aware that it was antagonistic to their ancestral faith. But, about this time they appeared to wake up to some understanding of the situation. A period of drouth was now experienced in the valley of the Minnesota. In 1842, and the years immediately following, the corn crop at Lacquiparle was a partial failure. This of necessity scattered the members of the church. A number went down to their friends living on the Mississippi, and did not return again. In the meantime, the introduction of "spirit water" all over the country, caused many to stumble and fall. Some of these cases of lapsing are recorded in other parts of this book. All through these years, there were many things to discourage the missionaries. But their hope was still in God, and they meditated a more extensive occupation of the field.

In 1846, Mr. S. W. Pond wrote from Oak Grove: "If the neighboring villages could be occupied, there would be more hope of doing good here."* Others thought that the opposition of the villages, where there was no mission, should by some means be counteracted.

In the autumn of 1846, at a meeting of the mission held at Traverse des Sioux, several important changes were decided upon. Dr. Williamson, on the invitation of the Indians, removed his family from Lacqui-parle to Kapo′-sia to commence a new station. Mr. Riggs and family went back to

* The Lake Calhoun band of Dakotas removed over to the Minnesota, about eight miles from Fort Snelling. The Lake Harriet station was consequently removed, and was occupied as Oak Grove by the brothers Pond from 1843. Mr. G. H. Pond still remains at the same place, having built up a church there among white people.

Lacquiparle, and Mr. Huggins removed to Traverse des Sioux to be associated with Mr. Hopkins.

About the same time, Mr. S. W. Pond received an invitation to settle at Shak-o-pee′, which he accepted; and the next year he put up a house, and removed his family thither, calling his station Prairieville, a translation of *Tin′-ta-ton′-we*, the Dakota name of the village. These changes left Mr. Robert Hopkins and Mr. G. H. Pond in charge of *Traverse des Sioux* and *Oak Grove.* Both these brethren, in connection with learning to speak the Dakota language, had been for several years pursuing a course of biblical and theological studies preparatory to preaching the gospel. They were licensed by the Dakota Presbytery, in May 1847, and ordained in the autumn of 1848, when the mission met at Kapo′-sia.

These, changes in the mission operated

favorably upon the Indians, in showing them that the missionaries could leave, if they thought it best to do so. At Laquiparle, a year after, Mr. Riggs wrote: "A uniformly good understanding has existed between the Indians and the mission since our arrival last fall. It was my intention from the first, to have them understand that my family were not so identified with this station, as to remain long in the face of any considerable manifestations of opposition. Our wood and our water must be free; our cattle and other property must be considered sacred; and our work of teaching and preaching the gospel must not be interfered with by the chiefs and soldiers."

About this time things began to assume a more favorable aspect in the mission. The dry seasons had passed by, and the corn crops were good again. Besides, for two years, buffaloes were abundant in the neighborhood of Lacquiparle. In the winter of 1847–8, the Indians were encamped about sixteen miles from the station, on the Pomme de Terre. Mr. Riggs spent every alternate sabbath at the camp. "Generally, I have succeeded," he wrote, "in securing a good attendance. Often as many as thirty have been present in a tent, and no more could well crowd in." At Traverse des Sioux, Mr. Hopkins wrote: "The average attendance on the sabbath service is about eleven." Several members of the Lacquiparle church had removed to Kapo′-sia, and they, with others who attended, made an interesting religious congregation. At Oak Grove, "two Christian women" are spoken of; and there was "less intemperance" than in previous years. Some men had even signed "the pledge of abstinence for a limited period." Thus, both the present opposition in many places, and the promise of a larger harvest in the future, seemed to call for a reinforcement of laborers.

In the Annual Report of the Board for 1848, it is said: "The Committee have been impressed with the desirableness of strengthening the missions; and they have accordingly designated two ordained missionaries, with their wives, to this field." They were the Rev. M. N. Adams and Rev. John F. Aiton. The former joined the station at Lacquiparle, and the latter commenced a station at Red Wing, formerly occupied by Rev. Messrs. Gavin and Denton of the Swiss mission. The Dakota name of this place was "*He-minne'-chan*"—literally, "Hill-water-wood," which very finely describes the peculiar wooded hill which stands out in the river just below the steamboat landing, at the present town of Red Wing. The next spring Mr. Joseph W. Hancock, from Saratoga Springs, N.Y., and his wife, were associated with Mr. Aiton at this station. In addition to the new men already mentioned, Rev. Joshua Potter and wife, with Miss Edwards, were transferred from the Choctaw to the Dakota mission. They came in the fall of 1849, and stopped for a year or so at Traverse des Sioux.

CHAPTER X.

JOSEPH RENVILLE.

1779-1846.

His childhood. — Taken to Canada. — Paddles his own canoe. — Interpreter for Gen. Pike. — Pike's letter to Wilkinson. — Renville a captain in the British army. — A trader of the Hudson's Bay company. — Transferred to the American. — His character, by Rev. E. D. Neill. — The tribute of Nicollet. — His connection with the mission at Lacquiparle as interpreter and translator. — Mr. Renville's hymns. — His translations of Mark and John. — Process of translation. — Tribute of Dr. Williamson. — Mr. Renville's French Bible. — Mrs. Renville. — Her profession of faith. — Her Christian death. — Mr. Renville a ruling elder. — His sickness and death. — Dr. Williamson's account of it. — His son Joseph

---

" For him that overcometh are
The new name written on the stone,
The raiment white, the crown, the throne;
And ' I uill give to him the morning star.' "

In the effort to plant the gospel among the Dakotas, the mission owed much of its success to the continuance and active co-operation of Mr. Joseph Renville, of Lacquiparle. It is, therefore, proper that a somewhat extended notice of him should here be given.

He was of mixed descent, his father having been a French trader of some reputation, and his mother a Dakota connected with the principal families of the Kapo′-sia band. His own story was, that he was born on the Mississippi River, a few miles below the town of Saint Paul, about the year 1779. His childhood was passed in the wigwam of his mother, who, as often happens, deserted her husband and went to live with one of her own blood.

The father, observing the activity of his son, took him to Canada when he was about ten years of age, and placed him under the care and instruction of a Romish priest. His instructor appears to have been both a kind and good man; and from him he received a knowledge of the French language, and the elements of the Christian religion. Before he had attained to manhood, he was brought back to Dakota land,

and was called to mourn the death of his father.

At that time, there was living in the country of the Dakotas, as the head of an English fur company, a British officer, by the name of Dickson. He, knowing that young Renville was energetic, employed him as a "voyager," or "runner." While a mere stripling, he paddled his canoe from the Falls of Poke′guma to the Falls of Saint Anthony, and followed the Indian trails from Mendo′ta to the Missouri. He distinguished himself as a "brave," and also, following in the footsteps of his father, became more fully identified with the Dakota people by purchasing a wife of the royal family, of which Little Crow was afterwards the representative.

The late Gen. Pike, of the U.S.A., then lieutenant, was introduced to Renville at Prairie du Chien, and was conducted by him to the Falls of Saint Anthony. This officer was pleased with him, and sought his appointment for the post of United States Interpreter. In a letter to Gen. Wilkinson, written at Mendo'ta, September 9, 1805, he says: "I beg leave to recommend for that appointment a Mr. Joseph Rénville, who has served as interpreter for the Sioux, last spring, at the Illinois River, and who has gratuitously and willingly served as my interpreter in all my conferences with the Sioux. He is a man respected by the Indians, and, I believe, an honest one."

"At the breaking out of the last war with Great Britain, Col. Dickson was employed by that government to hire the warlike tribes of the North-West to fight against the United States. From him Renville received the appointment of captain in the British army; and with Dakota warriors he marched to the American frontier." *

* "History of Minnesota by Rev. E. D. Neill."

After the war was over, we find him occupying a trading post at Lake Traverse, and receiving his goods from the Columbia Fur Company. This was about the year 1822. Fort Snelling was now being built, and occupied as a garrison; and, shortly after, the American Fur Company, of which John Jacob Astor was the head, not wishing any rivals in the trade, purchased the posts and good will of the other company, and retained their employees. Under this new arrangement Mr. Renville removed to Lacquiparle, and erected a trading house, inclosed by a stockade, in accordance with the custom of the times; and here he resided until his death.

Living, as he did, for more than half a century among the Dakotas, over whom he exercised the most unbounded control, it is not surprising that, in his advanced age, he sometimes exhibited a domineering disposition. But, as long as Minnesota exists, he should be remembered as one given to hospitality. He invariably showed himself to be a friend to the Indian, the traveller, and the missionary. Aware of the improvidence of his mother's race, he used his influence towards the raising of grain. He was instrumental in having the first corn planted on the Upper Minnesota. An Indian never left his house hungry, and they delighted to do him honor. He was a friend to the traveller. His conversation was intelligent, and he always communicated facts that were worthy of record. His post obtained a reputation among explorers, and their last day's journey to it was generally a quick march, for they felt sure of a friendly welcome. His eldest son, in 1837, was the interpreter and guide of Nicollet, that worthy man of science, who explored the country of the Dakotas in connection with Fremont. This gentleman, in his report to Congress, pays the following tribute to the father and son: —

"I may stop awhile to say, that the residence of the Renville family, for a number of years back, has afforded the only retreat to travellers to be found between Fort Snelling and the British posts, a distance of seven hundred miles. The liberal and untiring hospitality dispensed by this respectable family, the great influence exercised by it over the Indians of this country, in the maintainance of peace and the protection of travellers, demands, besides our gratitude, some special acknowledgment of the United States, and also from the Hudson's Bay Company."*

But, what is most worthy of record here, Mr. Renville was a friend to the missionary.

* For the gathering of much that is interesting in the early life of Mr. Renville, the author is indebted to "The History of Minnesota, by Rev. E. D. Neill."

The welcome which he gave to Dr. Williamson and party, has already been spoken of. "Upon the arrival of the missionaries at Lacquiparle, he provided them with a temporary home. He acted as interpreter; he assisted in translating the Scriptures; and removed many of the prejudices of the Indians against the teachers of the white man's religion."

In the Dakota Hymn-Book, prepared by the mission, and containing nearly one hundred and fifty hymns, twelve were composed by Mr. Renville. These were among the earliest hymns sung by the Dakota church; and a number of them deservedly continue to this day, the most popular, as they are the most expressive representations of song-worship. These hymns were generally set to French airs, which Mr. Renville and his family had learned from the "voyagers."

But the best work which he did for his

people, was the translation from the French of the Gospels of Mark and John. Very soon after the Lacquiparle station was occupied, in the summer of 1835, Dr. Williamson commenced holding religious meetings with the Dakotas. In the preparation for these services his plan was to obtain through Mr. Renville a translation of a chapter, or a part of a chapter from the Bible, to which he appended some explanatory remarks. The latter were written in French and all read to Mr. Renville, sentence by sentence, and written down as he gave the corresponding sentences in Dakota. Thus, besides the gospels already mentioned, a translation was obtained of a number of the Psalms and other portions of the Word of God. These were, at the time, invaluable to the members of the mission, not only as the means of giving religious instruction to the natives, but as affording them a better opportunity of learning the Dakota language than they could have had in any other way.

The writer joined this little group of translators in the autumn of 1837. It usually consisted of Mr. Renville, who sat in a chair in the middle of his own reception room, in which there was at one end an open fireplace with a large blazing fire, and Dr. Williamson, Mr. G. H. Pond, and myself, seated at a side-table with our writing materials before us. When all were ready, Dr. Williamson read a verse from the French Bible. This, Mr. Renville, usually with great readiness, repeated in the Dakota language. We wrote it down from his mouth. If the sentence was too long for us to remember, Mr. Renville repeated it. When the verse was written, some one read it over, and it was corrected; and then we passed to another, and so on to the end of the chapter. Translation-day did not often come more than once a week. That winter, the Gospel of Mark was finished, and printed in the following year. The translation of John was completed in 1841, and printed with other portions of Scripture in 1842.

The following tribute to his ability as a translator and interpreter, from the pen of Dr. Williamson, appeared in the Missionary Herald of 1846;—

"Mr. Renville was a remarkable man, and he was remarkable for the energy with which he pursued such objects as he deemed of primary importance. His power of remembering facts, and also words expressive of simple ideas, was extraordinary. In translating, he seldom took a book in his hand, choosing to depend on hearing rather than sight; and I have often had occasion to observe that, after hearing a long and unfamiliar verse read from the

Scriptures, he would immediately render it from the French into Dakota, two languages extremely unlike in their idioms and ideas, and repeat it over, two or three words at a time, so as to give full opportunity to write them down. He also had a remarkable tact in discovering the meaning of a speaker, and conveying the intended impression, when many of the ideas and words were such as had nothing corresponding to them in the minds and language of those addressed. These qualities fitted him for an interpreter, and it was generally admitted that he had no equal."

Years before there was any clergyman in Minnesota, he took his Indian wife to Prairie du Chien, and was married, in accordance with Christian usage, by a priest of the Romish church. Before he became acquainted with missionaries, he sent for a large folio Bible in the French language, and requested his employers in the fur-trade to send him a clerk who could read it. This Bible was printed at Geneva, Switzerland, in the year 1588, and had a latin preface by John Calvin. It was probably the first Bible owned by a resident of the country which is now the State of Minnesota. Some years after his death, I procured it, at the instance of Rev. E. D. Neill, from one of Mr. Renville's sons, for the Historical Society of Minnesota; but it was unfortunately destroyed in the burning of the mission houses at Lacquiparle, in March, 1854. On account of its historical value, all regretted its loss.

Mrs. Renville was the first full Dakota that joined the church. She was also the first Dakota who died in the Christian faith. Before she had ever seen a teacher of our religion, through the instruction of her husband, she had renounced the gods of the

Dakotas. When drawing near her end, Mr. Renville said to her, "You seem to-day to be failing."—"Yes," she replied; "to-day God calls me. I am remembering Jesus Christ, who suffered for me, and depending upon him alone. To-day I shall stand before God, and will ask him for mercy for you, and for all my children and all my kinsfolk."

Afterwards, when all her children and relatives sat around her weeping, she said, "It is the holy day; sing and pray." So they sang and prayed. "From very early in the morning," the chronicle says, "she was speeking of God, and telling her family what to do." Thus she died, "when the clock struck two." Some months after her death, Mr. Renville had a young woman, of about twenty years, given to him by her relatives, whom he married.

In 1841 he was chosen and ordained a

ruling elder; and from that time till his death he discharged the duties of his office in a manner acceptable and profitable, both to the native members of the church and to the mission.

He appears to have been by mental constitution a Protestant, rather than a Romanist. Of an independent mind, he claimed and exercised the right of private judgment in matters of faith. He declared to a Romish priest, then a guest in his house, his belief in justification by faith alone, and in the right and privilege of all to read the Scriptures.

But in the month of March, 1846, his time came to be gathered to his fathers. After a short sickness, his frame, never very strong, but very elastic and enduring, began to give evidence of a speedy decay. He knew that he was soon to occupy "his chamber in the silent halls of death," but he also knew in whom he had believed.

The following account of the death scene was written by Dr. Williamson, and published in the *Missionary Herald* for that year: —

"The evening before his decease, he asked me what became of the soul immediately after death. I reminded him of our Saviour's words to the thief on the cross, and of Paul's desire to depart and be with Christ. He said, 'That is sufficient;' and presently added, 'I have great hope that I shall be saved through grace.' About eight o'clock the next morning, which was the Sabbath, I was called to see him. He was so evidently in the agonies of death, I did not think of attempting to do any thing for him. After some time, his breathing became easier, and he was asked if he wished to have a hymn sung. He replied, 'Yes;' and after the singing, said, 'It is very good.' As he reclined on the bed, I saw a sweet serenity settling on his countenance, and I thought that his severest struggle was probably past; and so it proved. When the clock struck ten, he looked at it and intimated that it was time for us to go to church. As we were about to leave, he extended to us his withered hand. When we were gone, he spoke some words of exhortation to his family, then prayed; and, before noon, calmly and quietly yielded up his spirit."

His descendants are still living among the Dakotas. The son, who bore his name, died February 8, 1856, in the neighborhood of the Hazelwood mission station. Soon after his death I sent the following communication to the "Saint Paul Daily Times:"—

"The deceased was about forty-seven years of age, a son of Joseph Renville, who died at Lacquiparle some years since, and whose memory is identified with the past history of Minnesota. Inheriting from his father many noble and generous qualities, unfortunately for himself and family, the habits of the Indian trade, in which he was educated, were not such as enabled him to gain a comfortable livelihood by labor. After the death of his father, he removed with his family to the Mississippi, and for several years resided at Kapo′-sia, with Little Crow's band, many of whom were his mother's relatives. Soon after the cession of the Minnesota country to the United States, he, with a younger brother, and cousin of the same family name, removed up to the neighborhood of Fort Ridgley. When they came to attend a payment at the Yellow Medicine, he was already far gone in the disease which has just terminated his earthly career. Here, in the house of a younger brother, and with other relations, he found a temporary home, and a place to die. Through the kindness of friends and neighbors, they have not wanted. It has been pleasant to see that former kindnesses received from the family, when his father was a prince in wealth among them, have not been entirely forgotten by the Dakotas, but have been returned now to the son in his last sickness."

Of the eight children of Mr. Joseph Renville, senior, six are still living: three sons and three daughters. Two of the latter married Frenchmen, and have, consequently, connected themselves with the Roman Catholic church. The other four are members of our mission churches. Of John Baptiste Renville, the youngest of the family, and Daniel Renville, son of the second Joseph, a notice will be found in the chapter on Evangelization. They are both popular and effective preachers of the gospel to their countrymen.

CHAPTER XI.

1836–1868.

BELIEVING WOMEN.

Among the Dakotas the idea of home is wanting. — Girls not welcomed in the family. — Wives purchased. — Women the burden-bearers. — Women raise the corn. — Hard lot in life. — This lot accepted by them. — Reasons why women were more ready to change their religion than men. — Christianized women. — Mrs. Renville. — Catharine. — Rebekah and Amanda. — Mrs. Pettijohn. — Mrs. Titus. — Sarah Hopkins. —Ha′-panna.— Ite′-wa-kan-hdi-win. — Na-wang′-ma-ne-win. — Jenny Simon.

"*No sweeter is the cup,*
Nor less our lot of ill;
'Twas tribulation ages since,
'Tis tribulation still."

THE Dakotas, like other unevangelized nations, have no word for *home*. Their nearest approach to it is in *tee-pee*, a house, and *wa-kay-ya*, a tent. Indeed, with no fixed habitation for the most part, and the family herding together very much like cattle, the idea of home is wanting.

This state of things indicates somewhat the condition of woman among them. She comes into the world under a species of protest, every Dakota parent desiring rather to have boys than girls. She grows up into a condition of servitude. By the common custom of the nation, a wife is purchased, her price not varying greatly from that of a good horse. This is the honorable way of obtaining a wife: all other ways are dishonorable. By this custom, authority over a woman and property in her are recognized. And the man, having bought his wife,—although the custom of the country does not permit him to sell her to another, and thus reimburse himself,—he may put her away or leave her at his pleasure. He may also whip or beat her; for she is his "money."

In the nomadic and hunter life of the Indian, a proper division of labor requires the woman to be the burden-bearer. In the morning, the man must take his gun and go in search of game for the day's food, and this makes it necessary that the wife should carry the tent to the next encampment. Then, the hunter has wearied himself in the chase, and is coming home laden with venison; the woman is glad to meet and relieve him of his load. Besides, he has waded through swamp and stream, and run through thicket and woods, and his leggins and moccasins are wet and worn; the good wife will take them off for him, and rub, dry, and mend them for the next day's hunt. And since the woman is employed more about the teepee than the man, cutting and carrying home the wood has naturally devolved upon her. In the first instance the little corn-patch comes in simply as the supplement of the chase, and belongs to the woman's department. These divisions of labor, originating in necessity, become confirmed by custom; and when the corn-patch, which at first only gave food to the family for a month, grows into a larger field, furnishing provisions for much of the year, it is still cultivated with the hoe of the woman, while the man lounges around the teepee, or engages in playing ball or shooting the plum stones. It is not to be concealed nor denied that the lot of Dakota women is hard, even when compared with that of the men. And it is not strange that with such burdens of life they become prematurely old and haggard.

Do they desire to be relieved from these burdens? And will they welcome a higher civilization and the hopes of a better life, through the gospel of our Lord Jesus Christ? Hard as their present life is, even forcing them in many cases to commit suicide, they do not seem to be aware that there is any thing wrong in the customs of society by which these burdens are laid upon them. Indeed the Dakota woman feels it to be her privilege as well as duty to work out life on this line. She is doing no works of supererogation. It is right that she should cut the wood, and hoe and harvest the corn, and wait upon her husband. And among them an honest emulation often springs up, as to which one shall carry the heaviest burden, accumulate the largest pile of wood, dress the greatest number of robes, or raise the largest amount of corn.

It was not, therefore, with the expectation that thereby they would be eased of this life's burdens, that the Dakota women were found more ready to receive the gospel than the men. Condition had something to do with it, doubtless. Reverence previously developed had some influence in this direction. Besides, there were fewer obstacles in the way of the women. If a woman changed her religion and her gods, no one cared very much. It was "only a woman." In the estimation of the men, the national religion would not suffer much, if a few women abandoned it and embraced the faith of the gospel. Furthermore, while the internal change wrought by the Holy Spirit in the heart must be much the same, whether in a man or woman, the external change required in the former was not only different but greater than in the latter. The woman works already. It will not damage her to keep her house, and her person, and her children neater than when she was a pagan. There seemed to be no absolute necessity that she should change the fashion of her dress. It was not unseemly. Rather was it convenient and economical. So that if she kept herself from idols and from fornication, she did well.

If, however, a Dakota man became a Christian, he must not only abandon his ancestral faith, which bound him more strongly than the woman, for the very reason that he was a man, and had been inducted into manhood through the ceremonies of his religion, and must give up his liberty to have more wives than one; but it very soon came to be understood that the new doctrine required him to cut off his long hair, and to change his style of dress, which was not decent, and to go to work like a civilized and Christian man. And all this the gods forbade. He would do it at the peril of their displeasure. The *wakan'* men also forbade it, and to prevent it used all their power of bad medicine and all their arts of sorcery. So it was that in the first years of the Dakota mission, with the exception of two or three men of mixed blood, the church was composed of Dakota women alone.

In the remainder of this chapter, the reader will be introduced to individual characters, in whose life may be seen the power of the gospel to mould and elevate.

Next to Mrs. Renville, Catharine deserves to be mentioned. She was one of the first who joined the church from the Dakota village. Her name was *To-tee-doo'-ta-win*, or *Her Scarlet House woman.* Her husband had two wives. And as she was the one last taken, when she learned that polygamy was contrary to the ordinance of God, she at once said that she willing to be put away by her husband. She had been a member of the Order of the Sacred Dance; but on professing faith in Christ, she renounced that, and threw away her "medicine sack," which was regarded, by the medicine men, as a high crime. This subjected her to divers sorts of persecutions, which she bore patiently. There were times when all were forbidden to attend public worship at the mission. Then Catharine took joyfully the spoiling of her goods — the cutting up of her blanket.

She received the sabbath as a day of rest; and she more than once remained behind her company, when they travelled thereon.

In the first years of the mission at Lacquiparle, an effort was made to introduce spinning and weaving among the Dakotas. In these new branches of industry Catharine was a willing scholar. She spun and knit and wove garments for herself and household.

She was already a matronly woman, but learned to read among the first Dakota women, and entered heartily into all plans for her own and her people's elevation. Her children were coming up to manhood. She desired that they should be Christians. When an offer was made to have some young men or boys visit Ohio for the purpose of learning the American customs and language, she brought her oldest son, and wished he might be taken. Now she is an old woman, feeble and childish in many things; but she holds fast to her faith in Jesus Christ.

Rebekah and Amanda were among the earliest fruits of the gospel at Lacquiparle, and are both still living. The Dakota name of the former is *Wa-mna'-hay-za*, which means corn; and that of the other is *Ha'-pis-tin-na*, which is the name of the *third child* in a family, if that child is a girl. Mrs. Marble, one of the captives taken by *Inkpa-doo'-ta* at the time of the Spirit Lake massacre, was purchased by the two sons of Rebekah. They brought her to their mother's tent, where she was very kindly cared for until they could place her in the hands of white people at Lacquiparle. To the mother belongs a part of the honor of this rescue.

In like manner, when Mrs. Huggins was left unprotected during the terrible occurrances of August 1862, she was cared for tenderly by native Christian women. Amanda often sent milk to her children Letta and Charlie. She went down to the Yellow Medicine to get flour "for the white woman" who had sought their protection. "We have a white woman with us," she said, "and we keep her very carefully; we don't allow a young man to speak to her." Mrs. Huggins told how delicately her need of a shawl was supplied by a Dakota woman, who came up behind her and placed one on her shoulders.

Thirty years ago, in the little boarding school at Lake Harriet, under the care of Mr. Stevens, there were several bright eyed half-breed girls. One of these was Lucy Prescott. Her father, Philander Prescott, had taken her mother, years before, according to the custom of the country. In the summer of 1837, Mr. S. W. Pond solemnized their marriage in a Christian way. Mr. Prescott was killed in the outbreak of 1862. Lucy was educated in the mission school, and, when grown, she became the wife of Mr. Eli Pettijohn, and is now the mother of quite a family — a Christian woman.

Another of those girls trained up in the first years of the mission was *Jane Lamont'*. She was the granddaughter of *Cloud Man*, one of the chiefs of the Lake Calhoun band, and lived a number of years in the families of the Messrs. Pond. She learned to talk English as well as she did her mother tongue, but when she was examined for admission to the church, she desired to be interrogated in the Dakota language rather than in English, because her religious thoughts and experiences had passed through that medium. Jane Lamont became the wife of Mr. Star Titus, and is now a Christian mother guiding her household in the way of life, an influential member of the Presbyterian church at Shakopee.

Sarah Hopkins is the daughter of Catharine, mentioned above, and the wife of Robert Hopkins, one of our native preachers. She has, from early womanhood, been a most earnest and devoted Christian. When in health, she was an energetic worker in the Lord's vineyard. The years of her husband's imprisonment were hard years for her. She had her two boys to care for; and already had consumption fastened itself upon her. The years since have been a continued decline. But she meets the prospect of death very calmly. Rather is she, as she said, to the writer, a few weeks ago, *in haste to go*. She is "looking unto Jesus."

Ha'-panna belonged to the Lake Calhoun band. In the early days of the mission, the converts to Christianity were few. Public opinion was against them, as well as the native human heart, and many of them were called to endure persecution. But Hapanna was a bright example of Christian character. She was the only one, in a large and influential band of Dakotas, who seemed to belong to Christ; and much of the power and influence of the band were brought to bear against her.

One of her most bitter opposers was her husband. He tried all his art of persuasion to induce her to leave the new religion. He slandered her and threatened her; but it produced no effect. At last, he forbade her attending public worship on the sabbath. When she went, he followed her; and, several times, on her returning, he whipped her severely. Finding that this did not accomplish his object, he cruelly beat her with a heavy pipe-hatchet, so as to endanger her life. Then he left her. From these injuries she recovered, and lived a few years, ever an ornament to her profession. She died in 1854; and we feel sure that she lives with Jesus. Her husband subsequently became a Christian, and died about a year ago.*

Ite'-wakan'-hdi-win; or *Lightning-face woman.* When I first met her at the Crow Creek mission, I thought her one of the most uninteresting of Indian women. Of large frame and coarse features, with clothing uniformly dirty and ragged, and hair unkempt; and yet, as I learned her history, and became acquainted with her character, I admired, and, finally, loved her.

---

* This *sketch*, and the two following, have been furnished by Mrs. Mary Frances Pond, of the Santee mission, daughter of Rev. Robert Hopkins, whose missionary life is recorded in this book.

She was born near Lake Calhoun, where she lived until she was seventeen. About that time she became the wife of *Wazi'-kootay*, or the *Pine-shooter*, of Red Wing, and with him removed to that village. She was the mother of eleven children, four of whom died in infancy. The others were living when I first met her; but two of them have since gone to the spirit-land.

Previous to the revival, which followed the Indian trouble, in 1862, she was a most zealous heathen, devoted to the imaginary beings she had, from her infancy, been taught to worship. When the meetings for prayer were first commenced in the camp, she laid positive commands on her children not to attend. And to prevent their attendance, she often hid their moccasins, so that more than once they went barefooted through the snow. But when the Holy Spirit, as we trust, led her to

Christ, she embraced him heartily, apparently renouncing entirely all confidence in her idol gods. She was now so firm in her religious convictions, that when her youngest living child was taken sick, at Crow Creek, she did not call their conjurers to cure him, but with childlike confidence, "called for the elders of the church to pray over him." And when the little boy died and was buried, she seemed to feel that all was well with him; and to rejoice in the hope that he was with Jesus, and with his father, who had died only a few weeks before.

The old man was, in all external respects, the counterpart of his wife; but he had a great deal of poetry in his soul. He had been to her a kind and loving husband, even in the days of their heathenism; and she mourned for him while she lived.

Death came to her suddenly, and with as

little pain, perhaps, as it ever comes to mortals. It was in the early morning of July 23, 1867, that she was called. The swift messenger from the thunder-cloud bore her spirit from earth, summoning, at the same time, one of her daughters with her husband, her three grandchildren, and her sister, into God's presence. It was bidden to spare her youngest daughter and the infant in its mother's arms, the only other occupants of the tent.

We said, "God's ways are not as our ways;" and, the next day, we buried them on the hill, in three graves. No stone marks the spot; but memory will fail, before we forget our humble friend so suddenly called away.

My sympathies have been as strongly enlisted in behalf of *Na-wang'-ma-ne-win*, or *the woman who walks galloping*, as for any other member of our mission church. It is but little more than three years since I first met her. Then her tidy appearance and smile of quiet dignity attracted my attention; and I have found in her the elements of a noble woman. She was, I think, only sixteen when she was married, after the old Dakota custom, to *Sounding Heavens*, a young man of industrious habits and kind feelings, and who, but for Solomon's failing, would have made her a good husband. But "he loved many strange women." She has often said that, when true to her, he was just what her heart wanted.

Three years ago they were united in marriage by the solemn vows of our church ceremony. For two years they lived together in quiet happiness; and poor Na-wang′-ma-ne-win began to hope that all such troubles were ended. Her trial must have been greater than we can well imagine, when she found that she had trusted to be deceived. An abandoned Ponca half-breed was her rival. I shall not soon forget the look of hopeless misery with which she said, "I must go home to find that woman in my place in my own tent." I advised her to leave her husband until he was willing to do right, being sure that human nature could not bear with meekness what she would be called to endure. Since that time she and her little boy have lived with friends. Will praying ones offer one petition for her, and others in like circumstances, in Jesus' name, for she too loves him?

In the first years of the mission work, a young married woman came frequently to our house, in whom we soon began to feel a deep interest. She was inquiring how she might become better. This life she had come to look upon as real; and what she had experienced of its miseries, and the little glimmering of light that had entered her mind about the life to come, made her seek, with no ordinary interest, how she might secure the joys of heaven. So she learned of the salvation through Christ, and embraced him as her Saviour. Her name was *Ha'-pistinna*, which indicates that she was the third child in the family. At her baptism she received the Christian name of *Balbine*.

A few years after her profession of Christianity, her husband was killed by the Ojibwas, and Balbine, who had been living at Lacquiparle, went down to reside with relatives in the neighborhood of Fort Snelling. Through considerable opposition, she continued to live a Christian life, and after many years was married to Paul Ma'za-koota'-mave, who was twice elected President of the Hazelwood Republic. *Balbine* is one of the "honorable" Christian women who live in the neighborhood of Fort Wadsworth.

Jenny Simon has gone to the spirit land. She was the daughter of Simon, of whom mention is made in other parts of this book. Jenny was his youngest child, and when only six years old she was placed in the mission boarding school at Hazelwood. After the outbreak she was formally given by her parents to Mr. and Mrs. H. D. Cunningham, to be kept and trained up as their own child. From both father and mother Jenny inherited a strong will and a great deal of energy.

While on a visit to Ohio, in 1863, she was deeply impressed by what she heard and saw of the advantages of Christian civilization and the importance of religion. But it was not until two years after this that she became a Christian; then she appears to have had great sorrow for sin. "The sinfulness of her own heart," says one, "caused her to weep many bitter tears. When asked why she wept, she would reply, 'Oh, I am such a sinner!'" She felt, as she said, that she must give her heart to Christ *then*, or it would be forever too late. And she did then enter into the love and service of Jesus, and was soon thereafter received into the fellowship of the Plymouth Congregational Church of Minneapolis, when she was about eleven years old.

Those who knew her best say that Jenny was a finely developed child Christian. In the summer of 1867, as she seemed to be going into a decline, she visited her father's family in the neighborhood of Fort Wadsworth. There, in the tent, in the dusk of the evening, I met her. I had not seen her for several years, and she had grown beyond my knowledge. I said in English, "Who is this? You look as if you could talk English." She replied, "This is Jenny;" and then told me that she had come up on a visit, hoping her health would be benefited thereby.

But the change did not arrest the progress of the disease. The winter that followed was a severe one, and through it she continued to approach the shadowy land. But to her it was not a land of shadows. She said, "I love all my friends here, but I love Jesus more. Don't be afraid to tell me when you think I am going to die. I *know* Jesus, and I shall go and live with him." So she fell asleep on a Sabbath morning of May, 1868, at Fort Wadsworth. Chaplain G. D. Crocker said her death was peace.*

These specimens of Dakota Christian women are given to show that the gospel had, from the beginning, a prevailing influence upon them. They were easily accessible to

---

* For many of the statements in this narrative of Jenny, the author is indebted to a communication from Mr. and Mrs. Cunningham.

the teachers of religion, and were more disposed than the men to change their faith in the gods of their people for the more intelligent and life-giving faith of Jesus Christ.

CHAPTER XII.

1837-1862.

PERSECUTION.

The first reception of the gospel by the Dakotas. — Their own religion antagonistic. — *Men* must not become Christians. — Opposition to schools and Sabbath worship. — Taking "the spoiling of goods." — Killed by witchcraft. — Case of Simon. — His former standing. — Changes his dress and habits of life. — Form of persecution — "the man that made himself a woman." — New form of trial. — Honors and temptations. — Spirit water. — Simon falls. — Repents, and falls again. — "Simon will yet return." — Much ashamed. — Simon restored. — His record in the outbreak.

"*Yea, and all that will live godly in Christ Jesus shall suffer persecution.*"

The proclaiming of the gospel among a heathen people will always, sooner or later, produce opposition and persecution in some form. The Dakota mission enjoyed several years of prosperity before the leading men began generally to understand that the religion of Christ was antagonistic to their own superstition. But by and by young men and honorable men, — or such as were honored among their own people, having taken many scalps of enemies in battle, and thereby acquired the right to wear a corresponding number of eagle's feathers, — came over to the side of education, civilization, and the religion of Christ. Then the chiefs and braves in various villages began to resolve that the book must be tabooed, that the schools must be stopped, and that the Dakotas must not become Christians.

In those years, when the opposition was most effective, 1842–1848, the "soldiers," or law-making power among the Dakotas, often interfered with the mission schools, and sometimes with the attendance at the house of God. On several different occasions, at Lacquiparle, men were stationed on the road to the mission with orders to stop all persons who were going there, whether young or old. The children were, of course, afraid, and staid away from school until the guard was discontinued; which usually was done in two or three days. Many of the women staid away also from the sabbath worship, but several times native Christians took the spoiling of their goods rather than stay away. The guard cut up their blankets and then let them pass on. At the mission stations on the Mississippi and lower Minnesota, the soldiers' lodge often broke up the schools, and kept them for months together from re-assembling.

In addition to all this, it was not an uncommon thing for men who had either embraced the new religion, or were understood to be favorable to it, to die very suddenly and very mysteriously. It was generally supposed that they were put out of the way by "bad medicine," or by sorcery. The ability to put to death in this way was claimed by many of their pow-wows.

But the nature and force of this opposition, as brought to bear upon their own people, will be best understood from a single example, that of *Simon Ana'wang-mane.* He was of good Dakota connections, had earned glory on the war-path, and had recently married into a family the members of which long opposed the gospel. He learned to read and write in the first years of the mission at Lacquiparle, though he never became as good a scholar as some others. He became a convert to Christianity about the beginning of 1840. The energy and independence which had characterized him on the hunt and the war-path, were carried into his new relations. By dressing like a white man and laboring with his hands, he showed his faith by his works.

This was all contrary to the customs of his people, and very soon brought on him a storm of opposition. He built for himself a cabin, and fenced a field, and cultivated it. For this his wife's friends opposed and persecuted him. No man in the village had more Dakota honors than he had; that is, no one had helped take more scalps of the enemy, and hence no one had a right, according to custom, to "soldier-kill" him; that is to kill his horse, break his gun, or cut up his blanket. But now no one was so poor as to do him reverence. And as he passed through the village, going to his work, he was laughed at, and the children often said, "There goes the man who has made himself a woman." The men who before had honored him, as a Dakota brave, now avoided him, and called him no more to their feasts. But these forms of opposition Simon met bravely, and was made stronger thereby. And for several years, his consistent and energetic course, as a disciple of the Lord Jesus, gave us great joy.

But about the beginning of the year 1844, Simon with his family went down to the then new mission station at Traverse des Sioux. The Indians at this place, although even more opposed to the new religion than were those at Lacquiparle, nevertheless treated Simon very differently. They honored him and invited him to their dog feasts. They praised him, they told him that he was a good fellow that he had taken many Ojibwa scalps, and so they wanted him to drink "spirit water" with them. How much Simon resisted their importunities is not known, as he never apologized for his conduct. He fell. He degraded himself. He was ashamed. He avoided the missionaries. He put off his white man's clothes, and for some time was an Indian again. Then for a while he appeared very desirous of shunning the way of temptation; but he was drawn away. His appetite for "spirit water" returned, and the desire to obtain horses by trading in it led him farther astray.

We mourned sadly over his fall; and he was suspended from the communion of the church. "But," in the language of the record of 1847, "sickness in his family and other misfortunes led him to reflect upon his past backslidings, and brought him to consecrate himself anew to the service of Christ. He acknowledged that he had sinned knowingly, and regarded this as a great aggravation of his guilt.

But Simon repented and returned only to fall again; and he appeared to go down deeper than before. For years he seemed to be working iniquity with greediness. Yet, during all this time we prayed much for him, and often talked with him, urging his return to the path of life. And something seemed to say, "Simon will yet return." Sometimes we obtained a promise from him, that he would attend church again. And sometimes he came; but he was so much ashamed that he could not be persuaded to enter, but would sit down on the door-step. So he came up gradually, getting more and more strength and courage. And so, in 1854, our hearts were made glad in welcoming him back to the fold of the good Shepherd. On the 21st of March, eighteen days after the mission houses were burned at Lacquiparle, the following record was made: —

"Last Saturday Simon came up from Dr. Williamson's place and spent the sabbath with us. He desired to be restored to the privileges and fellowship of the church; and Dr. Williamson wrote, "I know of no reason why he should not be." Accordingly the brethren were called together sabbath morning, and, after considerable conversation with him, we agreed to restore him." "For two years," one writes, "his course has seemed to be upward." And since that time he has witnessed a good confession before many witnesses, as a ruling elder, and recently as a licensed local preacher.

When the outbreak of 1862 occurred, Simon and his family were living in a brick house near the Hazelwood mission station. Subsequently Little Crow and the whole camp of the hostile Indians, removed up to that part of the country, and the Christian Indians were all obliged to leave their houses and to go into tents. Afterwards their houses were all burned. Then the camp moved farther up the Minnesota, and all were obliged to go along. It was at this time that Simon brought Mrs. Newman and her children to Fort Ridgley, as detailed in another chapter. This woman, though not a professing Chistian herself, said when she reached Simon's house, and heard them sing, and then saw them kneel down to pray, she felt safe! This was a valuable testimony in favor of Christianity.

CHAPTER XIII.

1843-1854.

GREAT SORROWS.

Mission party.—Toiling up the Minnesota.—Thomas L. Longley.—Reaching the traverse.—Bread stolen.—Building a log-cabin.—Going to bathe.—Mr. Longley drowned.—Buried under an oak.—Stricken hearts.—Black Eagle's sympathy.—Robert Hopkins.—Another great sorrow.—Gathering to make a treaty.—Fourth of July.—Mr. Hopkins drowned.—The body found.—Oaks of weeping.—Mrs. Hopkins returns to Ohio.—Mr. Hopkins' youth.—Efforts to obtain an education.—Teaching colored children.—His mental characteristics.—Desire to do good.—The third great sorrow.—Stations at Pay-zhe-hoo′-ta-ze and Hazelwood.—The ides of March.—Smith Burgess Williamson.—His Bible reading.—Is crushed under an ox-sled.—God makes no mistakes.

"I was dumb, because Thou didst it."

EARLY in the month of June, 1843, a missionary company might have been seen toiling up the Minnesota in a small keel boat. It consisted of Mr. and Mrs. Riggs with two children, Mr. and Mrs. Hopkins, and Thomas L. Longley, besides two or three men whose business it was to propel the boat.

Miss Jane S. Williamson and Miss Julia Ann Kephart had been of their company from Ohio to Fort Snelling. There they stopped for a time, with the family of Dr. Williamson, then residing near the garrison. Mr. Riggs and family were returning from the East, where he had been to superintend printing in the Dakota language, at Boston and Cincinnati. Mr. and Mrs. Hopkins were natives of Southern Ohio, who had been recently married, and were now on their way to join the Dakota mission. Mr. Longley, a brother of Mrs. Riggs, was a young man from western Massachusetts, who had just reached his majority, and had come by invitation to spend a year in helping to erect buildings at a new station. This station, as finally selected, was at Traverse des Sioux.

The voyage was not an unpleasant one, the party reaching the Traverse in good health and spirits. The only accident remembered was the loss of a loaf of nice light bread, which the women had raised on the boat with dificulty, and stopped to bake it by the way in a Dutch oven. While they slept, it was taken from a box that stood inside of the tent. When the call was made the next morning to breakfast, it was discovered that they had nothing to eat.

Some obstacles were thrown in the way of commencing the new station, by the Indians, but they were not serious; and Mr. Riggs and Mr. Longley proceeded to erect a small log-cabin. Mr. Hopkins and his wife had gone up to spend a year at Lacquiparle, and Mrs. Riggs had accompanied them, to bring down Isabella, who had been left there a year before in the keeping of friends.

Six weeks passed away, and the fifteenth of July came. Mrs. Riggs and the little ones had come back from Lacquiparle, accompanied by Mr. Alex. G. Huggins and his sister, and Mr. Isaac Pettijohn. It was Saturday, and they expected the cabin to be so far finished that day that they could leave their tents and occupy it. After noon Mr. Longley proposed to go and bathe in the Minnesota River. Mr. Huggins and Mr. Riggs went with him. The river was not well known to any of the party, and they naturally went to the boat-landing.

Near that place there was a strong whirling current driving into a very deep hole. Only a few moments after he had entered the water, it was observed that Mr. Longley was in trouble. One of the others plunged in and swam to his relief, but failed of giving help, and barely succeeded in regaining the shore. We gathered along the bank, and stretched our eyes over the water, but he whom we all loved was gone! The Indians assembled at the place, and efforts were made all that afternoon and the morning following to find the body, but without success. As that long sabbath wore to a close, the lifeless body drifted ashore; and we took it up, washed it, and, wrapping it in a clean linen cloth, buried it under an oak near the unfinished cabin, just as the sun was setting. We could not do otherwise than go and tell Jesus.

It was a great sorrow. It would so sadden the heart of his father and mother, away off in the hill country of New England! How could we tell them that they would see their darling boy no more? It seemed as if our own stricken hearts could receive no comfort. And for many a long month afterward, the water where he was drowned, flowing on so carelessly, really seemed frightful.

One day, when we sat nursing our sorrow, an old Indian, Black Eagle by name, came in and counselled us to "cry it out." "Even a goose," he said, "when its companion is shot, flies around the place and makes a great outcry. A deer also, when alone in the world, cries out for the lost ones. In like manner, we, children of nature, wail out our sorrow when our friends die. But it is not so with white people; they mourn in secret." The lesson of the old Indian man was not unheeded.

We now pass to another great sorrow, in 1851. Many changes had been wrought in the Dakota mission. Mr. Robert Hopkins, as already stated, had been licensed and ordained as a minister of the gospel by the Dakota Presbytery; and he was now, with Mr. Huggins, occupying the station at Traverse des Sioux. It was again the month of July, and Indians and white men were gathering at Traverse des Sioux. The Commissioner of Indian Affairs, from Washington, Hon. Mr. Lea, was there, and had associated with him, Alex. Ramsay, Governor of Minnesota. They were about to make treaties by which the claim of the Dakotas to a large tract of country would be transferred to white men. This was a year of flood in the valley. The Minnesota had spread out over all the low bottoms, and quite surrounded the mission houses, which stood on a small elevation. The Fourth of July was to be celebrated by rejoicing and feasting by that mixed multitude. The morning came, and while Mrs. Hopkins prepared their customary meal, Mr. Hopkins went to bathe. He told no one; but, quietly placing his clothes on the stones of the little bluff bank, just below the mission houses, he went in and walked out a short distance on a ridge of ground, and then, as it is supposed, stepped into deep water, from which, not being able to swim, he could not recover himself! He had been seen from a distance, by an Indian, going into the water; but he thought no more of it. The breakfast waited, and he came not. The wife grew uneasy. Where had he gone? When search was made, his clothes were found; but they told a tale which could not be misunderstood. Much unsuccessful search was made for the body; but it was finally caught by a fishing-net, stretched for the purpose, along the edge of the wood. So he was taken up and buried under the oaks, by the side of the one who had drowned eight years before. Soon after this, the land here came into the possession of white men, and the place was laid out in town lots. On this account, after a few years, it was thought best to take up these remains from beneath the *oaks of weeping*, and transfer them to another place, selected and laid out as a cemetery.

Mrs. Hopkins, with her three children, returned to her friends in Ohio; and, several years later, became the second Mrs. G. H. Pond. One of these children, now Mrs. Edward Pond, has for several years been connected with the Dakota mission on the Missouri. So it comes to pass that, "in the place of the fathers are their children."

When young, Robert Hopkins obtained only a common school education; which, in those days, in Ohio, embraced spelling, reading, writing, and arithmetic. When he arrived at early manhood, he determined to qualify himself, by his own exertions, for preaching the gospel. Accordingly, he commenced studying the Latin language, at Hillsboro', where he hired a room and boarded himself. Seeing a number of colored children about the village, who were growing up in ignorance and vice, because they were excluded from the public schools, he invited them to his room, procured books, and devoted a portion of his time to teaching them to read. Having in this way secured their confidence, and that of their parents, he was enabled, after a short time, to assemble a considerable number of them, on the Sabbath, for religious instruction.

His health failed, and he went home to work on his father's farm. Then again he recommenced his studies at South Hanover College. But he was again obliged to stop. Then he decided to give his life-work to the Dakotas.

Mr. Hopkins' perceptive powers were not above the average; and hence he acquired some kinds of knowledge with difficulty. But his memory was retentive, and his judgment sound. His piety was intelligent, living, and active. In him a strong desire to do good to his fellow-men was controlled by a determination in all things to obey God. When he knew what was duty, he did not hesitate to do it. His desire to preach Christ to the Dakotas was very great. Often, even in winter, he walked ten, fifteen, or twenty miles, to tell a few families the way of salvation. He was characterized by great earnestness. His prominent defect was his lack of prudence or caution. And this was probably the cause of his death. But his work was done, and his Master saw fit, in this way to call him home.*

On the third of March, 1856, a great sorrow came to the mission station at Pa-zhe-hoo′-ta-ze. When the country on the Mississippi and Minnesota had been ceded to the white people, and it became evident that the Indians would, in a short time, be re-

* See letter of Dr. Williamson in the "Missionary Herald" for 1851.

moved to their reservation in the upper country, Dr. Williamson selected a place near the mouth of the Yellow Medicine for a new station. Thither he removed his family in the autumn of 1852.

The *third* of *March* had already become associated with trouble; for it was on this very day of the month, in 1854, that the mission houses at Lacquiparle were consumed by fire, and the families reduced to great straits. A result of this burning was the removal of the station to Hazelwood, only two miles distant from Dr. Williamson's place. But the nearness of friends did not prevent the coming of sorrow. *Smith Burgess Williamson*, in this spring of 1856, was about fourteen years of age, a stout, manly, quiet boy. It had been noticed that he read his Bible more during the winter previous than usual, and his friends then hoped he was under the softening and constraining influences of the Holy Spirit; but no one knew of his having reached a hope in Jesus. This third of March, he was engaged in hauling wood with a yoke of oxen and a heavy ox-sled. How he fell under the runner no one knew; but the oxen came homeward, with his body dragging under the sled. *His young life was crushed out.* But his sorrowing parents and friends could still look upward and say, "God makes no mistakes."

CHAPTER XIV.

1835—1854.

LESSER TRIALS.

Trials. — Unreasonable demands. — Indian begging. — War parties. — Eagle Help. — Killing mission cattle. — Station commenced at Traverse des Sioux. — Sleepy Eyes and Big Walker. — Opposition. Cattle killed. — Drunkenness. — Missionary remonstrance. — Gray Leaf's reply. — Drunken visitors. — Opposition at Lacquiparle. — School stopped. — More cattle killed. — Trials from apostasy. — New station at Yellow Medicine. — Hard times. — Mr. Hunter and Mr. Jacques. — Winter journey. — Terrible snow-storms. — Frozen feet. — Every thing left. — Reaching home. — Childlike trust. — Help from Lacquiparle. — Mission buildings burned. — Native Christians help kindly. — Proofs of sympathy. — Hon. George Grinnell's letter. — So He causeth to triumph.

"*It was no path of flowers,*
Through this dark world of ours,
Beloved of the Father! thou didst tread;
And shall we in dismay
Shrink from the narrow way,
When clouds and darkness are around it spread?"

In the first years of the Dakota mission there was both a great abundance and a great variety of trials. It will be the object of this chapter to bring some of these together, and to show that out of them all the Lord delivered us.

The Indians were often very unreasonable. They did not, and perhaps could not, understand the motives which actuated the missionaries in coming to live among them. "It must be that they are here for the purpose of making money. At any rate, they ought to pay for the logs they used in building their houses, and the rails that fenced their fields, and even for the hay they cut, and the grass which their cattle cropped on the great prairies."

As soon after going to Lacquiparle as possible, Dr. Williamson and Mr. Huggins built for themselves log-houses. The Indians said it took a great many of their trees to make them. Besides, the missionaries were better clothed and better fed than they were; and why not give a portion to them? So they came and danced the "begging dance." They danced outside and they danced inside of Dr. Williamson's unfinished house. The Doctor was a merciful man, and very kindly disposed towards them. He would give clothing to the naked and food to the hungry to the full extent of his ability; but he could not see that it was right to pay able-bodied men for dancing. They were stronger than he was, and could take what clothing and food he and his family had; but he would not give it to them in such circumstances. They went away very angry, but seldom afterwards troubled the missionaries by dancing to them the "begging dance."

Another form of trial came to the missionaries in the frequent war-parties. From time immemorial the Dakotas and the Ojibwas had been enemies. A peace was made between them only to be broken by one side or the other. In the spring of 1838, the Ojibwas had violated their pledged faith. They had come and deceived and murdered the inmates of three Dakota lodges, as detailed elsewhere. To avenge this, in the spring following, Eagle-Help, one of the Dakota men who had first learned to read and write his own language, made up a war-party. The members of the mission felt it their duty to oppose their going, and refused to give aid and encouragement to them in such an enterprise, even by grinding their corn for provisions by the way. They tried earnestly to dissuade Eagle Help from going on the war-path. They said, perhaps unwisely, that they would feel it their duty to pray that the party might not succeed in taking any scalps of their enemies. This was very easily made to mean that the missionaries would pray that they, the Dakotas, might be killed. They were of course greatly offended; and as they went out on the war-path, they killed two of the mission cattle. A few weeks after they returned, having had a very wearisome and unsuccessful march, and then of necessity they must kill another. But notwithstanding the ill-feelings produced by this unpleasant conflict, it had some effect in stopping war-parties from Lacquiparle.

The commencement of the new station at Traverse des Sioux, in June, 1843, was attended and followed by an unwonted amount of trials of various kinds. Sleepy-Eyes, the old chief, and Big Walker, and the greater part of the principal men, received our proposition to stop among them favorably; but there were some opposed to us. The very next day after our conference with the Indians, there passed up through that place a chief soldier and very energetic man, whom we had before known by report as strongly opposed to giving up their ancestral religion and customs. He told the sons of the trader that he would soon come back and put a stop to our building. But that night, four miles out from the Traverse, he was killed by drunken comrades.

The opposition, however, did not all die with him. The only team of the mission, at this place, was a single yoke of young cattle. These hauled the logs for a cabin, and seemed to be quite a necessary part of the establishment. But when corn-gathering came, and the Indians wanted fresh meat, these oxen were shot as they were feeding out on the prairie. Winter came on, and another single ox was purchased, as it was hardly possible to get along without a team of some kind. He drew the wood and rails for the station; and it was hoped he would be available in putting in a spring crop, both for the mission and the Indians. But, before that time arrived, he went where other good oxen go. A parcel of drunken Indians came one night and demanded the key of the stable. It was of course refused; whereupon they broke in the door and helped themselves. Remonstrance in such a case was useless, if not dangerous.

About this time, drunkenness was becoming exceedingly prevalent among the Dakotas on the Mississippi and Minnesota. A few whiskey shops constituted Saint Paul; Indians could obtain *fire-water* easily. For several years, indeed, the trade in it was carried on briskly, notwithstanding the efforts of the commandant at Fort Snelling to prevent it. Indians not unfrequently died of drinking, and more were killed in their drunken quarrels.

"In the month of February," writes one of the missionaries, "a man drank very freely, and lay down to sleep, but did not awake again. But this only made some the more determined to drink on. Shortly after this I was called to a dog feast, when I took occasion to remonstrate with them. If an enemy had come in the night, I said, and had killed and scalped one of your number, on finding him in the morning, would you have embraced and kissed him; or would you not rather have taken his life and danced around his scalp? But here is an enemy that you have found and brought into your lodges; he has killed one, and another, and another; and yet, the more of you he kills, the more you love him, and the more do you press him to your lips."

Gray Leaf, the brother-in-law of Sleepy Eyes, replied: "What you say is true; we all know it is bad; we know it has killed many of us; it has cut up our tents, and driven our women and children into the woods; it has killed our dogs and our horses. We know all this, and some of us do not wish to use it; but when we are called to a feast, and our hearts are all glad, if then a little spirit-water is passed around, we cannot be so unmanly as not to drink."

For the next year or two, drunkenness was still on the increase. And the visits to the mission houses, of Indian men in a state of intoxication, or pretending to be under the influence of spirit-water, were always annoying, and, sometimes, frightening. It happened that the last night of 1844, the men at the Traverse des Sioux station were necessarily prevented from reaching home until after midnight. During their absence, Big Walker, in a state of intoxication, came and tried to open the door. But not succeeding, he left, saying he would return with his gun and break it open. At another time, an Indian man, who was always ugly, and of whom the women were always afraid, came in quite drunk and asked for food. Some cold Indian rice was given him, which he did not greatly relish. After slobbering over it awhile, he commenced to feed the women of the mission with his spoon, and they did not dare refuse.

One sabbath, when twenty or thirty Indian men were in different stages of intoxication, they made an attempt to drink *min'-ne-wakan'*, *spirit water*, in the *tee'pee-wakan'*,* *spirit house*, at the Traverse; and were only prevented from doing so by some of their own number.

At Lacquiparle, during these years, the opposition to education and Christianity was greatly increased. The soldiers forbade all persons from attending school and religious meetings at the mission; and, to effectually enforce this prohibition, they sta-

* The Dakota name for church.

tioned guards along the paths. These guards also visited the mission houses morning and evening, and cut up the blankets of several women whom they found there. They also forbade the missionaries from taking any wood, except such as was already cut down. In addition to all this, they continued to cripple the mission by killing their cattle. Little Crow, at this time chief of the band living near Saint Paul, on a visit to Lacquiparle, encouraged them in these forms of opposition. And, as the result of all this, Dr. Williamson writes: "In two successive years, they killed, each year, twice as many as they left us. They killed our best horse also; and it was necessary to put a yoke on our two remaining milch cows to haul our firewood."

But trials and discouragements came to the missionaries, from the apostasy of those who had professed to be Christians, which were harder to bear than any of the foregoing that came from the heathen party. When, during these years of opposition, the half of the full-blooded male members of the church fell into sin, Christ was wounded in the house of his friends. One of these, who formerly endured with meekness much persecution, on account of his embracing the gospel, and for several years appeared well, apostatized; first by neglecting the means of grace, and then selling and drinking spirit water, and finally by deliberately taking part in idolatrous ceremonies. Another repeatedly broke his promise to abstain from strong drink, and then ran away with his brother's wife.

A third was one of the young men who had been in Ohio, and had made a profession of Christianity there. He was, at that time, young, but appeared well. In those years, no Dakota man read his Bible more, or seemed to be a more humble Christian, than the younger Simon. But he fell away, and was never recovered. Twenty years after, he was wounded at the battle of Wood Lake, and died a prisoner.

The case of Abel Ite′-wa-wi′-ni-han, or *Fearful Face*, was still more sad. His wife was not true to him, and he, moved with jealousy, shot a man with a barbed arrow. He was then pursued by two relatives of this wounded man, one of whom he shot in the arm with a ball. Some time afterwards, they formed a conspiracy against Abel, and killed him. Heathen men said these evil deeds were permitted because the young men forsook the religion of their ancestors.

In the autumn of 1852, Dr. Williamson removed his family from Kapo′-sia to his newly-selected station of *Pay-zhe-hoo′-ta-ze*, near the Yellow Medicine. The house which he had built was in quite an unfinished state when the cold weather came on. The walls were covered on the outside with split clapboards, and the space between the studs was filled in with mud. The roof was of composition, but was only partly finished. It was a two-story house, sixteen by thirty feet, with no partition, and many cracks through which the winter winds whistled. It was almost the last of October when the family reached this unfinished house; and winter came on that year very early, and was terribly severe.

Some potatoes had to be brought from Lacquiparle, and then the teams were to go down to Traverse des Sioux for flour and other needed articles. November was an uncommonly severe month; and not until the last day of that month were Andrew Hunter and Jacques ready to start for the winter's supply of provisions.

They took one yoke of oxen and three horses, attached to sleds which had been rather clumsily made. They reached the Traverse in safety, and were loaded and ready to start back on the tenth of December. On the fifteenth day of the month they had made fifty miles, or half the distance home, and had reached the house of the trader at Little Rock. "On the thirteenth," says Dr. Williamson, "commenced the most terrible series of cold and stormy days I remember to have known." From that to the end of the month the average of the thermometer at sunrise was sixteen below zero; and the average of the greatest warmth in those eighteen days was only a little more than four degrees above. "But this gives only a faint idea of the severity of the weather. The only three mornings when the mercury was above zero, it sunk, as the day advanced, so as to be below in the afternoon, the snow falling at the same time. Two of these were the most terrible days I ever knew; the wind blew a tempest, and drifted the snow so thick that, at times, a house could not be seen at a hundred yards' distance, and made drifts in one day often not less than ten feet deep.

On the morning of the fifteenth, they left the trader's house, which was the only inhabited dwelling between Traverse des Sioux and the Yellow Medicine. That day they reached a little wood ten miles off, where they encamped. Here, by continuous snow-storms, they were detained a whole week. Two of their horses, through want of food and the severity of the weather, were unable to travel further. At this place about half their load was abandoned. To the next point of wood near the road was a distance of twelve miles, and they were three days in making it. Mr. Hunter's feet had been badly frozen the second day after they left the Traverse; and, in these nights of sleeping in the snow without a fire, Jacques met with the same misfortune. Although they had abandoned all their loads except about three hundred pounds, this condition of their feet, together with the snow drifts, storms, and weakness of their teams, prevented their advancing more than about three miles farther until the last day in the year.

That night they decided that, to save their lives, they must abandon every thing. Jacques made a little hand-sled; and the next morning he bound on it their bedding and some provisions, together with an axe, a Bible, and the papers and letters. Mr. Hunter needed help to get up and walk; but after trying it a little he was able to go alone. Thus they started, hoping to reach that day an unoccupied house at Patterson's

Rapids. But night came on, and they were unable to reach the house, but found a ravine where they slept, sheltered from the wind. During the night a fresh snow fell, and the next morning they found it three feet deep on the level, and not hard enough to bear up even their little hand-sled. At this place they were obliged to leave their bedding and Bible and mail: they took nothing but the axe and a few biscuits. In two or three hours, having travelled about as many miles, they reached the house they had hoped to find the night before. Here they rested, for it was the sabbath. They made a large fire to keep themselves from freezing, and, spreading some hay on the floor for a bed, they lay down to sleep, Mr. Hunter, in his more than childlike helplessness, saying his child-prayer, —

"Now I lay me down to sleep;
I pray the Lord my soul to keep;

If I should die before I wake,
I pray the Lord my soul to take."

The next day, in cutting a hole in the ice on the river to obtain water, their axe slipped from them. They had sixteen or eighteen miles to travel that day before reaching the mission; and they were now in no condition to lie out without bedding and without fire. In that case they must have perished. But as Providence would have it, they reached the mission at eight o'clock that night, perfectly exhausted. They carried home a sad tale; but Dr. Williamson and his family greatly rejoiced to see them.

"Three weeks had passed since Mr. Hunter's feet were first frozen; and they had been often frozen subsequently; so that when he reached home there was no natural feeling in any part, and it was impossible, on opening them, to distinguish between the dead and live flesh." He was crippled for life.

How shall the mission family get through the winter? When these men returned they had been living for six weeks on potatoes and hominy. Their teams were lost, and the provisions, which they had been hoping and praying for, were left on the prairie and destroyed by wolves. At this time their "corn was reduced to less than a bushel, and the potatoes were too few to last until the weather could be expected to moderate." But two days after this, a small quantity of provisions arrived from Lacquiparle, sent by the missionaries. It was carried the whole distance of thirty miles on hand-sleds, the snow being too deep for horses. In addition to this, fish were abundant the latter part of the winter. So they thanked God and took courage. And on the first day of April following, we have this record: "Our provisions have lasted so much better than I expected that I am often reminded of the widow's oil and meal. We thank God that he counts us worthy to suffer as well as to labor."

On the 3d of March, 1854, as already stated, the mission buildings at Lacquiparle, except the church, were all burned down. This included also the stables and hay. In the efforts made to extinguish the fire, almost nothing was saved. From the room occupied by Miss Spooner, now Mrs. Drake of Cincinnati, quite a number of the movable articles were rescued. Two barrels of corn were saved. Our books, except about a dozen, were consumed. After the fire, a part of a barrel of salted beef was found in the cellar, cooked; and about two fifths of the potatoes in the cellars were found to be still fit for use. The mission family went into the church for shelter, and their Indian neighbors brought them bread to eat. They acted nobly. "I never supposed," said the writer, "that I should be dependent upon an Indian for a decent suit of clothes; but it is even so. My best coat and pants have been furnished me by Lorenzo Lawrence. On Monday Dr. Williamson, hearing of our misfortune, came up, bringing numerous articles of food and clothing for our necessities. We are now as comfortable as we can be in the circumstances. We saved one chair and an old bedstead. Our Indian neighbors have offered us nothing but their 'best.' And we know that, with such a friend as our Father in heaven, we shall not want any good thing."

Several months afterwards it was said by the Secretaries in Boston, that Mr. Riggs had received proofs of sympathy, unexpected but most grateful, from the friends of missions in all parts of the country. In illustration of this statement, it is proper to introduce the following letter: —

"GREENFIELD, MASS., May 30, 1854.

"REV. MR. RIGGS AND MRS. RIGGS: —

"Dear Christian Friends: Personally I am a stranger to you both. In Mrs. Riggs I recognize the daughter of my intimate friend, the late Gen. Longley. I have felt much, perhaps an unusual interest in the mission to which you are attached. Your recent affliction by the loss of property and many comforts, by fire, cannot but awaken my sympathies. It was from the Lord, and will be borne submissively, even cheerfully. He will educe good from this temporal calamity. He will bring out of it compensating benefits.

"Accept the small sum of ten dollars, which I inclose for your own personal use. And may the Lord bless you and your family, and the cause you have in charge.

"I am respectfully, Your friend,

"GEO. GRENNELL."

So He always causeth us to triumph.

CHAPTER XV.

1849–1862.

LATER PLANS.

Enlargement of the mission. — Encouragement at Lacquiparle. — Opposition elsewhere. — Influence of the so-called school-fund. — Dark pictures. — Mr. Potter's impressions. — Prospects more hopeful. — A new treaty talked of. — Mr. Hopkins' difficulty. — Treaties of 1851 — Deaths in the mission. — Others withdraw from the service. — Influence of the mission on the white settlements. — Michel Renville. — Dr. Williamson removes to Pay-zhe-hoo′-ta-ze. — New station at Hazelwood. — Station at the Lower Agency. — Mission chapels.

"*Lengthen thy cords, and strengthen thy stakes.*"

LET us now resume more especially the thread of our missionary narrative, which in a former chapter was brought down to the close of 1848. It will be remembered that considerable additions had been made to our effective force. Never at any period, before or afterwards, had we so many men and women in the field. But, notwithstanding these additions, the work progressed slowly and against many obstacles.

In the next years, we had more encouragement at Lacquiparle. The Dakota services on the sabbath were well attended; the week-day and sabbath schools were comparatively prosperous; and there were several accessions to the church. About the first of the year 1849, the first recorded effort to enlist the native members in the work of propagating the gospel was made here. The author then wrote: "To-day we held a meeting, at which I presented the claims of other heathen, and the obligations we are under to aid, as God enables us, in carrying the gospel to them." The result of this effort was about ten dollars in cash, and ten pairs of moccasins, which were afterwards turned into money. But there was still opposition among the heathen party, which sometimes showed itself in discussing the question, whether they would drive us away or not.

It was, however, among the lower Indians, — those on the Mississippi and lower Minnesota, — that a strong organized opposition grew up. They were not altogether insincere in their invitations to Dr. Williamson and Mr. Pond to form new stations at their villages; but they were influenced mainly by selfish considerations. It was, they thought, profitable to have a missionary to write letters for them. A few had, doubtless, been actuated by higher motives. They were really desirous of availing themselves of the benefits of education. But the spreading of the mission, and especially its large reinforcement, excited their apprehensions, and were, in part, the cause of the active and determined opposition which followed. The more powerful and more real cause was the accumulated "school-fund."

In the treaty made with these Indians, in 1837, there was a provision for the application of five thousand dollars, annually, for the support of schools. The agent who was instrumental in making the treaty, Maj. Taliaffero, expended a few thousand dollars in this way. But, as he very soon gave place to a new man, and the Indians spoke against the plan, the money remained unexpended and accumulating from year to year. Now, it amounted to more than fifty thousand dollars. The traders who had unsettled balances due them were interested in having this money paid directly to the Indians, and so encouraged them to oppose its use in the work of education. Only a little of it was so applied; but that little aroused the opposition of the Indians and unprincipled white men; and measures were taken to stop all the schools at Red Wing, Kaposia, Oak Grove, and Prairieville; and the influence was felt at Traverse des Sioux and Lacquiparle.

About this time, the discouragements seemed to be greatly multiplied. The annual report of the mission, adopted in September, 1849, gives an exceedingly dark picture. The small number who attended the religious meetings at all the stations, except Lacquiparle; the shutting up of schools; the number of defections in the church, amounting to two fifths of all the members who were living; the stealing and killing of mission cattle; the wars carried on between the Sioux and Ojibwas; the flooding of the Dakota country with "spirit water," and the great annoyances, and often dangers, to which the missionaries were subjected from drunken Indians carrying their knives and guns; the effect of their annuities, and especially of the so-called "education fund;" and the general state of society in a community of savages, — all these were great obstacles to the planting and progress of the gospel.

"Christianity," the missionaries said, "cannot flourish among a people living in the lowest state of barbarism. It may be said that the civilization of the Indians would be the natural result of their conversion to Christianity. But so long as the native converts form only a very small minority, and they chiefly women, it is next to impossible for them to rise much above the general level of the society in which they live. In the present state of things, no Dakota can have in his possession a cow, or even a pig, or chicken; and whatever the wishes of individuals may be, they are compelled, by the force of circumstances, to live with and live like savages."

"Those who are disposed to listen to our advice, we have persuaded to build houses, fence and plant fields, and try to live like white men; and when they have attempted to do so, we have aided them as far as was in our power; but both we and they have lost our labor. If they have built comfortable houses, others occupy them; if they have a sufficiency of food, others eat it; and if they accumulate a little property, it is begged or stolen from them by others, until they become discouraged, and return to their skin tents, and to that poverty which is their only security from the attacks of thieves and beggars. Their situation is worse than Lot's in Sodom; for they can extricate themselves from it only by going out of the world." So, at this time, wrote the older missionaries. And yet they were not altogether discouraged, but cast themselves and their work "on the arm of the Mighty God of Jacob," and on "the promise of the Holy Ghost to be sent down from heaven, in answer to believing and earnest prayer."

Mr. Potter "found the contrast between

the Dakotas and the Choctaws particularly striking;" far greater, indeed, than he had anticipated. In July he wrote from Traverse des Sioux: "I consider the Dakotas as accessible to the gospel only to a very limited extent. And the great question is, 'How shall we get the ear of this people? How shall we induce them to hear with such a disposition that the truth will be likely to do them good?' In general they look upon the missionaries as aggressors. They say, 'You came uninvited. You never even asked our consent to settle here. You are among us like robbers. You occupy our lands; you destroy our timber; you pasture our grass, and drink at our streams. True, you say you came to instruct us; but we do not desire your instruction, and we will not receive it. We wish you gone, and we have told you so: why don't you go?'" This, it must be acknowledged, was putting the case very strongly, but there was much truth in the statement. Mr. Potter saw things so much in this light that he did not feel it his duty to remain among the Dakotas, and, at his own request, was transferred to the Indian mission in western New York.

The next year the prospects beame more hopeful. About the beginning of 1850, a church was organized at Kaposia, the station occupied by Dr. Williamson. It consisted of seven Dakota women and one of mixed blood, besides several white persons. Six of the seven Dakota females had been members of the church at Lacquiparle. At Oak Grove, a church was organized about the same time, which consisted of three Dakotas and five white persons.

During this year there was much talk, at all the Dakota villages, about a treaty which they expected the government to make with them. Indeed, they could do little but talk about this. The prospect of such an event took away from them the ordinary incentives to labor to better their own condition, and made them afraid to have any one else help them. Mr. Hopkins puts this in a forcible way: "I suppose," he says, "the majority of the Indians believe that we are expecting pay for the aid we give them, and that our hope of obtaining it hangs on the expected treaty. This is an exciting topic. Every thing connected with the making of a treaty is deeply interesting. What place will the half-breeds occupy? They have received more than the full Indians in the former treaty with a part of the tribe. Some say, 'Now they must have nothing at all.' All, I suppose, agree that the missionary shall have nothing; but the fear is that neither the missionary nor the government will agree to this. If my word would satisfy them, I would set their minds at rest; but it is of little use to speak for one's self on this exciting topic. The people keep the subject on their minds, and are often engaged in balancing accounts. 'They have taken grass from our prairies, water from our streams, stone from our quarries, and wood from our groves; and they have occupied our land, a large piece for a garden, besides what their cattle have grazed. Occasionally they have ploughed some for us; and they have built for us a few little houses; that can't more than balance the account!'" So much did Mr. Hopkins desire to put this obstacle out of the way, that he drew up a formal paper which he signed before the Governor, declaring that he would receive nothing for any aid which he had given them.

The expected treaties were made in the summer of 1851, with the four bands of Dakotas occupying the Minnesota country as far west as Lake Traverse, which lake was in the western line of the purchase. Provision was made for a reservation on the Upper Minnesota, which was stricken out by the senate of the United States, and the Indians were only permitted to occupy that part of the country at the will of the President.

This year of the treaty was eventful. Besides the change already mentioned, Mrs. Hancock of Red Wing died in the early spring previous. "She was glad that she had come to the Dakotas, but regretted that she had not done more good among them." And in the first months of the next year, Mrs. S. W. Pond was gathered home to the spirit land. "She was a noble woman; very quiet and retiring, very pleasant and truthful. No one who became acquainted with her could help admiring her character as a woman and a Christian."

And while the laborers were falling by the way, and being translated to the beautiful land above, the result of the treaties on the mission was still farther to reduce their numbers. Mr. G. H. Pond and wife withdrew from the service of the Board, and gave their labors henceforth to the white people who were settling around them; and not long after, Mrs. Pond was taken up to the Master. Mr. Huggins and Mr. Pettijohn and their wives retired from the mission work. And a year afterwards, Mr. S. W. Pond, Mr. M. N. Adams, and Mr. J. W. Hancock went into the home service.

We may pause here for a moment to speak of the filling up of this new land by white settlers, and the effect of the pre-occupation of the field by the gospel messengers, No sooner was it known that the Senate had ratified the treaties made with the Dakotas in the summer of 1851, than multitudes flocked to the west side of the Mississippi. Every one sought for the most desirable location. Town-sites in great abundance were selected, surveyed, and platted; and corner lots ran up to extravagant prices. Men went everywhere seeking and occupying the fine prairie farms which adjoined the woodlands. Villages and communities grew up as by magic. All over the country were seen the same selfishness, the same speculation, the same jumping of claims. Hence the state of society in a new country is very undesirable. The communities must be organized; the discordant elements must be fused and made accordant; the selfishness must, in part at least, be suppressed and overcome. What can do this better than the gospel of Jesus Christ? And here it was, already on the ground, prepared to do its blessed work. At Red Wing and Oak Grove, at Shakopee and Traverse des Sioux, there were men to mould the ingathering populations, — make them into families of Christ.

It must be acknowledged that the enlargement of the mission, described in this chapter, did not fulfil the earnest desires of the Board and its friends. God had another way of accomplishing his work among the Dakotas. And yet it should not be thought that the expansion was without its influence for good in the future. Those long years of trial, of patient and faithful but seemingly unsuccessful working, spent by the brethren among the lower Dakotas must be read in the light of that after scene in the Mankato prison. Some good seeds planted then, and long lying unproductive, sprung up at last and bore fruit unto eternal life. Then too, as we have seen, the work of Foreign Missions was dovetailed, here as elsewhere, into that of Home Evangelization.

During these years of excitement and change, no very marked progress of God's truth is recorded. Still some additions were made to the churches, several of them "men with small families;" and thus "the number of praying households was increased."

In 1852, Mr. Adams wrote from Lacquiparle: "The attendance on the sabbath services has increased to about fifty." And in the next year Mr. Riggs wrote: "Three Dakotas have recently been admitted to the church, and the young men give us much encouragement. Across a ravine from the mission houses stands a hewed-log house, covered with bark. Formerly it was farther off and was covered with shingles. Years ago it was occupied by

Mr. Joseph Renville. It has since been the residence of his sons. Now it is occupied by Michel Renville, the third son, and the youngest but one of eight children. He was for many years a most reckless fellow, the scapegrace of the family. When a boy in Mrs. Pond's school he threw a slate at her across the school-room. But years have passed by, and Michel has come to man's estate. He has a wife and two children, and 'behold he prayeth.'" So there was encouragement enough to keep up our faith in God.

The treaties of 1851 had now gone into effect, and Dr. Williamson had removed from Kaposia, on the Mississippi, up the Minnesota to the Yellow Medicine. The number of laborers in the Dakota field had been greatly reduced; and the winter of 1853–4 had been exceedingly severe, both for the Indians and the missionaries; but in the early spring Dr. Williamson wrote: "I have never seen any time when the prospect of successful labor among the Dakotas was better than it is now." And a few weeks after this a church was organized at his new station of *Pay-zhe-hoo'-ta-ze* or Yellow Medicine, consisting of seventeen persons, twelve of whom were natives.

The experience of previous years had seemed to lead naturally to concentrated effort as the most likely to be successful. Hence, after the mission houses at Lacquiparle were burned down, and Secretary Treat's visit to the mission, it was concluded to remove that station to the neighborhood of Dr. Williamson's. It was first called New Hope, but afterwards Hazelwood. Nearly all the native members of the Lacquiparle church gathered around the new station.

And now for a brief period, the word

of God prevailed, and the number of disciples was considerably increased. Quite a neat mission chapel had been erected at the Hazelwood station, which was often filled to overflowing with earnest worshippers. The same was true of the house at Dr. Williamson's station, which was used both for a school and for religious meetings. In addition to them, Rev. John P. Williamson had organized a church at the Red Wood Agency, and, without aid from the treasury of the Board, had built a nice church building, which was dedicated only the winter previous to the uprising. And "Bunyan's Pilgrim's Progress," translated into the Dakota language, sterotyped by the Tract Society in New York, and received and read extensively by the native readers, was the emblem of the progress of the gospel among the Dakotas.

CHAPTER XVI.

1857.

SPIRIT LAKE TROUBLES.

The value of missions. — Spirit Lake settlement. — Scarlet End and his band. — Deep snows, and game scarce. — Quarrel with the white people. — The massacre. — Four women taken captive. — They go to the westward. — Mrs. Marble purchased by Spirit Walker's sons. — Brought to the mission stations. — Mrs. Noble and Miss Gardner still in the hands of their captors. — Paul and John Other-day sent for them. — Mrs. Noble killed. — Miss Gardner delivered. — More trouble. — Great fear. — Scarlet End's son killed. — Sherman's battery arrives. — Great gathering of Indians. — Dakotas required to punish Scarlet End. — A soldier stabbed. — The Indian prisoner escapes. — War expected. — A party sent out to find the Spirit Lake murderers. — The report of the Prudential Committee.

"*Cross against corselet,*
Love against hatred,
Peace-cry for war-cry!
Patience is powerful;
He that o'ercometh
Hath power o'er the nations."

"THE indirect value of missions has been illustrated in a most unexpected manner, the only two persons, who escaped the barbarity of the Spirit Lake murderers, having been rescued, at great peril, by men who had learned humanity from our missionaries." So wrote the Prudential Committee of the American Board, in their annual report for 1857.

Spirit Lake is the name given to a group of beautiful lakes lying in Iowa, near the southern border of Minnesota. About two years previous to the time of which we speak, a white settlement had been commenced there; and in the early spring of 1857, there were living in that region some six or eight families, besides several single men. A small party of Dakotas, the principal men of which were *Inkpa-doota*, or Scarlet End, and his sons, belonging to the band of *Leaf Shooters*, had been in the habit of hunting on the Little Sioux River far down into Iowa. This winter they had gone down there as usual. All over that country in the months of February and March, the snow was very deep; and the Indians found hunting difficult and unproductive. In the sparsely settled county south of Spirit Lake, they had greatly annoyed the white inhabitants. But on reaching this settlement, an open rupture with the white people was brought about by causes which it is not necessary to detail here. *Inkpa-doota* and his clan carried their murderous work through the entire settlement, killing about forty persons, and taking four women captive. The Indians seized the cattle, provisions, and clothing of the white people and departed. But the snow being very deep — too deep for travelling, their camp remained in the neighborhood for some time. The news of the massacre was carried to Fort Ridgley, and a detachment of soldiers was sent to follow and punish the Indians. But the white soldiers made their way with difficulty through the deep snow-drifts. They did not see the savages, though they did not themselves escape being seen. The Indians went westward with their captive women, one of whom, not being able to walk a log which was felled across the Big Sioux, was there killed.

While in this region west of the Big Sioux, they came into the neighborhood of some families from Lacquiparle, who were out on their spring hunt. Two young men, sons of Spirit Walker, named respectively Sounding Heavens and Gray Foot, went to Scarlet End's camp, and traded for one of the women. They had their choice, and this choice fell on Mrs. Marble. They took her to their mother's tent, who was a Christian woman. There Mrs. Marble was furnished with good Indian clothes, and well cared for by these young men and their mother. They took her to Lacquiparle, and sent word to Hazelwood and Yellow Medicine that they had a white woman, whom they wished to return to her friends.

Dr. Williamson and the writer went up to bring her down, and found her at the trader's house, with the wife of Sounding Heavens, busily engaged in making a white woman's dress for herself, the materials for which the Indians had furnished. She was asked if she wished to return to her friends among the white people. She did not know; she had found friends who were kindly caring for her and supplying all her needs. But, on farther considering the matter, she was willing to go, and was accompanied to Hazelwood and Yellow Medicine by Sounding Heavens, Gray Foot and their father. The agent, Mr. Flandreau, generously rewarded these young men, giving them $500 in gold and an obligation for $500 more. It was a good deed done, and deserved a handsome acknowledgment.

When Mrs. Marble left Scarlet End's camp, there were two white women left,

— Mrs. Noble and Miss Gardner. The agent lost no time in making arrangements for their rescue. Three Indian men were selected and sent on this difficult and responsible business; of whom Paul was the chief, and John Other-day the second, whose tact and energy were a sufficient guaranty of success.

They were absent several weeks, but found the camp of hostile Dakotas, and, not without some danger to themselves, succeeded in their errand. Very recently, in a letter written by these men to the President of the United States, they speak of this work in this wise: "Great Father! We cannot be deceiving you, when we say that we regard ourselves as white men. Scarlet End rebelled and killed white men and took their women captive; but, because you told us to go after these women, we took our lives in our hands, sought them for you, and delivered them to you." Unfortunately Mrs. Noble had been killed a few days before our men arrived at their camp. Miss Gardner they brought to the mission, where she was dressed again in white woman's clothes; and then, by the agent and her deliverers, she was taken down to Saint Paul. They were all received with acclamations by the Governor and citizens, and the Dakotas were liberally rewarded.

The trouble was not yet over. Scarlet End's people should be punished. How, and where, and by whom should it be done? The following statement of the excitement and dangers which were passed through during the months that followed, is taken chiefly from a letter written by Dr. Williamson for the Missionary Herald.

"The Dakotas in this neighborhood were greatly alarmed, as soon as they heard of murders about Spirit Lake. Though they had no sympathy with the murderers, and spoke of their deeds with horror, they evidently feared that, in some way, they might be involved in the difficulty. In the spring and early part of the summer, various circumstances increased this alarm; such as the terror of the white settlers; the firing of a party of militia on an unoffending party of Dakotas; a report that a large body of Yancktonais were coming here to demand of the annuity Dakotas satisfaction for lands claimed by them, and sold by the said annuity Indians; and lastly, the fact that several expeditions of soldiers had gone to hunt the murderers, but accomplished nothing.

"A knowledge of all these things made it manifest to the Indians about us, and to ourselves also, that our remaining here might be attended with danger. They generally seemed to expect that we should flee. But for our own sakes, and the interests of the mission, as well as the Indians, it seemed manifestly our duty to stay. The danger might become such that I should think it best to send my family away, but it would be better for me to remain and be killed here, should that be the will of God, than to flee."

About this time it was pretty well ascertained that one or more of the Spirit Lake murderers were in White Lodge's camp, which was only two or three miles from the Yellow Medicine Agency. This intelligence was conveyd to Agent Flandreau at Red Wood, who immediately sent to Fort Ridgley for a detachment of soldiers, and desired that he might be joined by a few of the most energetic and trustworthy men of the Hazelwood Republic. John Other-day, Enos Good-hail, and others performed their part well; and owing to their presence and aid, one of the murderers was killed and his wife taken prisoner.

The excitement in the neighborhood now became very great. The Indian women came running to tell the news, and advised us to flee and hide, as many of them did. The Indian men gathered down at the agency, all armed to the teeth. A conflict was expected between the Indians and white soldiers, if not between the Indians themselves. Mr. Flandreau appeased them by releasing the woman, saying that he had taken her only that he might know who she was.

"The Yancktonais, whose visit had been expected for some time, were now reported to be near at hand, and all armed for war. So great was the alarm that the members of the Hazelwood Republic, assembled at Mr. Riggs' with their double-barrelled guns, and kept watch all night;

as much for mutual assistance in defending themselves, as to protect him and his family. The agent also engaged a picket guard of twenty Dakota men, besides the government employés, who were all armed."

This war-party did not, however, arrive for some days; and in the mean time another "scare" was got up by the report that Scarlet End and some of his party had been seen at Lacquiparle, coming to avenge the death of his son. Major (afterwards Gen.) T. W. Sherman's battery was known to be on its way up from Fort Snelling, and a messenger was sent to hasten its coming. In the mean time several hundred Yancktonais warriors arrived. The night before Major Sherman came, "the danger was thought to be imminent, and I asked," says Dr. Williamson, "of my Dakota neighbors, a guard for my house. Three men came and watched through the night."

The arrival of Sherman's battery "had little effect in giving security, and but for the prudence and moral courage of the commander himself, would have increased the danger." The Yancktonais warriors counted the fine horses and mules belonging to the United States troops, and evidently thought that it would not be difficult to cut off the whole company of white soldiers. The number of Dakotas now in the neighborhood had been greatly increased by the arrival of the two thousand northern Sisitonwans, who had come down expecting to receive their annuities.

Three thousand Dakotas, gathered here for various reasons, had all pitched their tents on the beautiful little prairie which lay between Major Sherman's camp on the Yellow Medicine and the station occupied by Dr. Williamson. "Mr. Cullen, the Indian Superintendent, who came up with the soldiers, was instructed by the department at Washington, to require of the annuity Dakotas that they pursue after and punish the Spirit Lake murderers, and to withhold their annuities until this should be done. This requirement the Indians regarded as unjust, and they were very reluctant to engage in the work."

In this camp of about five thousand Indians there was a great scarcity of provisions, which greatly increased the danger of an *emeute*. While negotiations were going on, a young Dakota man made a very insane attack upon the camp of Major Sherman, and stabbed a soldier. He was demanded and delivered up. Would this bring on a conflict and endanger the lives of the missionaries? Mr. Riggs took his family away for a few days down as far as the Lower Agency. Dr. Williamson was so situated that he could not do this.

Major Sherman could not send him a guard, but would give him protection in his camp. Friendly Indians could not protect his family. Neighbors assured him that the hostile bands were about to attack the camp of white soldiers, and that the only chance of safety for him and his would be in their getting out of the way.

In this state of uncertainty about the future, Dr. Williamson saw the hundreds of tents, which stood in sight from his house, "coming down, as if swept by a hurricane, and the Indians moving off in great haste." He then thought it would be wise to take his family to Major Sherman's camp for protection. But before this could be accomplished, he was told that it was too late; that the attack would be made immediately. Shut up to staying at home and trusting in God, it was with joy that he saw these same conical tents again spreading themselves on the prairie about a mile and a half distant. There would be no war that night!

"On one occasion, while the officers were holding a council with the Indians, the young fellow who had stabbed the soldier broke away from his guard and ran directly towards the council. The guard fired low for fear of hitting some one in the council. Several shots took effect in his feet and legs; but, fettered and wounded as he was, he managed to make his escape to his own people. There was some firing of guns on the Indian side also; and, to avoid a battle, by the advice of Mr. Riggs, who was in the council, the prisoner was suffered to escape." The wounded soldier was now getting well, and the Indian would have been released in a few days.

As they took him to their camp, they made a halt not far from the house of Dr.

Williamson, when he and Dr. Daniels, the Indian physician, walked over to see his wounds. As they made their way through the crowd, Dr. Williamson heard just behind him the exclamation, "That knife!" He turned quickly and saw a large butcher knife, in the hand of a woman, raised above his head. She was a sister of the young man who was wounded, and had drawn the knife to plunge it into Dr. Williamson, but a man standing by had caught her hand. "The danger, which I had not feared," said Dr. Williamson, "was past."

Various councils with the Indians resulted in sending out about one hundred Dakota men to find and punish Scarlet End's people. They did, perhaps, all that could have been expected. Little Crow, who was chief of the party, brought back an exaggerated report of what they had done in firing upon the Spirit Lake murderers; and so they obtained their annuities. But Scarlet End's people were not properly punished. And the chastisement they received came not from white soldiers; and hence the Dakotas were confirmed in their low opinion of the bravery of our troops. If that work of punishment had been properly followed up, the great outbreak might not have taken place.

The Prudential Committee, in their next annual report, say: "The excitement among the Dakotas, growing out of the Spirit Lake massacre, has passed away. It operated injuriously for a time in several ways; but the value of the gospel to these Indians stands out more clearly and palpably than it ever did before. Godliness is seen to be profitable for the life that now is, whatever may be its value for the life that is to come."

CHAPTER XVII.

1862.

THE DARK HOUR.

Communion Sabbath at Hazelwood. — August 18th, 1862. — The massacre at Red Wood. — The news carried to Yellow Medicine. — Indian council. — John Otherday delivers a party of white people. — Indians offer to protect the missions. — The missionaries leave. — Houses locked up. — On the island. — The several families get together. — The final departure. — A wounded man. — Dreary nights. — Mr. and Mrs. Moore. — Out of food. — Killing a cow. — Having the picture taken. — Dangers unknown. — Starting for Fort Ridgley. — Seeing Indians. — A dead boy. — The garrison in distress. — The party turn out and go around the fort. — A night of fear. — Situation of Ridgley. — The circuit made successfully. — Four men leave to go to New Ulm. — All are killed. — Forsaken houses. — Provisions found in them. — The Lord delivered those who trusted in Him. — Keeping the Sabbath. — Otherday reaches Saint Paul. — His reception and testimony. — Mr. Mattock's testimony.

"*Far down the ages now,*
Much of her journey done,
The pilgrim church pursues her way,
Until her crown be won.
The story of the past
Comes up before her view;
How well it seems to suit her still —
Old, and yet ever new."

During the twenty-seven years since the commencement of the Dakota mission, we had seen many dark hours, but none quite so dark as this. The day before was the sabbath. The Hazelwood church had engaged in celebrating the Lord's Supper; in which, being joined as was our custom by the church at Pay-zhe-hoo′-ta-ze, about fifty native members participated. That proved to be the last communion ever celebrated in our "holy and beautiful house," the mission church.

Monday came, the 18th day of August, 1862. All was quiet about Hazelwood and the Yellow Medicine. The volcano had burst forth at the Lower Sioux Agency, about forty miles from us. The killing of white people had commenced early that morning, and had been continued all day long, on both sides of the river. Many were making their escape from the almost indiscriminate slaughter, and finding refuge in Fort Ridgley. A company of soldiers, in command of Capt. Marsh, consisting of about fifty men, came up to the ferry, hoping to stop the *emeute;* but they were only fuel for the flame, one half being slaughtered on the bank of the river, and the others escaping to the fort, without their arms.

The news was carried up by men on fleet horses; and not long after noon, it is said, the Indians at the Yellow Medicine had gathered in council to debate the question what they should do. Some favored killing the white people, but the more part advised letting them escape, and. taking only the spoil. In this council was John Other-day, who lifted up his voice against violence and bloodshed, and then left to care for and pioneer the more than sixty white persons of the agency to a safe place. He did his work nobly. The next morning, by daybreak, he and his party were started across the prairie to Hutchinson, the nearest town on the frontier where they would probably find safety.

That afternoon some of Dr. Williamson's neighbors carried the word to the mission. But the sun was near his setting when it was told at Hazelwood. Antoine Renville brought the strange story: "The Indians and white people are fighting at the Red Wood." It appeared, however, like an idle tale, and was not believed. No: perhaps a drunken row had occured, and an Indian had killed a white man. Nothing more! So we suggested. At least the story was greatly exaggerated. But, not long after, Simon and Paul, with others of our neighbors, came in; and all were very much excited. They believed the report. It was being confirmed by additional testimony, they said.

Thus the evening came on. A messenger had passed up in haste to carry the news to the villages above. Two Indian men had come down from Red Iron's village. They brought Mr. Jonas Pettijohn's family, who were on their way moving to the neighborhood of Saint Peter. These men heard the story and started back home. When the night set in, strange Indians were seen flitting around the stables. Some of our horses disappeared before we were aware of the danger, and the others needed to be guarded. As Mr. Pettijohn was coming in the twilight with his last load, having a double team which belonged to the mission, he was met by two Indian men who appropriated the horses. After nightfall, two young Indians were sent down to the Yellow Medicine, who brought back word that the stores were already surrounded by multitudes of Indians, and would be broken into very soon.

At this point in the progress of events, there came to some of us an experience of fear. It was the first realization of real danger. *What should we do?* Our Dakota neighbors said they would protect us and ours; and so they came with their double-barrelled guns to stand guard. But by and by squads of Indians began to pass down from the villages above, and the danger seemed to become more imminent. The Indian men, whose counsel we much valued, began to be alarmed, and knew not whereunto all this would grow. "Could these men protect us?" we naturally asked. They would *try*, at least until the morning. Then, in the language of a chronicle of that time, "We sang, 'God is the refuge of his saints,' commended ourselves to our Father's safe keeping, and the most of us retired to rest. An hour or two was passed, in peaceful slumbers by some, in nervous anxiety by others."

Finally, after midnight, our friends strongly advised us to leave and go to a place of safety. We had too many young women to run the risk of staying; and our remaining might endanger our neighbors also. And so those who had gone to sleep were awakened, and, with hardly a thought whither we should go, we started, taking little besides the clothes we wore. The houses were locked up; but the locks were broken and the houses rifled by the early dawn. As we passed down into the woods behind our mission premises, twenty white persons, young and old, aided and hastened on by our Indian neighbors, the question would come up, "Is this flight necessary?"

We were guided along, through the woods and the tall wet grass, and by daylight were safely paddled over to a sequestered spot on an island in the Minnesota. There we waited to see what the day would bring forth. A few hours told us that we had acted wisely in leaving, but not so wisely in not taking provisions for a journey to the settlements. While we were there an Indian woman, one of our church-members, brought a bag of provisions that had been put up but forgotten. Blessings be upon her! We had started from home with three horses and a double wagon and a buggy; but two of our horses were taken from us before we left the island. Fortunately our friends from Pay-zhe-hoo′-ta-ze, who had left in the early morning, had brought away with them two teams, one of horses and the other of oxen, and, by the help of Indian friends, they had succeeded in getting them safely across the river. They had also driven along some of the mission cattle, and had a partial supply of provisions.

When the sun was declining towards the west, "we took up our line of march," says the chronicle before quoted, "each carrying a bundle, having left on the island the only trunk brought by the party. For a mile or so, we followed up ravines, with difficulty keeping our footing on the side hills which we chose for safety. Reaching the prairie, we came to one of the two teams in charge of Mr. Andrew Hunter, Dr. Williamson's son-in-law. The little baggage which we had was transferred from our shoulders to the wagon, and the feebler ones were provided with seats, while the stronger ones walked on. Soon we came to the remainder of the party, — Dr. Williamson's family and half a dozen persons from one of the government saw-mills, who had cast in their lot with them."

Not long after the final starting, a white man was discovered following with some difficulty. It proved to be a Mr. Orr, who had been shot and stabbed that morning at his trading place near the mouth of the Chippewa. "It seemed a marvel that he had been able to walk so far; and room was immediately made for him in a wagon, though it curtailed that of others. Our journey was rendered unpleasant by a fiercely driving rain-storm, from the soaking effects of which we did not recover until the next day, though it had the good effect of obliterating our trail."

"Night came on, and we lay down on the hard earth to *rest*, with bed and covering both scant and wet. And in the dawn of the morning, we sought our Heavenly Father's protection, and went on our way, having had but little food, as cooked provisions were scarce, and we dared not kindle a fire for fear of attracting attention." *

Wednesday night, the second one out, was a very dreary one. A slow, steady rain continued to fall through all the long

* Narrative of the trip written soon after by Martha T. Riggs, now Mrs. Morris.

night, which completely saturated every article of clothing. All who could do so crawled under the wagons, as if they would afford some shelter. The children cried to go home. They were told we had no home. And then came over us the feeling that our life-work had been in vain. True, we did not then even dream of the extent of the massacres and the wide destruction of property. But it seemed as if this rebellion must sweep over and destroy much of the civilization which we had labored for so many years to produce. The standard of the cross, too, would be thrown down, and our church-members scattered, perhaps much demoralized.

These were sad thoughts; but they were in keeping with the feelings of the whole party. As we were trying to start in the morning, Mrs. Moore thought, such was the discomfort, that *it might be as well to die as to live.* Mr. and Mrs. Moore were a newly married couple from New Jersey, who had come to Minnesota on their wedding tour, and were stopping at Hazelwood mission station. It was to them a sad experience, and one which no one would care to have repeated.

"In that comfortless rain, we drank some milk, ate a crust or two, and travelled on through the long, wet swamp-grass, and the swamps themselves. By noon of that day, which was Thursday, we came near a little wood, where we stopped for the remaining half-day, killed a beef and luxuriated on meat roasted on sticks held over the fire. We also baked bread in quite a primitive style. The dough being first mixed in a bag — flour, water, and salt the only ingredients — and moulded on a box, it was made into thin cakes about the size of one's hand, and placed on forked sticks over the fire, to bake if possible, and to be smoked most certainly." *

At this place Mr. Adrian J. Ebell took a stereoscopic photograph of the company. As Mr. Mattocks, of Saint Paul, afterwards remarked, it was strange that a company who were fleeing from the Indians should stop to have their picture taken. Mr. Ebell was a young artist from New Haven, who had only a few days before come up to the mission for the purpose of obtaining stereoscopic views, and had managed to bring away with him a part of his apparatus.

How great our danger was, while stopping at this place and on the previous days, we never knew. We had, however, several times crossed the trails of parties who had passed out to the settlements to murder and plunder. Afterwards we learned that one party of this kind had started with the

---

* Martha Taylor Riggs' Narrative.

determination to follow us, and they were prevented from doing so by one of our special friends, *Peter Big Fire*, who went with them until after they had passed our trail. Then he feigned lameness, and returned home. Poor fellow! Although he stated this on his trial before the Military Commission, he was not believed, but was condemned for starting out with the raiding party. After nearly two years' imprisonment, he and some others were released by President Lincoln, on a representation of the facts.

Up to this time we had not progressed well. We were trying to make our way, without a road, through an unknown part of the country, and frequently embarrassed by lakes and marshes. Hence, we decided on making our way to the old Lacquiparle road, and going in to Fort Ridgley, if possible. While stopping at the aforementioned road for dinner, Dr. Williamson and his wife and sister overtook us. They had staid until the day after we left; and thought to stay through the uprising, but were persuaded by their neighbors to leave. From this place Mr. and Mrs. Hunter rode over to the white settlement on Beaver Creek, where was their home; but they saw only some Indians, who told them to hasten to the fort.

After holding a council, we pursued our journey, with the intention of reaching Fort Ridgley that night. We felt ourselves in danger, and thought if we were only inside the garrison we should be safe. "The men shouldered their arms, the daylight faded, and we marched on. In the mysteriously dim twilight, every taller clump of grass, every blacker hillock, grew into a bloodthirsty Indian, just ready to leap on his foe. All at once, on the crest of a hill, appeared two horsemen, gazing down upon us! Indians! Every pulse stopped, and then throbbed on more fiercely. Were those men, now galloping away, sent by a band of warriors to spy us out; or had they seen us by accident? We could not tell. The twilight faded, and the stars shone out brightly and lovingly. As we passed along we came suddenly on a dead boy, some days cold and stiff. Death seemed to come nearer; and, as we marched on, we looked up to the clear heavens, beyond which God dwells, and prayed him to keep us."

The garrison at Fort Ridgley were sending up rockets, as signs of distress; but we thought they might be signals to direct our way thitherward. We sent forward a messenger, who returned with the word that the Indians had been fighting them all day; many of the outbuildings were burned, and the fort was filled with women and children.

The commandant of the post said: "If you can go on, go; if not, come in here." Having set our hearts on reaching safety there, some of our company turned out very reluctantly. But, as we had fears that we might be followed, and there were signs of danger where we were, we hastened our steps. We went, striking our way out on the great prairie.

"Ah! if night of fear and dread was ever spent, that was one. Every voice was hushed, except to give necessary orders; every eye swept the hills and valleys around; every ear was intensely strained to catch the faintest noise; expecting momentarily to hear the unearthly war-whoop, and see dusky forms, with gleaming tomahawks uplifted. How past actions came back, as haunting ghosts! How one's hopes of life faded away, away, and the things of earth seemed so little and mean compared with the glorious heaven beyond! And yet life was so sweet, so dear; and, though it be a glorious heaven, this was such a hard way to go to it — by the tomahawk and scalping knife! O God! *our* God! must it be? Then came something of resignation to death itself; but such a sore shrinking from the dishonor, which is worse than death; and we could not but wonder whether it would be a greater sin to take one's life than thus to suffer." In this strain wrote one of the younger members of that company.

Fort Ridgley stands upon a high point of land formed by the intersection with the Minnesota of a little stream coming in from the north, the Minnesota here running south-east. This creek, for several miles up, is deep wooded ravine. A quarter of a century ago, it bore the name of "the Lone Tree," so named from a prominent tree then standing near the common crossing. The prairie on either side is undulating, and generally dry, except in the wetter parts of the year. Many years before, we had been accustomed to travel a road which crossed the stream spoken of about three miles above the fort. Could we find that old crossing in the darkness of the night? In that wooded defile near the fort the hostile Indians were encamped; so that our safety depended upon our getting around quietly, and under cover of the night. As God would have it, we made no mistake in our course. We came directly to the sought-for place of crossing; and, while hunting the ancient road among the growth of willows, the company was startled by a sound near by, which seemed as though it might be the shouting of an Indian calling his fellows. It was probably only the cry of a fox. Thus we travelled on through the night, not without thinking often of our interrupted work;

it seemed as if our hopes were all blasted.
"So the night wore on, until two hours past midnight, when, compelled by exhaustion, we stopped. Some slept heavily, forgetful of danger, past and present; while others sat or stood, inwardly fiercely nervous and excited, but outwardly calm and still. Two hours passed: the weary watchers awakened the weary sleepers, and as quietly as possible the march was renewed."

We had now gotten fairly round the fort; and as the sun arose on that Saturday morning, four of our company — one an Irishman, and three Germans, who belonged at New Ulm — renewed their last night's request to leave. We saw the sheen of their guns in the morning sun, an hour afterwards, as they approached the woods of the Minnesota. Poor fellows! They were even then going into the jaws of death. The Indians, who had fought yesterday at Fort Ridgley, were this morning passing down to attack New Ulm. We heard the reports of the guns by which they were all killed, but knew it not then. We travelled safely on, for God kept us! Although not far from danger, — all day long in sight of burning stacks and buildings where Indians were killing white people, — it came not nigh to us. We felt ourselves comparatively safe; and "Jehovah hath triumphed; his people are free, are free!" seemed to ring through the air.

The houses along our road were all deserted. The people had left in great haste, as in many places we found the dishes on the table. In these deserted houses and corn-fields, we found an abundance to satisfy our wants.

Finally, on sabbath morning, we reached a place where the settlers had gathered together in the road in considerable numbers; and there we stopped to keep the day of rest. We now felt safe, and could breathe freely; and it was eminently fitting that we should unite in the worship of our God, who had brought us safely through this "great and terrible wilderness." "Towards evening," one writes, "my father held divine service, which was almost the only outward reminder that it was the Lord's Day. People were coming and going, — bustle here, there, and everywhere, — so different from our last quiet sabbath at home."

Personally, few had more cause for gratitude than we had. The report had gone abroad over the land, that the missionary company were all killed; and during this long week of suspense, many of our friends were in great agony about us. "Why, we thought you were all killed!" was the greeting that we received. Mr. John Moore, of

Red Lion.—" Gospel," etc , chap. 18.

Clayton, New Jersey, had gone to Philadelphia every day, to hear what the telegraph would tell of his brother and wife. While he was sending a message to the proprietor of the Merchants' Hotel, of St. Paul, to *spare no effort nor expense to obtain the bodies of his dear friends*, they stepped ashore at that place. The hotel-keeper sent back the telegram: "I have obtained the bodies."

On the same morning (August 19th) that the mission party started from Hazelwood, John Other-day left the agency at the Yellow Medicine, with a party of sixty-two, — twenty men and forty-two women and children, mostly government employés. "There was for them only one chance of escape, and that was as one to a thousand against them." So said John Other-day.

"They forded the Minnesota River; and, when on the other side, Mr. Goodell, the superintendent of farming, wanted to go to Fort Ridgley. Other-day objected, and said they must go to Hutchinson and Glencoe in order to be saved." Seven days after, John Other-day arrived at St. Paul, where he received the congratulations of many citizens, and in the evening was introduced to a large audience assembled for the organization of a home guard. He stated that he was a Dakota Indian, born and reared in the midst of evil, without the knowledge of any good; but he had been instructed by the missionaries, had become acquainted with the sacred book, and there learned his vileness. He was a member of Dr. Williamson's church, and his religion had taught him what to do. When he heard of the trouble at the Lower Sioux Agency, knowing that it was not in his power to prevent it, he thought the best thing he could do was to attempt to save the white people at the Yellow Medicine. "With sixty-two men, women, and children," he said, "without moccasins, without food, and without a blanket, I have arrived in the midst of a great people, and now my heart is glad. This deliverance I attribute to the mercy of the Great Spirit."

Rev. John Mattocks, of St. Paul, writes: "John Other-day says it was the gospel of Jesus that made him protect these white people. He wrote his address in my study, and it was translated by Rev. G. H. Pond. It was a noble testimony to the gospel, and a large audience of citizens appreciated it. This has done more for missions than any event during the whole history of the Dakota mission."

CHAPTER XVIII.

1862.

THE RESCUE.

The Sioux outbreak. — Its extent. — The opposing forces. — Indians still successful. — Birch Coolie. — The captives. — Simon brings Mrs. Newman and children. — Lorenzo brings Mrs. DeCamp and others. — The church Bible. — Hope for the other captives. — Wood Lake Battle. — Burned mission buildings. — Camp Release. — A hundred white women and children. — Tears of joy. — Mrs. Huggins cared for by Walking Spirit. — Patient waiting. — Starting for Red River. — The party of rescue; Enos, Lazarus, Robert, and Daniel. — Glad deliverance. — Counter revolution. — John Renville. — Paul, the President of the Hazelwood Republic. — The Christian Indians. — Mr. Pond's statement. — Rewards of government.

" Weak, sinful, blind, to Thee we kneel,
Stretch dumbly forth our hands, and feel
Our weakness is our strong appeal."

" But out of them all the Lord delivered."

THE Sioux outbreak of August, 1862, was commenced with the determination to carry fire and sword through all the white settlements of Minnesota, even to Saint Paul, the capital. For nearly three weeks, the Indians had it all very much their own way.

All over the country they met with but little effective resistance. True, they did not succeed in taking either Fort Ridgley or Fort Abercrombie; but the troops in these places were sore pressed; and possibly a little more personal daring, on the part of the Indians, would have made them masters of the situation. They were repulsed also at New Ulm and Hutchinson, but these places were afterwards abandoned. In two weeks, fifteen or twenty of the frontier counties of Minnesota were almost depopulated. How many white persons were killed in these raids will never be known. At the time there was a great tendency to exaggerate. When everybody was fleeing, and hostile Indians were seen in black stumps and shaking grass, it was natural to estimate the number killed at twelve or fifteen hundred. But a more careful inquiry, during the months that followed, led to the conviction that the victims of that massacre were not more than six hundred; possibly they were less than five hundred.

But it was terribly fearful; and made more so by the fact that many of the men, from these fleeing and murdered families, had enlisted and gone south to help quell the great rebellion, of which the Indian outbreak was an offshoot. Some of these fathers and brothers and sons were in the regiments then organizing at Fort Snelling. There was, of course, hurrying to and fro; and parts of regiments were sent into the field imperfectly equipped. By the last of August, twelve or fifteen hundred troops had reached Fort Ridgley, in command of Col. Sibley. But the Indians still asserted their superiority by gaining a victory over some two hundred of these troops, who had been sent up to the Lower Agency, as a burial party. These poor fellows defended themselves bravely; but when relieved by the rest of the command the camp at Birch Coolie presented a horrible spectacle of dead horses and dead men scattered about, and often partly covered by the suddenly made earthworks.

A loud cry was now coming up from every part of the State; and when we remembered the wives and daughters who were still in the hands of the hostile Indians, this cry became a bitter wail! How can they be delivered?

While still waiting at Fort Ridgley for the army equipments necessary to meet Little Crow, now at the head of the rebellion, some captives were brought to our camp. Simon, one of the elders in the Hazelwood church, brought down Mrs. Newman and her three children. This woman had left the teepee of her captors and sought protection in Simon's family; and she said she felt safe when she found herself in a teepee where they prayed and sung hymns of praise to the Great Spirit! When Little Crow ordered the camp to be removed from the vicinity of Hazelwood up to the mouth of the Chippewa, Simon fell behind, and finally, leaving his own family to take care of themselves, he and one of his sons placed Mrs. Newman and her children in a little wagon, and succeeded in bringing them safely to Fort Ridgley.

About the same time, Lorenzo Lawrence left Hazelwood with canoes; and, hiding by day and travelling by night, he brought Mrs. DeCamp and three children, and Mrs. Robideaux with five children, together with his own wife and five children, and reached the fort in safety. Mr. DeCamp had been mortally wounded in the battle of Birch Coolie, and had been buried only a day or two when his family arrived. Lorenzo Lawrence brought with him also the Hazelwood

Church Bible, presented by Charles, Landgrave of Hesse. On one of the fly-leaves was written by a Christian Dakota, eight days after the outbreak commenced: "The remnant that are yet alive expect to go with the tribe to the British Settlement, trusting in our God that deliverance will yet come to the wanderers."

"We have many captives," they said, in a letter sent to Col. Sibley. The deliverance of those above mentioned not only caused great gladness in our camp, but gave us hope that God would enable us to rescue the rest. Indeed, this was to us the first evidence of that counter revolution which was brought about by the daring and energy of the Christian Indians, and which resulted in the release of nearly all the captives. It was the first lifting up of that dark cloud of almost despair, which had been settling down upon the missionaries in reference to the gospel among the Dakotas.

After much delay the white troops moved up the Minnesota valley; and on the 23d of September was fought the battle of Wood Lake, by which Little Crow's forces were put to the rout, and the backbone of the Dakota rebellion was broken. The gods had fought — "the stars in their courses fought" — and the Wa-kan′ of the Dakotas had failed them in the day of battle. Little Crow and Little Six, and the hostile party generally, fled to the broad prairies of the west, and to the British settlements in the north. We passed up through the Reservation, and found it burnt and desolate. We looked upon the blackened remains of our churches and mission houses. The hostile party had set fire to every house belonging to a Christian Indian on the upper Reservation. This was done for the purpose of committing them to the necessity of fighting and fleeing with the others. But although it was sad to look upon the destruction of our old homes, we did not stop to drop a tear over them, for we knew not yet what would be the fate of the hundred captive women and children who were still in the hands of the Indians.

When our own and the enemies' dead were buried, and our wounded properly cared for and sent back to Fort Ridgley, we pressed on; and, three days after the battle of Wood Lake, reached a point nearly opposite the mouth of the Chippewa River, which we named "Camp Release." Here was a camp of about fifteen hundred Indians, who had thrown up breastworks to protect themselves from the hostile party, when the separation took place. And here we found nearly one hundred white women and children, who had been about six weeks in captivity, some of whom had been shamefully abused. Before the sun went down this company, poorly clad and sunburnt, were delivered into our hand. As they came up in little groups, brought generally by the loyal Indians, who had obtained them from their captors by purchase or persuasion, strong men were moved by the sight, and tears ran down many cheeks for very joy. Some said it was the gladdest day of their life. This was also a day of deliverance to many families of half-breeds, who had been under the necessity of remaining in a state of partial captivity.

But some of those who were known to be in captivity, were not there. Among these was Mrs. Josephine Huggins and her two children. Mr. Amos W. Huggins was the son of one of the oldest missionaries of the American Board among the Dakotas.

He was, at the time of the outbreak, employed as government teacher at Lacquiparle, where he was killed on the 19th of August.* His wife and two little ones went to the teepee of Walking Spirit, where they were cared for and protected from violence. "How thankful I was," says Mrs. Huggins, "when I went in and met a kind welcome from the chief's wife. Here I found food and rest for myself and children. I was so tired, so sad, that I did not try to speak or ask for any thing; but she seemed to understand how I felt, and kindly, even tenderly, supplied my wants."

---

*Mr. Huggins was the author of quite a number of our most popular Dakota hymns; and during the last year or two of his life, he is known to have entertained the idea of especially fitting himself to preach the gospel to the Indians. His death was not supposed to be the result of any personal ill-will; but it was considered as a necessary step in the plundering of his house. It was done by men from another place, in the absence of the Christian Indians of his village.

The chief was not at home; but when he came, Mrs. H. says, "He talked to me very kindly, and made me understand that I was to stay in his house, and when he could, he would take me to my friends." And then she adds: "My poor, weary heart felt comforted. This old man was my friend and protector! For the next six weeks, I found a home in Walking Spirit's family. True, I was a captive, in an enemy's country, longing for deliverance, subject to many inconveniences, many hardships. But the chief and his wife were kind to me, and made my troubles as light as possible. Here I learned patience. Here I gained strength and courage. My husband's Bible was my daily companion, and I felt that God, as a loving father, was ever watching over me and my fatherless little ones."

This personal narrative of Mrs. Huggins

is exceedingly interesting; but we must pass on to its closing part. "Several days before we started," she says, "they told me of a great number of white soldiers who were down below somewhere. They said that Mr. Riggs and Dr. Williamson were among them. I did not understand the half of what they told me. I could only conjecture and wish and wonder. Walking Spirit told me, several times, that, if Mr. Riggs and Dr. Williamson sent for him, he would take me and the children in a wagon, and go." But, although the writer had a deep personal interest in Mrs. H., and had received the most earnest entreaties from her friends to procure her release, if possible, hitherto no such message could be sent to Walking Spirit. Accordingly, he and the whole village started up north. He said to Mrs. Huggins: "You can go or stay, as you like best." "I was perplexed and distressed," she says. "What could I do? Could I contrive any way to go to the soldiers below? I shuddered to think of my danger, should I try to go unprotected. Ought I to make an effort to get some one to go with me? I believed Walking Spirit would have taken me down if he had dared to do so. 'I will go,' I said. And he said they would take care of me; that I should not walk, but ride. His wife said, 'Yes; you and the children shall ride.'"

That night, after receiving the captives at Camp Release, Gen. Sibley very readily adopted the plan suggested, of sending some reliable Indians after Mrs. Huggins. They overtook the fleeing party about eighty miles to the north-west. Mrs. Huggins says of the flight: "We travelled on for four days, over beautiful prairies, and in sight of beautiful lakes. Sometimes I felt cheerful, and sometimes very sad and desponding. Charlie was growing weaker every day. How hard it was to think that my darling might die from the exposure!

"Early one morning, a man came to us with some news. The chief's wife told me something about white soldiers, and about my going, and then asked me if I was glad, — if I wanted to go. I felt bewildered. I did not know what to think. Hardly knowing what I said, I answered, 'I don't know.' She laughed heartily, and said, 'I guess she don't want to go.' About noon we camped, and our folks began to bustle about, making room in the tent, and placing down robes for visitors. They said some one was coming; but I did not understand who it was. I thought they must be distinguished persons, to call forth such preparations. The family were all seated to their liking before the visitors entered. Oh! how my heart did bound with delight and surprise when I saw Enos Good-Hail and Lazarus Rusty, and, in a moment, Robert Hopkins and Daniel Renville! They were looking so pleased and happy, I felt sure they had good news for me.

"After they had shaken hands with us all, and seated themselves, Enos drew two letters from his pocket; one for me, and one for Walking Spirit. Mine was from Mr. Riggs. The chief's was from Gen. Sibley, written first in English, and then translated into Dakota. Here, then, was deliverance!"

With Mrs. Huggins and her children, these men brought two German girls and a half-breed boy. The mother of one of these girls was in our camp; and when the daughter was taken to her, having still another one, she knew not where, she clasped her in her arms, and, looking up wishfully, said, "Mr. Riggs, where is the other one?"

Paul, Elder in one of the Mission Churches.
"Gospel," etc., p. 319.

When, at the commencement of the outbreak, the missionary party abandoned their homes and their flocks, to seek some shelter from that storm of blood, John B. Renville and his wife, who is a white woman, desired to go also. But, for certain reasons, they decided to remain. God had a work for them to do then and there. As John Otherday's white wife decided his course, and secured the safety of that company of sixty white persons, so John B. Renville's white wife strengthened him to initiate the counter revolution; and together they formed a nucleus around which the Dakotas who desired to be loyal might rally.

Beyond all controversy, Paul Ma′-za-koo-ta′-ma-ne, elder in one of the mission churches, and President of the Hazelwood Republic, was the most energetic and fearless in his opposition to the rebellion; and under his leadership the white captives were delivered. But Paul would not have been what he was, the eloquent and successful denouncer of the course pursued by the hostile party, except for the quiet and firm support which he received from Mr. Renville and others. It was exceedingly gratifying to know that all that was done to help white persons to make their escape, to deliver the captives, and to weaken the power of the hostile party by forming a loyal one, was done by Christian Indians, and such as were under their influence.

On this point the testimony of Rev. G. H. Pond is important. It is taken from an article, furnished by request, and recently published by the Historical Society of Minnesota. Infidelity had charged that the missionary work among the Dakotas was a failure, and that the so-called Christian Indians were at that time the worst enemies to the whites. Mr. Pond asks,

"Where is the evidence? Were not those *Christian* Indians, at least by profession, who rescued companies of our people from death, and conducted them, through perils, to a place of safety? Were not those *Christian* Indians who sacrificed their all and risked their lives to protect individuals? Were not those *Christian* Indians who effected the deliverance from bondage and death, or treatment worse than death, of hundreds of captives at Camp Release? Did not the leaders of that band bear *Christian* names, given to them in the holy ordinance of baptism?"

There was one exception to this, and only one — George Spencer's friend, Wa-kin′-yan-ta′-wa, who was a pagan Indian. Doubtless he had something to do in inaugurating the rebellion, but he nobly protected Spencer, and cared for him, and on that account was cleared by a military commission, which investigated his case in the spring following the outbreak.

The government of the United States has recently ordered the disbursement of a sum of money to those who aided in the escape and deliverance of white people. This action was procured by the efforts of Bishop Whipple. In this distribution quite a large number have participated; from John Otherday, who received two thousand dollars, to Zoe, the Indian woman, who carried the forgotten bag of bread to the missionary party on the island, whose portion was fifty. Thus the gospel among the Dakotas is disabused. It did not prevent the uprising of 1862; neither did the gospel in the South prevent the Southern Rebellion.

CHAPTER XIX.

1862.

CAUSE AND CONSEQUENCE.

The uprising. — Trouble at Yellow Medicine. — Agent Galbraith. — Breaking open the warehouse. — Difficulty adjusted. — Soldiers' lodge. — Causes of the outbreak. — Bad faith. — Changing annuities. — Southern war. — Incidental and direct influences. — Enlisting soldiers. — Heathenism against Christianity. — Consequences. — Condemned to be hung. — Hurried trials. — False principles. — Excited state of feeling. — The path of righteousness. — Wicked wish. — False philanthropy. — Justice beautiful. — Vengeance is God's. — The gospel extended.

"*Surely the wrath of man shall praise Thee.*"

As "affliction cometh not forth of the dust, neither doth trouble spring out of the ground," so this uprising came not without cause. So suddenly and unexpectedly did it come upon us that at the time we were at a loss to divine the reason; nevertheless, while some of the causes were more superficial and born of the occasion, others were deep-rooted and had been long working.

Indications of trouble had been from time to time manifesting themselves; and they were more serious than the usual insubordination and unrest which show themselves especially at the times of the annual payments.

A month or so before the outbreak, the agent had some trouble with the Indians at the Yellow Medicine. The Sisitons from Big Stone Lake and Lake Traverse had gathered at the agency, at the ordinary time of receiving annuities. Agent Galbraith told them that he had not sent for them, and could not engage to feed them until the annuity money arrived. He would distribute among them some provisions then; but desired to retain the most of what he had on hand for them until the time of making the payment.

Of course, this was not quite satisfactory to the Indians. The money ought to have been there then. They had come with their wives and children a hundred miles, and could not well go back and come again. So they staid and starved, and that was not quite satisfactory. Under these circumstances, they concluded there could not be much harm in their taking some of their own flour and pork. So a company of the men went to the warehouse, and two of the young braves battered in the door, and they began to carry out the provisions. At this point of the proceedings, the officer in command of a small detachment of soldiers sent up from Fort Ridgley for the occasion, made his appearance and turned the muzzle of his howitzer on the crowd. Though no shot was fired, this scattered the Indians, who immediately removed their camp three miles further off.

The agent was somewhat alarmed, and feared a conflict between the Indians and white soldiers. An hour after, when the author rode down to the agency, he said: "If there is any thing between the lids of the Bible that will produce harmony, I wish you would apply it." I answered that I would try, and went immediately to the camp of Standing Buffalo. That afternoon the principal men were gathered at the agency in council. They told Major Galbraith that they had nothing to eat; that the young men had broken open the store-house under the insanity of starvation; and they authorized him to have the door repaired at their expense. It was evident that no punishment could be inflicted with safety; so the agent accepted their apology and gave them some provisions. Soon after this the Sisitons left for their cornfields.

Some months before, there was formed at the Lower Agency what they call the Soldiers' Lodge. This organization, whenever established, is the acknowledged governing power among the Dakotas. Ordinarily it is resorted to for protecting the buffalo hunt; but now it became a war-council, under color of seeking redress from government for grievances. It is not strange that some persons afterwards claimed to have perceived the coming storm in the cloud-shadows that went before.

However, to understand fully these events, it is necessary to look deeper for the causes, and not only to study the Indian, but our relations to him. The whole Indian system, as adopted and acted upon by our government, seems to be unwise. We have, in our treaty-making, assumed that the various Indian tribes occupying our territories are independent nations; whereas they are wanting in all the elements of sovereignty, having no government, and consequently no power to compel the fulfilment of treaty stipulations. Not capable themselves of making and enforcing laws for the protection of person and property, it became our duty as a great Christian nation to act towards them the part of guardian, making them amenable to law and bringing them under the controlling influences of a Christian civilization. This we failed to do. Besides, the Indian Department has for years been proverbially corrupt and corrupting. When one administration became famous for corruption, and grew rich on Indian "stealings," we expected that the change of parties would bring in more honest men and a better policy. But in this we were too often disappointed. The policy and practice grew worse and worse. Thus the Dakotas had many complaints to make of wrongs, real and supposed.

A second cause of the uprising was the unwise attempt of the new Republican administration to change money annuities to goods. In the autumn of 1861, ten thousand dollars' worth of goods were sent to the Dakotas of the Red Wood Agency, and the same amount to those at the Yellow Medicine. It was proposed to the Indians to be glad on account of these goods; but they were not. They were afraid to receive them. And it turned out that these amounts respectively were taken from their money annuities of 1862. As this gave so much dissatisfaction, the Department was obliged to retrace its steps; but in doing this a delay was caused of six weeks in the time of payment. The money came to Fort Ridgley after the uprising had taken place. It was too late!

But the outbreak will not be fully accounted for until we have linked it with the Southern rebellion. Under any ordinary circumstances, the annuity Dakotas were not so foolish as to break a lance with the United States government. They knew too well the power of the white people. But now, in addition to their numerous grievances, they were excited to war by mere sympathy with war existing. The very hearing of battles fought excites in certain minds a desire to join in such scenes. This operates very powerfully upon warlike Indians.

Besides this indirect and accidental influence exerted upon them by the fact that we were in a state of war, there were influences more direct and positive. When a battle occurred between our forces and the rebels, in which the latter had the advantage in any respect, our Indians were sure to learn the fact, and, oftentimes, with exaggerations. Frequently, such men as Paul and Simon and Lorenzo and Enos and Joseph would come to inquire whether it was so — that their Great Father was so badly whipped; whether it was true that he was likely to be driven away, or captured and killed; whether the South would overrun the North, and make slaves of us all.

By and by, the white men and half-breeds on the Reservation were asked to enlist. To Indians who were disposed to be disloyal this had a meaning. They argued that now their Great Father must be in a great strait for men; and now was the time to strike, when only women and children and old men were left in the settlements. They could now make their way down to Saint Paul, and repossess themselves of the good land of their fathers, for which they had been so poorly remunerated. If there had been no Southern war, there would have been no Dakota uprising and no Minnesota massacres!

And last, but not least, among the causes which produced the Sioux outbreak must be mentioned *the antagonism of heathenism to Christianity and civilization.* Mr. Pond, in the article from which I have already quoted, says: "They hoped to be able to roll back the providential wheels of Almighty God." Such had been the opposition of the medicine men and the war prophets to the religion of Christ, that they only wanted "an opportunity to rise, and re-establish by violence the waning power of the Ta′koo-wakan′, and to return wading through the blood of Christians, if need be, to the homes of their pagan fathers."

But now the uprising was checked. Little Crow and Little Six and all the leaders in the rebellion, with the most guilty of their followers, had fled, taking with them many who were not so guilty. Between four and five hundred men, with their families, including the most loyal of that part of the Dakota nation, had given themselves up, or otherwise had fallen into the hands of our troops. A military commission was organized, before which, during the next month, seven eighths of these men were brought, to prove their innocence or to be condemned as guilty. Of those who were thus brought to trial, about fifty were acquitted, three hundred and three were condemned to be hung, and twenty were to be imprisoned from one to five years.

In looking back upon the work of condemnation accomplished by that commission, two things are very apparent. 1. In the majority of instances, the trial was so brief and hurried, that the facts could not possibly be ascertained. It is to be remembered that forty cases were finished in one day; and there were other days when over thirty were disposed of. 2. The principle, that all participation in the outbreak was worthy of death, acted upon by the commission, was a very wrong one. In many cases, persons acknowledged that they had been present at some battle, as at Fort Ridgley, New Ulm, Birch Coolie, or Wood Lake. If a man was present at one of these places with a gun and ammunition, and had fired off that gun, there was one law of condemnation for him. In addition to this, it was held that a half-breed might be forced to go to these battles, but not a pure Indian.

In considering this action of the military commission, as it has now become a part of history, it is necessary to remark, that the action and the principles on which it was based, were the result of the highly exasperated state of feeling which existed in the minds of all white people on the border against all Indians. "They are Indians," was regarded as a sufficient justification of hasty and superficial trials. Six months afterwards, when men came to discriminate, that same commission would have conducted the trials more properly, and the majority of the findings would have been quite different.

But here again we are reminded that God's thoughts are not as our thoughts. His plan embraced the end, and these condemnations were doubtless necessary to accomplish that end.

Let us endeavor to understand what is the path of righteousness. On the one hand, the border troubles so far maddened a large class of persons against Indians, that they demanded their extermination; and, of course, they were ready to indorse even such wrongs and barbarities as those committed by Col. Chivington on the Cheyennes and Arapahoes. Persons who have had friends killed and scalped, or barbarously treated by Indians, are not likely to discriminate between the innocent and the guilty. To them an Indian is an Indian. In many minds all are regarded as guilty; or if some have not participated in actual murders, it is only because they lacked opportunity. Even the little children are looked upon as devils in the process of growth. It surely cannot be wrong to crush young vipers. A Yankee woman was once heard wishing that the Mississippi River would suddenly rise and drown a whole camp of fifteen hundred Dakota women and children. It is very easy to perceive that justice and right are not here.

On the other hand, it is difficult for those who are at a distance from the scenes of these massacres, to make a proper allowance for the sufferers. The men who have passed through the horrors and deaths of Andersonville, and those only, know what is meant thereby. *We* have heard of those things only by the hearing of the ear. So one needs to have seen whole households murdered, women taken captive and ravished, houses burned, and a whole country laid waste, in the space of a few days, as only Indians can do it, to properly sympathize with the border population, at the time when these men were tried and condemned. In some good men there is discovered a species of sentimentalism, indicated often by the use of the phrase, "The poor Indian!" which unfits them for judging correctly of Indian criminality. In their view Indians have been wronged and cruelly treated, and therefore are measurably justifiable in their attacks upon the whites.

In order to arrive at right conclusions in regard to Indian crime and punishment, it is needful that we find the middle way. Indians are neither so bad nor so good as these different claims would represent them.

In fact they are found to be possessed of all the evil traits of character which inhere in our fallen humanity. Also all the native goodness, which is common to man, not dependent for its development on the humanizing influences of Christian civilization, is found in them. To us they are barbarians. But what makes us to differ from them? Chiefly are we indebted to the Bible for our superior intelligence and more civilized habits. And yet, with all these advantages, the late war has shown the white race to be capable of systematic cruelties which throw the barbarities of Indian massacres into the shade.

Without doubt the Dakota uprising in 1862, was wicked as well as insane. It was a crime as well as a blunder. And justice demanded that a proper punishment should be visited upon the guilty. Soon after these events the author wrote: "All through these Indian troubles, I have been teaching myself the lesson that *vengeance belongeth unto God*. But I have, nevertheless, come to see a *beauty* and a *fitness* in justice which I never saw before. For those who have committed murders the proper punishment is death. I have no sentimentalism on this point. When thirty eight Dakotas were hung at Mankato, in those last days of 1862, I performed my part with no feeling of hate or vindictiveness, but rather of sorrow, but with the feeling also that righteousness required it, that justice was exalted thereby."

So also thought President Lincoln when he had the rolls of the military commission examined, and those selected who were shown, by the evidence, to have participated in individual murders, or to have violated white women. All who belonged to these two classes he ordered to be executed. And the Indians who were executed, while they exculpated themselves individually, acknowledged the justice of the sacrifice. "A great many white people have been killed," they said: "it is right that some Dakotas should suffer."

Such also, it would seem, was the thought of God. The demands of public justice were to be met, and the sacredness of human life vindicated. And in addition to this, the gospel among the Dakotas was to prevail as it had not done before. When they should cry unto the Lord in their trouble, he would deliver them from their distresses.

CHAPTER XX.

1862–1863.

THE MORNING LIGHT.

White man against the Indian. — The gospel against heathenism. — God conquers. — Education desired. — The prison a school-room. — Great progress. — The camp at Fort Snelling. — Demand for books. — Twenty-five years' work. — Change of religion. — Robert Hopkins. — His previous record. — Misapprehended testimony. — His condemnation. — God's plan. — Hopkins becomes the religious teacher. — Round Wind reprieved. — The influence of the executions. — Dr. Williamson. — G. H. Pond. — God's wonderful work.

"Through all depths of sin and loss,
Drops the plummet of Thy Cross;
Never yet abyss was found,
Deeper than that Cross could sound!"

It has been already stated that the ancestral religion of the Dakotas was opposed to the religion of Christ. It was also opposed to Christian civilization. It has been said also, that the conflict which they inaugurated and carried on so furiously, was regarded by themselves as a conflict between the gods. In one aspect, the question was, "Shall the Indian or the white man rule?" But in another and more important one it was, "Shall the kingdom of Christ be set up among the Dakotas, or shall the *worship of stones* be continued?" So especially thought those three hundred and thirty prisoners, who were wearing chains on their ankles in Mankato in the winter of 1862–3. And they regarded the question as having been settled by the events of the last few months. The power of the white man had prevailed; and the religion of the Great Spirit, or the white man's God, was to be supreme. In acordance with this conviction, they were now ready to listen to the messages of God's word; and they were ready also and desirous to avail themselves of the book-education which the great part of them had before rejected with scorn.

Very soon after these prisoners were removed to the vicinity of Mankato, Dr.

Williamson and his sister, Miss Jane S. Williamson, who were then making their home at Saint Peter, visited the prison and distributed some slates, paper, and pencils. In the prison were eight or ten young men, who had previously learned to read and write their own language. To them materials for writing were peculiarly acceptable, as they had then been imprisoned five or six weeks, and the time passed heavily. But when these men commenced writing for their own relief and amusement, it was found that many others wished to learn. From that time all the elementary books that could be anywhere procured, were in demand; and the young men who were at all skilled in the books, became the teachers of classes of ten or fifteen each. During the whole winter that followed, any one going into the prison in the daytime could see these groups scattered all over, around little fires, made on the earthen floor, and all diligently engaged in learning to read and write. It was, indeed, a strange sight. And the desire to learn was so contagious, that almost every man in prison, except a few who were too old, and some who had very sore eyes, made the attempt. Their progress too was very rapid. In less than three months, the majority of them had learned enough to be able to write letters down to their families, who were that winter kept at Fort Snelling. In the month of March following, the author visited the prison, carrying a package of about four hundred letters up to them from the camp; and about the same number were sent down by him on his return.

With little or no instruction, except what they gave each other, many of them were soon able to read fluently, and to write a beautiful hand. Here was a fact that could not be gainsayed. So far as their religion was concerned, the genuineness of their professions might be doubted and disbelieved; but here was a conversion which commanded belief. These men, only a few months before, were determinedly opposed to education. They would not permit their children to go to school. Now they have taken hold of it with an enthusiasm which is amazing. And not only do they learn themselves, but they write down to their wives and children and their other friends, exhorting them to learn also. So the camp at Snelling, in like manner, is turned into a great school, and almost every tent is a class-room. Every boy and girl and man and woman, who had learned before, is almost by force turned into a teacher, and labors in this work without reward. The demand for elementary books in the Dakota language suddenly became so great that it was necessary to have some hundreds printed in Minneapolis.

Thus was the number of Dakota readers of the Bible greatly multiplied in a few months, and that at no outlay to the mission except for the books. Twenty-five years of labor had preceded; the language had been reduced by patient and persistent work to a written form; and books had been prepared to meet the demand as it progressed. But here was a revolution in letters, which asked us only to stand still and see what God was working out!

There was, besides, a revolution in their minds of more significance than their educational progress. Indeed, there was a revolution of which their desire for education was only one exponent. The gods whom they and their fathers had worshipped and trusted, had failed them. The god of the waters and the god of the prairie, the god of the storm and the god of the woods, the god of motion and the stone god, together with the so-called medicine men and the war-prophets — all these had failed to deliver them. The spell was broken, and they turned now to Christianity.

Among the prisoners was Robert Hopkins Chaskay, a man thirty two or three years old, quite tall, and good looking. He was one of the civilized band of Indians, and an elder in the Pa-zhe-hoo-ta-ze church. His wife, Sarah, a devoted Christian, has already been mentioned. Hopkins was quite impulsive, and possessed a great deal of energy. He had, at the commencement of the outbreak, guarded Dr. Williamson and his family while they remained, and aided them in making their escape. Evidently he had no sympathy with the rebellion, and had no knowledge of it until it burst upon them. But after the white people had all been helped away from the neighborhood of the Yellow Medicine, Hopkins, being curious to know the extent of the war, went down to the Lower Agency, and thence to Fort Ridgley and the neighborhood of New Ulm. Looking at this part of his course, it seemed unfortunate that he had not remained at home. He was now where he might be led into some wrong path; and, at any rate, his being there might be taken as evidence against him. When passing through the settlement, he and one or two others came to a deserted house. He went around the house, fired off his gun, and came back, saying, "I have killed!" This was told before the military commission, in the absence of Hopkins. They understood that he had killed a human being; it was only an ox. Nevertheless, this was the reason for his condemnation, and he would have been executed, if his friends had not interested themselves in his behalf. Indeed, other efforts not succeeding, a letter written by Miss Jane S. Williamson to President Lincoln alone saved him. God, who makes no mistakes, had a work for him to do in the prison, as he had for Joseph in the land of Egypt.

When the new religion was sought for by the prisoners, Hopkins was there to explain to them the Christ of God, and the way of salvation through faith in his dying for us. Dr. Williamson commenced visiting them and preaching to them regularly on the sabbath. Before the executions there was manifested more than usual religious interest; and one old man, whose name was on the list to be executed, came forward on the sabbath preceding that event and desired to be baptized. It is proper to say he did not then know that he was in that black catalogue of thirty-nine. Two days after, he and the thirty-eight others were taken out of the common prison and placed in a room by themselves, and more securely chained. Round Wind, for that was his name, said that he was ready to go to the "spirit world," for he believed in Christ the Saviour. He did not, however, die with the rest, but was pardoned by a telegram from President Lincoln, which came only the night before the executions took place. The old man attributes his salvation directly to God. The fact was, he had been condemned on the testimony of a German boy, who declared that he was the man who killed his mother. The boy was mistaken. Round Wind was several miles off when the boy's mother was killed.

The executions made a profound impression upon all in the prison; and fear undoubtedly had a powerful effect upon them. They knew that their remaining pagans would not save them. If they became Christians, as the missionaries urged them to do, would that deliver them? Perhaps. Something like this may have been the process of thought in their minds. It would not be strange. Then, too, the unexpected deliverance of Round Wind may have pressed in this same direction. But, whatever was the moving cause, fear or hope, or *both combined*, one thing was certain: they now received the preached word of the Lord as hungry men take food.

The sabbath immediately after the executions, which was the last in the year, the prisoners were all permitted to come out into the prison yard, where the author preached to them. Dr. Williamson, having spent the previous week with the condemned men, was worn out, and had returned home. In the prison yard the fresh snow lay nearly a foot deep; but these men, chained two and two, came around the speaker and stood during the whole service. By this time many of them had learned to sing, and they did sing with spirit some of our most moving Dakota hymns. They opened also their ears to the truth, and it was to them evidently "good tidings of great joy."

Dr. Williamson continued to preach to them through the winter, usually walking up from Saint Peter, about fourteen miles, on the Friday or Saturday before, and staying until Monday or Tuesday. These men have since frequently spoken of that self-sacrificing work of Dr. Williamson. They had always believed the missionaries had some selfish motives in preaching to them. But that laborious winter's work, performed under the peculiar circumstances, satisfied them of their benevolent designs.

During the next five or six weeks, the religious interest continued to increase. The greater part of the prisoners were what we called Lower Indians, who had formerly resided in the villages near Fort Snelling. Ten years before, they had known the Pond brothers, who had come to the Dakota country at so early a day, and labored with and for the Indians until their removal to the upper Minnesota. When the question was, "Shall we change our religion?" these men naturally remembered their teachers of other days, whose instructions they had then refused. They wanted to hear what the Messrs. Pond would now say to them. It was in answer to this call that Rev. G. H. Pond went up, some time in February, and spent a week in the prison with Dr. Williamson. The men had begun to ask to be baptized into the faith of Jesus, the Son of the Great Spirit. Day after day the number desiring to make a profession of this new faith increased. The circumstances were unfavorable to a very satisfactory examination of each individual. As on a former memorable occasion, they asked, "Can any man forbid water, that these should not be baptized?" Taking advice of Rev. Marcus Hicks, who was then the pastor of the Presbyterian church in Mankato, and giving special instructions on the nature of baptism as the initiatory rite into the Christian church, when each one of that multitude asked, "What doth hinder me to be baptized?" the brethren answered, "If thou believest with all thine heart, thou mayest." And there were added to the church that day more than two hundred souls!

CHAPTER XXI.

1862—1863.

THE ADVANCING DAY.

Sympathy between the camp and the prison. — Women most disposed to receive the gospel. — The incomprehensible. — John P. Williamson. — His moral heroism. — His labors in the camp. — The good work of the Lord. — Bishop Whipple and the Episcopal mission. — The Lord's Supper in prison. — Three things prayed for. — That chain. — The prisoners taken to Davenport. — Singing Old Hundred. — The penitential Psalm.

"*And the Leaves of the Tree are for the healing of the Nations.*"

THE religious awakening which commenced in the prison at Mankato, extended to the camp at Fort Snelling. There was, indeed, a kind of electric sympathy existing between the two places. Communications were numerous and frequent. Many of the same influences which were operating on those in prison, were equally powerful in the camp. The women, too, being more easily impressed than the men, were more disposed to accept the gospel. Another advantage which the women had, was that they had not generally been so much under the influence of their ancestral superstition. One woman, writing to her husband confined in prison, said to him: "You have been a great *wakan'* man; what do you think of it now?" The question had reference to the man's faith, and intimated her own past unfaith in those things, as also her present belief in the new religion.

At the time the outbreak occurred Rev. John P. Williamson, son of Dr. Williamson, born at the Lacquiparle mission station, was absent in Ohio. He had graduated at Marietta College and Lane Seminary; and, after preaching awhile to white people, had commenced a station at the Lower Sioux Agency. The summer previous, he had there erected a mission chapel, and organized a small church. It seemed quite providential that he was away, as the work of death commenced near and at his boarding-place. But when the news of this rebellion reached Mr. Williamson, in Ohio, he immediately started back, and, as soon as practicable, identified himself with this Dakota camp, as its religious teacher. There was something very noble in his thus casting in his lot with those who were then hated and despised. The older missionaries could afford to bear shame and reproach for the sake of Christ and his cause among the Dakotas. It was little to them, if men despised them. Their life had been given to this work, and they had no other young life to spend. But he was young, — he could have occupied a desirable position in one of the Ohio or Indiana churches. Hence, his choice to labor among the Dakotas, in such circumstances, was a manifestation of moral heroism. But the Master has richly rewarded him! During that first winter he was permitted to rejoice in a glorious work of grace among the lowly.

As in the prison, so in the camp, the school and the church occupied the time. Every evening, and often during the day, men and women and children were crowded into tents and engaged in prayer and praise. Hard by the camp stood a large one-story warehouse, the upper part of which, immediately under the roof, was procured for holding religious services. Often that room was packed, away under the roof, with old and young, met to praise and pray to the God of our fathers; and of many it will be said: "This Indian was born there." More than one hundred were added to the church in the four or five months they were kept at Fort Snelling.

The Episcopalians also shared in this work. Two years before the outbreak,

Bishop Whipple had established a mission at the Lower Sioux Agency, and placed Mr. Hinman in charge. He, with a lady teacher, had providentially escaped to Fort Ridgley on the morning of August 18th. Friendly relations and kindly intercourse have ever prevailed between that mission and ours. It would be pleasant to be able to say that they used no measures to proselyte from our schools and communion. But that could not be expected of the High Church party, who do not acknowledge any other true Christian organization. While they have, from the beginning, used books prepared by our missionaries, singing our Dakota hymns and reading our translations of the Scriptures, they have, in their publications and public speeches, altogether ignored our work among the Dakŏtas.

In the month of March the author went up to Mankato and spent ten days with Dr.

Williamson in the prison. At this time the Lord's Supper was first administered to them. The prison was a low building made of large logs on a vacant lot between two houses. The sides were only about four feet high, and there was only room for all the prisoners to lie down. The ground floor was covered with straw, except where the little fires were kept burning. Along through the middle of this low room, three or four guards were stationed. At this time, the prisoners were enjoying more liberty than during the early part of their confinement. Some had their chains removed from their ankles; others were still wearing them, but were not fastened to a fellow prisoner; while some still remained as they had been.

Of their own accord, during this meeting, the prisoners drew up a paper which declared that they had agreed together to pray for three things. The first was their freedom, "the removal of that chain." The second was that God would give them a country again, where they and their families could have a home. And the third was for a "sacred house," or church.

All through the services on this occasion, there was great interest manifested; and every thing was done decently and in order. Even the changing of the guards caused very little interruption. The only exception to a very orderly communion was that one old man, as he took the bread and wine,—home-made currant wine,—prayed audibly that that chain might be taken off. The minister remarked that there were other stronger chains than that binding us, the chains of sin, which the Master was able and willing to take off, and to bring us into the perfect liberty of his children.

In the spring of 1863, soon after navigation opened in the Mississippi, both the prisoners at Mankato and the occupants of the camp at Fort Snelling were removed. The majority of the latter were taken to Crow Creek on the Missouri, and the former were placed in one of the military camps near Davenport, Iowa.

A writer for the Saint Paul Press said of the prisoners, as they descended the Minnesota and Mississippi, that they were much engaged in religious worship, carrying their prayer meetings far into the hours of the night. And as the boat, which conveyed away these two hundred and seventy chained Indians, passed St. Paul, they were singing the words of David to the tune of Old Hundred. The following is a pretty close translation of the first part of that Dakota hymn:

Jehovah, have mercy upon me,
For thine own mercies sake;
Thy loving-kindness is very great,
Therefore place me in thy heart.

My sin has been against thee only ;
So that if thou shouldst condemn me —
If thou shouldst punish me —
I would esteem thee just.

I know mine own iniquity —
The foolish things I've done ;
From these do thou me cleanse,
And wash me thoroughly.

For blotting out transgression
Not any thing is able ;
The blood of Jesus only
Shall cleanse away my sin.

CHAPTER XXII.

1863–1866.

DAVENPORT AND FORT THOMPSON.

Three years of trial. — The scouts' camp church. — Crow Creek Agency. — Dry summers. — Work and temptation. — The gospel progressing. — Elders class-leaders. — Mr. Williamson's church. — Mr. Pond teacher. — The prisoners at Camp McClellan. — How treated. — Escape meditated. — Hopkins prevents it. — The prisoners make trinkets. — Education continued. — Religious services. — Hopkins released. — The prison a theological school. — A test question. — Native doctoring. — Cause of disease. — Conjuring, or powwowing: is it consistent with Christianity? — The opinion of the mission. — The question discussed. — Reasons for continuing it. — Many sick. — Christ healed the sick. — Question submitted to the elders. — Their decision. — Belief in the power of prayer.

"*So hearts that are fainting*
Grow full to o'erflowing,
And they that behold it
Marvel, and know not
That God, at their fountains
Far off, has been raining."

THE next three years were still years of trial for these Dakotas. About thirty or forty families were retained in Minnesota, and the men employed by the military as scouts and messengers. They were half-breeds and such full-blood loyal Indians, as had signalized themselves in behalf of white people during the outbreak. These families had no permanent residence or planting-grounds, but were removed from place to place under the direction of military commanders. By this contact with soldiers, they would naturally suffer much, morally and religiously. Besides, their circumstances were not favorable to progress in education. And yet, it is a matter for thanksgiving, that the majority of the professing Christians in this camp held fast to their integrity. The church organized among them was called the Church of the Scouts' Camp, and embraced a large share of those who were church members before the outbreak.

Fort Thompson, or Crow Creek Agency, was on the eastern bank of the Missouri, about 240 miles above Sioux City. Among the twelve or thirteen hundred persons taken to that place, there were but few men. The two next seasons proved to be very dry, so that neither corn nor potatoes were raised anywhere in that region of the Missouri. This was very disheartening to the Indians, and resulted finally in their removal to the Niobrara, in the summer of 1866. But although there was no corn in the field, and no herd in the stall or on the prairie for them, many more of them became Christians, and their children almost all learned to read and write in their own language, and some made good proficiency in English. Doubtless with truth, it was stated that, up to a certain point, few white communities were educated better than that.

"Starvation was followed by disease, and in the three years of their residence at Crow Creek, over three hundred died. The women made themselves hewers of wood and drawers of water for all the white settlements in the territory. The trenches of the army and the cellars of the farmers were dug with their hands; the woodyard of the steamboat, the saw-mill, the cornfield and the kitchen were all familiar to the Santee women, as places for finding employment; and, with sorrow for the morals of our fellow countrymen, we may add that to many of them the soldiers' barracks were, alas! too familiar. At the same time that the Lord, by sword and famine, was driving hundreds to the truth, the devil used his seductive arts to keep them away.

"The feeling that God had visited them for their sins, universally felt and often openly acknowledged, led to a national repentance and general profession of Christianity, with the hope that God would avert his wrath and be gracious to them. However, in many cases the work was not one of personal conviction; and the heart, not being renewed by the Spirit, the prospect of a present supply of their daily wants was sufficient to lead such still farther down to destruction." *

Mr. Williamson's church, at this time, numbered about 250; and, as the greater part were women, he found it expedient to appoint "deaconesses," whose special duty it was to conduct prayer meetings and to take charge of classes of women. As the members of the Dakota mission were members of Presbytery, the churches organized were on the Presbyterian model; but in this particular of classes they were on the Methodist plan. The *Hoonka'yape*, or elders, occupied very much the position of class-leaders. Some plan of this kind was found to be needful, both for the instruction and proper watch and care of the members.

*Rev. John P. Williamson.

In the work of education at Crow Creek, and since at Niobrara, Mr Williamson has been efficiently aided by Mr. Edward R. Pond, son of Rev. G. H. Pond, formerly a missionary to the Dakotas. In the autumn of 1868, Miss Julia A. La Framboise joined this station as teacher. Her maternal grandfather was *Sleepy Eyes*, a chief of the Dakota nation, always friendly to the white people. Miss La Framboise was educated in mission families, and afterwards graduated at the Female Seminary of Rockford, Illinois.

The Indian prisoners at East Davenport were kept at Camp McClellan, a recruiting post of United States volunteers. They were confined in a wooden fort, which was surmounted by a guard walk, and inclosed about an acre and a half of ground. Within were four long buildings put up hastily, and with green lumber, having, of course, an abundance of cracks to let in the air. For a while the Indians were pretty closely guarded; but by degrees they gained the confidence of their keepers to such an extent, that their chains were all taken off and the guard reduced to those who kept the door. In the summer of 1864, about ninety more were brought down. They consisted of whole families, men, women, and children, who had delivered themselves up to our troops at Pembina. None of them had been tried by military commission, and, consequently, were not under condemnation.

The women and children were allowed to go out of the prison during the daytime at pleasure. The men were called out to cut wood, carry up water from the river, and, in general, to do the work of the camp. When a new officer and new troops came to guard them, the freedom of the prisoners was abridged, and they were treated with more severity. But, after a few weeks' acquaintance, the Indians gained the confidence of their keepers, the prejudices of the soldiers wore away, and they came both to pity and respect the red man. Often a dozen Dakota men would be permitted to go out on a deer-hunting excursion, with but a single white soldier accompanying them. During hoeing and harvest times, squads of prisoners were sent out to the farm-houses around, with or without a guard. Thus they had frequent opportunities to run away, but they never made the attempt. It is said that, at one time, an escape was meditated by a few; but a rumor of the intention reaching Hopkins, he and others represented to the parties concerned that an attempt of this kind would probably not be successful; that it would result in their all being more severely dealt with, and perhaps they would again be reduced to chains; and, finally, that it would put off the time of their hoped-for release.

While the prisoners were at Davenport they were not idle, but often drove a brisk trade in rings, birds, fishes, crosses, and other ornaments which they made from the muscle shells of the Mississippi; and also in moccasins and bead work, and in bows and arrows. With the money they made in these ways they supplied themselves with some of the luxuries of life, and also with books and materials for writing. At one time they purchased more than a hundred Dakota Testaments, some of which, with expensive binding, cost from one to two dollars each. At another time, they appropriated the entire earnings of a week, amounting to nearly ninety dollars, to reimburse expenses incurred in efforts to obtain their liberation.

The educational and religious movement

that commenced in Mankato was continued in East Davenport. Night and morning, as they returned, were witnesses of their devotions. Sometimes they gathered all together, and at other times their worship was conducted in the different houses. They read the Scriptures; they sung and prayed. Besides, they had their regular times, during the week, for prayer and exhortation. The sabbath services were always kept up and well attended. In the absence of the missionaries, Robert Hopkins was the acknowledged religious leader. Although then not formally licensed to preach, he was known among white people as the preacher. By order of President Lincoln, he was released in the autumn of 1864, but remained at Davenport until the spring following; and during his whole stay in the prison he was the teacher of religion. He thought it hard that for no crime he should be condemned and imprisoned, and so long separated from his wife and boys; but it was the Lord's will, and the work he did for his people was the Lord's work; and he was comforted thereby.

In the first two years which succeeded their removal from Mankato, Dr. Williamson spent a considerable part of his time with the prisoners. During these years the author visited them twice, staying ten or fifteen days each time, and was with them the last winter of their imprisonment. On two different occasions, they were rejoiced at seeing and hearing Mr. John P. Williamson, who came to them from their friends at Crow Creek. Mr. Alfred L. Riggs, also a son of the mission, who was then preaching at Lockport, Ill., came down once and again to give them instruction in singing. It was intended to make the prison a religious educational training school; that on their release, these men should be prepared to carry the gospel to the regions beyond. That these efforts, under God, were not unsuccessful is shown by the fact that three of the men who were in prison are now preaching the gospel as licentiates, and two as ordained ministers, co-pastors of the native church at Niobrara.

The gospel among the Dakotas should not fear to be subjected to the same tests as are applied elsewhere. How did it meet and grapple with their ancestral customs?

Among all nations disease and death are common. The heathen die as fast as Christians, perhaps faster; and when sickness comes into a family, it would be inhuman not to make some efforts to alleviate and cure. This feeling belongs to our humanity. It is greatly influenced and shaped, but not created, by the Christian religion. Among the Dakotas, and probably all Indian tribes, the method of treating the sick is that known to us as powwowing, or conjuring. By them it is called Wape'yape, or renewing.

Disease, they say, is caused by spirits. The gods are offended by acts of omission or commission; and the result is that some spirit of an animal, bird, or reptile, is sent by way of punishment, and the man is taken sick. The practice of "renewing" must accord with the theory of disease. It will not be met by roots and herbs, or medicines, properly so called, but by incantations. Hence, the Indian doctor must be a Wakan' man; that is, he must be inhabited by a god, which will enable him to cast out demons from others. The process includes chants and prayers, and the rattling of the sacred gourd-shell, as well as the application of the mouth of the conjuror to the diseased parts, to suck out the cause thereof.

"This operation is continued for hours, and sometimes day after day and night after night, with brief intervals for smoking. The process sometimes effects a cure very soon. At other times, more powerful demonstrations are deemed necessary. The doctor ascertains the sin which has been committed, and the god offended which has inflicted the disease. Then he makes an image of the offended god and hangs it on a pole, which, at a particular time in the powwow, is shot by three or four persons in quick succession. As the image falls to the ground, the god in the doctor, leaping out, falls upon the spirit represented by the image, and kills it. The sick one is now expected to recover. But his recovery is not absolutely certain. After repeated experiments, the doctor often discovers that the Wakan′ which has inflicted the disease is more powerful than the one which inspires him." * He can then do no more. Another doctor, with a mightier Wakan′ than his, must be obtained, or the sick person must die. Every effort of these native powwows must be paid well for, usually in advance. Hence, it is a lucrative profession, and one that will not be easily displaced. Will Christianity modify or abolish this system of conjuring?

From the commencement of the Dakota mission, we had never taken any fancy to powwowing. It appeared to us that such terrible screeching, and groaning, and singing, and rattling, and sucking, would make a well man sick, rather than a sick man well. This was education. An Indian did not think so. But soberly, we thought it was not a civilized and Christian way of ap-approaching a sick person. We had, also,

* Rev. G. H. Pond, in the Minnesota Historical Society's Annals for 1867.

an opinion about it as wrong and wicked, thus to come in contact with the evil spirits, over the suffering body of one sick. Hence, Dr. Williamson always refused to practise medicine in a case where the conjurer was also employed. And it had been pretty generally understood, that we regarded the Dakota system of treating the sick as inconsistent with a profession of Christianity. Still the question could hardly be considered as finally settled.

In October of 1865, the question came up for discussion and settlement in the prison on this wise. During the summer, when no missionary was with them, a number of men had yielded to various temptations. Some had drunk beer, and, perhaps, something stronger, to an extent that they could hardly be called sober. Some had been hired by white men to dance an Indian dance, and others had either powwowed or been the subjects of the powwow. In the adjustment of these cases, one man, admitting that he had practised as a Dakota conjurer, claimed that it was right. His fathers practised in this way, and were often successful in healing the sick. He grew up in this system of doctoring, and had also practised it with success. He was not skilled in any other mode of treating disease. The white people had their medicine men. No one was willing to see a friend die without making some efforts to prolong his life. It was merciful; it was right. Jesus Christ, when on earth, healed the sick and cast out devils. Besides they — the prisoners — were in peculiar circumstances. More than a hundred had died since their imprisonment. And the white doctor, who was appointed to treat the sick, cared not whether they died or lived. Indeed, they thought he would rather have them die. When a good many of them were sick and dying with the small-pox, he had been heard to say that his Dakota patients were doing very well! Thus they were under the necessity of endeavoring to heal their own sick by the only method in which they were skilful. This was the argument.

The missionary would not decide the question, but referred it to the elders. After two weeks, they signified their readiness to give the decision. When they were come together for this purpose, they were told that the gospel of Christ moulded the customs and habits of every people by whom it was received. There might be some wrong things in a national custom which could be eliminated, and the custom substantially retained; or the custom might be so radically absurd and wrong that it could not be redeemed. In that case, Christianity required its abandonment. It was for them, with their knowledge of the teachings of the Bible, and the requirements of Christ's religion, to decide on the character of this custom of their fathers.

There were twelve elders. Very deliberately each one arose, and stated his opinion. Two thought the circumstances were such that they could not altogether give up their ancestral method of curing disease. They were shut up to it. But ten agreed in saying that the practice of conjuring was wrong, and inconsistent with a profession of the Christian religion. They said the notion entertained by the Dakotas, that disease was caused by spirits, they believed to be erroneous; that sickness and death, they now understand, come not out of the ground, but by the appointment of the Great Spirit; that the system of conjuring brings men into contact with the spirits of evil, and tends to lead them away from Christ. This decision was a finality in the prison on that point, and is accepted throughout the mission churches.

As a sequel to this, may be mentioned a story told by Mrs. Pond at Niobrara. They had read in James, "Is any sick among you? let him call for the elders of the church; and let them pray over him: and the prayer of faith shall save the sick, and the Lord shall raise him up." One of the elders was quite sick, and the disease was quite obstinate. They practised on the advice of James. They gathered together and prayed over him; and this they did many times. Finally, the man recovered; and they said, when speaking of it, "Why, he ought to get well; for we have had four prayer-meetings with him."

CHAPTER XXIII.

1835-1869.

CIVILIZATION.

Influence of the mission. — Mr. Lynd's testimony. — The Bible the great civilizer. — Condition of the Dakotas as regards civilization. — Stone knives. — The plough and the hoe. — Missionaries worked. — Indians build cabins. — Women taught to spin, knit, and weave. — First weaving done in Minnesota. — Untoward circumstances. — Influence of "the Dakota Friend." — Seed long sown germinates. — Government influence. — Progress in civilization. — Nucleus of civilization. — The Hazelwood republic. — The Constitution. — The first signers. — Building a chapel. — Advance in agriculture. — More houses built. — Government aid. — Brick houses. — Another civilized band. — Labor lost in the outbreak. — God gathers up the fragments, and prepares for higher developments. — A government of law needed. — Indians can be civilized.

"Stronger than steel
Is the sword of the Spirit;
Swifter than arrows
The light of Truth is."

"The influence of the mission among the Dakotas has ever been of a direct and energetic character. The first efforts of the mission were directed more to the Christianizing than to the civilizing of the Sioux;

but, of late, the missionaries, though their exertions in the former respect are not at all abated, have been more earnest in their endeavors to teach the Indians to plant and to till." Their work "has been a ceaseless and untiring effort to promote their welfare." These are the utterances of James W. Lynd, a young man of education, who was a member of the Senate of Minnesota, and who spent a number of years among the Dakotas, studying their language and customs, and was killed on the first day of the outbreak at the Lower Sioux Agency.*

On the statement of Mr. Lynd, that "the first efforts of the mission were directed more to the Christianizing than to the civilizing of the Sioux," one of its members remarks: "Our previous efforts in that

*Mr. Lynd had in the course of preparation a book concerning the Dakotas, the fragments of which only were recovered, and are now in the keeping of the Historical Society of Minnesota.

direction were bringing forth fruit in the later years of the mission." That uncivilized heathen nations should *first* be civilized, and *then* Christianized, is a sentiment of the past. Now it is coming more and more to be acknowledged, that *the Bible is the great civilizer of the nations.* Modern missions have carried with them the plough and the hoe, and all the materials of civilization. So, at least, it was in the Dakota mission.

The habits of the Dakotas, in regard to labor, were decidedly against progress in civilization. All the man's education has hitherto been to make and keep him a hunter and a warrior. He may take furs, and kill game, and go on the war-path; but the planting and hoeing of the corn, the cutting of the wood, and dressing skins, with the carrying of burdens, and other hard work necessary in a hunter's family, belong, of course, to the woman. And while all this is the woman's work, the implements employed will be of the rudest and most ineffective character. In planting and tilling the ground, nothing was used but a very heavy club-hoe. The wood also was cut with a round-eyed axe, such as no white man would be willing long to use.* But, as the men were taught by precept and example that labor was honorable, these barbarous implements gradually gave place to better models. The plough, too, was

* There is evidence that the Dakotas, prior to their intercourse with white men, used stone axes and stone knives. Their name of Mille Lac was Isan-ta-mde, or Knife Lake; and, from their dwelling there, they are called *Isanyatee*, corrupted into *Santee*. On that lake they found the stones which they could make into knives and axes. In 1674, a party of Dakotas are said to have visited the Jesuit mission at Sault St. Marie, where "a Cree Indian insulted a Dakota chief by brandishing his knife in his face. Fired at the indignity, he drew his own stone knife from his belt, and shouted the war-cry."

introduced. As early as the spring of 1835, we find the Messrs. Pond aiding the Indians with the plough to prepare their corn patches for planting. It soon came to be understood by them that ploughing the ground not only made planting and hoeing easier, but was a guaranty of a better crop. A few years after this, those Indians who resided near Fort Snelling received, through treaty stipulations, the aid of farmers at their several villages. But, as these farmers did the work for the Indians, instead of teaching them to do it themselves, it was difficult to see that they were really advanced in civilization.

The missionaries, on the other hand, working without pay from government or the Indians, were careful to see that their efforts were mainly in the line of teaching them. Seldom were they disposed to plough a patch of ground, unless the man held the plough or drove the team. And so, by and by, as years passed on, one and another of the young men came out more and more on the side of labor. By degrees, it came to be less dishonorable for a man to work. The missionaries worked; and they were not common Frenchmen, — the menials of the traders. When the first Dakota man at Lacquiparle put on pantaloons, and fenced and ploughed and planted a field, and, with some assistance, built a log-cabin, he brought upon himself a storm of persecution. But, bearing it bravely, others followed his example. "Two Indian men built log-cabins for themselves," is the record of 1842.

And while the men were thus slowly led to regard labor as manly, and to begin to take their share of bearing the burdens of life, it was thought equally necessary to teach the women certain things. At the Lacquiparle station, about the close of the year 1839, we find this record made: "A part of the forenoon is devoted to teaching the girls to sew, spin and knit." And again: "Mr. Huggins, about the beginning of cold weather, made a loom, and a few of the women spun the filling and wove six or eight yards of cloth." About a year after this, Dr. Williamson wrote: "The females who attend school spend half their time in learning to spin, sew, knit, and weave. Within a year the Indian women, with some aid, have spun and wove twenty yards of flannel and blanketing." This was probably the *first spinning*, certainly *the first weaving* done within the limits of the State of Minnesota.

The history of the next dozen years of missionary effort, in the line of civilzation, may be told in few words. A combination of circumstances, the chief of which was the partial failure of the crops at Lacquiparle, produced a scattering of the Indians from that place. There arose about this time, moreover, a strong and determined opposition to both the religion and the civilization of the white man. The resolution to stand by the ancestral faith was general, extending all over that part of the country, and it could hardly be said to be broken in upon, until the treaties of 1851 had been made and ratified. Indeed, with quite a large majority of that people the settled purpose not to change their religion and the customs of their fathers was manifest up to the time of the outbreak in 1862, and as already intimated was one of the chief causes of that outbreak.

"The Dakota Friend" may be mentioned here, both as a civilizing agent and an evidence of progress. This was a small monthly newspaper published by the mission, partly in English and partly in Dakota, and edited by Rev. G. H. Pond. By many of the readers in the Dakota language its appearance was hailed with joy. But changes in the working force of the mission and other circumstances made its discontinuance necessary in 1852.

The teaching of the mission, which had been continued wherever practicable during all those years of opposition and discouragement, began to produce manifest fruit, soon after the occupancy of the Reservation on the Upper Minnesota. Two Indian agencies were then established, one near the Red Wood, and the other at the Yellow Medicine. The payments of the Dakotas residing above, being made at the latter place, there was a tendency to drift from Lacquiparle and other villages towards that point. Dr. Williamson had already removed from his station at Kaposia, near Saint Paul, up to the Yellow Medicine, or Pay-zhe-hoo-ta-ze. And when the mission houses at Lacquiparle were burned in the early spring of 1854, it was thought best, after consultation, to remove that station down to the same neighborhood. The plan of concentrating the working force in that neighborhood embraced in it, from the beginning, the idea of collecting the civilized and Christianized Indians together for the purposes of mutual protection and higher progress. In the carrying out of this plan, all the Christian men who joined the new station were to adopt civilized habits of dress and to make for themselves houses and cultivate fields.

In the summer of 1856, this matter had so far progressed, that it was deemed necessary to form a civilized band which should elect their own chief or president. On the 29th of July a constitution was adopted and signed by seventeen men, eight of whom were half-breeds. They called themselves "The Hazelwood Republic." Besides the president, they were to elect a secretary and three judges; the duty of the latter officers to be the arbitrating and deciding of all disputes between man and man.

In this constitution they professed their faith in the one God, as opposed to the many gods of the Dakotas, and their desire to regulate their lives by the teachings of the word of God. They professed their earnest desire for education, and pledged themselves to the support of schools. They were to conform themselves to the habits of white people, to live in houses, cultivate fields, and keep stock; and for all injuries done by any one to the person or property of another, restitution or remuneration was to be required. They abjured the Dakota modes of life, and pledged themselves to work for the elevation of their people. They would be obedient to the laws and to the officers of the United States government, and would ask the agent to recognize them and their families as a separate band. This is the substance of their mutual covenant. The agent readily acceded to their request, and treated them thenceforth as a separate organization.

Among the men who first signed this constitution are the names of Paul and Simon, Lorenzo Lawrence, Joseph and Enos, Robert Hopkins,* and the Renvilles, whose record in the the outbreak, as well as before and since, is an honorable one. Many of these men, and others, built for themselves houses, some of which were log-cabins and some frame-houses. They also contributed liberally in work and money

* The Indian namesake of Mr. Hopkins, the missionary who was drowned.

to the erection of the Hazelwood church, a neat frame building capable of accommodating about one hundred persons. At the front was a bell-tower, which below served as vestibule, and in which above swung a clear-toned bell, that called the people together to worship God. The entire cost of this building was about seven hundred dollars.

Dr. Williamson's station was two miles from Hazelwood, and that much nearer the Yellow Medicine. In the year 1857, he writes, in regard to the progress in civilization in his neighborhood: "The advance in agriculture and house building is greater than in religion and letters. Last year, for the first time, the Dakotas of this neighborhood raised more corn and potatoes than they needed for their own consumption during the year. They have sold many bushels of each, and some have yet to spare. There are now in the neighborhood fifteen Dakota families living in log-cabins, and two in framed houses. None of our male members, who have wintered here, now live in tents, and but few of the female members. The cabins consist of a single room, but have one or more glass windows, and nearly all of them a stove."

About this time, the United States government, in fulfilment of treaty stipulations, commenced expending considerable sums of money for the Indians on this Reservation, for purposes of civilization. The men who would have their hair cut, and put on pantaloons, should have fields ploughed and houses built for them; and they would be furnished with work-cattle, wagons, etc. The battle against their Indian prejudices having been already well fought by the mission, the government came up as an ally to lead on to victory.

As building timber was not very abundant on the Reservation, brick was introduced; and, in the next four or five years, the prairies around the two agencies were well dotted over with one and a half story brick houses, which were erected by the Department, and occupied by Dakota families. "During the past summer," wrote Dr. Williamson, in November, 1860, "the United States government have erected for the Indians in this neighborhood not less than a dozen brick houses."

In the mean time, there was formed a civilized band at the Red Wood Agency, on the model of the Hazelwood Republic, the members of which, in the outbreak, did good service to the white people. But no other band or portion of a band adopting civilized habits, making fields, and living in brick or frame houses built for them by the agent, embodied in it so much of the educational and religious elements as the Hazelwood Republic.

When, after the outbreak of 1862, we looked upon the burnt dwellings and desolated fields on the Upper Minnesota, and saw the people imprisoned or scattered abroad, it was hardly possible not to regard the efforts which had been made, through long, weary years, to civilize them, as having been a failure. The labor seemed to be lost. But, since that time, it has become quite apparent that God, who rules over all, means not only to "gather up the fragments, that nothing be lost," but, by building deeper and broader, to erect a better and more abiding civilization.

Although poor, and giving little external evidence of progress in respect to property, there are now many more of those Santee Dakotas who are prepared for and desirous of being introduced into the status of civilized men, than there were previous to the rebellion. What is now wanting to bring them up into thrift and independence is that they have, like all other classes of people in this country, the protection of law, and that they be likewise subjected to the wholesome restraints of a just government.

Belonging to the same human race, and being very much like other heathen, the Indians are capable of being civilized and Christianized. But give them a chance, and hold out proper inducements to them. Make it possible for them to become men, and help them to become such; not by feeding and clothing them, except for the present necessity, but by showing them that work is honorable and remunerative, and that the law of labor is one from which no people are exempted; and, above all, by leading them through education and religion up to the knowledge and experience of a higher life.

CHAPTER XXIV.

1835–1869.

EDUCATION.

Schools. — The place of education in the mission work. — The missionaries generally engaged in teaching. — A goodly list. — Teaching in the vernacular; also in English. — School at Lacquiparle. — Boarding-schools at Lake Harriet and Hazelwood. — Native teachers tried. — Preparation for schools. — Education carried on by their own efforts. — High School at the Santee Agency. — Lessons learned by our experience: 1. Learning to read in Dakota easy. — 2. Reading Dakota a step in education. — 3. Its great advantage as a preparation for learning English. — 4. English boarding-schools not the best means to accomplish the great ends. — 5. Teaching the vernacular necessary to evangelization. — 6. A people should be elevated together by common schools. — The government plan defective. — Thought education needed. — Books already printed in the Dakota language.

"*The entrance of thy word giveth light.*"

SCHOOLS occupy a very important place in the missionary work. In some missions among the Indians, the school is the first and almost the sole agency used; and this is in accordance with the common theory that the heathen should be civilized and educated before an attempt be made to Christianize them. Among the Dakotas the school was always subordinate to the preaching of the gospel. But it was, nevertheless, always regarded as a most important and indispensable auxiliary.

To this work of school teaching all the members of the mission gave their time; some for longer and some for shorter periods, some partially and some almost exclusively. Among the women, the first teachers at Lacquiparle were Miss Sarah Poage, afterwards Mrs. G. H. Pond; Mrs. Mary A. L. Riggs, and Miss Fanny Huggins, afterwards Mrs. Jonas Pettijohn; while at the Lake Harriet station, during those first years, were Miss Cornelia Stevens, afterwards Mrs. Gavin, and Miss Cordelia Eggleston, afterwards Mrs. S. W. Pond. Then came Mrs. Agnes Hopkins, now the second Mrs. G. H. Pond, Miss

Julia A. Kephart, and Miss Jane S. Williamson, who has given her life to the blessed work. Still later came Miss Amanda Wilson, Miss Lucy Spooner, now Mrs. Drake, and Miss Mary Spooner, now Mrs. Worcester, both of Cincinnati, Ohio; and Martha Ann Cunningham, now Mrs. Rogers. And connected with the boarding-school, which will be noticed hereafter, were Mr. and Mrs. H. D. Cunningham, Mrs. Anna B. Ackley, Miss Ruth Pettijohn, Miss Eliza Huggins, and Miss Isabella B. Riggs, now Mrs. Williams, of the North China Mission.

The teaching done at the various stations, in the day-schools, was mostly in their own language. It was found to be the most productive teaching. Reading, writing, and arithmetic were the branches taught. They learned to read their own language easily; and that knowledge we found to be helpful in learning English. At the same time, the English language was taught to all who desired it; but the results were not very encouraging, except as the children were gathered into boarding schools or taken into mission families.

During the first half dozen years of the mission, the day-school at Lacquiparle was prosperous, and only occasionally met with opposition. And even when at other stations the schools were tabooed, and teaching was stopped, it went on with but slight interruptions there. At one time, about one hundred pupils were reported in all the schools, fifty-four of whom were readers.

When, in 1854, the Hazelwood station was projected and occupied, a small boarding school was a part of the programme. Nearly twenty years before, Mr. Stevens had started such a school at Lake Harriet. It was continued for several years, and was the means of educating some half-breed girls, who made wives for white men, and did good in the world. And in the years that followed, something was done in this line by taking children into the various mission families, and teaching them the English language, and giving them the advantage of Christian family culture. Some did not turn out as well as we hoped; but of several the missionaries could say, "These are our jewels."

But the time seemed to have come when more should be done in that line, and when greater results might be expected therefrom. Rev. M. N. Adams, when at Lacquiparle, had gathered the nucleus of a school; and when the station was removed to Hazelwood, a building was erected for that purpose, and the children placed in charge of Mr. and Mrs. H. D. Cunningham. It was successfully carried on until the outbreak.

Previous to the trouble in 1862, we had

at various times employed native teachers with encouraging success. The desire was to bring the means of education within the reach of all the Indians in that part of the country, and to encourage and stimulate all to avail themselves of its advantages.

With a system of notation in which there were no silent or redundant letters, it was easy for a Dakota to learn to read and write his own language. The missionaries had given much time and labor to the preparation of suitable elementary books, as well as hymns, translations of Scripture, and other means of instruction. When trouble came, and turned the minds of many of the Dakota people to education and the new religion, all this previous preparation was found to be just what the wants of the people required.

Since that time education has made rapid progress, and that with little effort and expense from us. Their teachers have been from among themselves. The ability to read and write has come to be valued among the Santee Dakotas on the Missouri River in Nebraska, and the settlements on the Coteau des Prairies, near Fort Wadsworth.

All that has been required of the mission for the last few years has been to furnish books, some of which the Indians have purchased, and some they have received as a gift. The school taught by the missionaries themselves at the Santee Agency is of a higher grade. It is a day-school. The teaching is chiefly in the English language. All who are instructed here have previously acquired the ability to read and write in their own tongue. This school is expected to raise up teachers, not only for their own community, but for the bands of Dakotas who have as yet received no instruction.

Our experience in prosecuting the work

of education among the Dakotas for a period of thirty-three years has taught us the following lessons: 1. That teaching Indians to read and write in their own language, when they are willing and desirous to learn, is very easy. One of the Cherokee delegation, which I met in Washington a year ago, said, that to read Cherokee was so easy that every one learned without going to school at all. In the Dakota language it has been found not quite so easy as that.

2. The ability to read and write in an Indian language is of itself a great step in education. It gives the man an understanding of what letters mean. It is to him a process of culture. He is not now the ignorant, superstitious man he was before.

3. The Dakota scholar, by having learned the art of reading in his own tongue, which he understands, is thereby able more intelligently and vigorously to take hold of the

English, which he does not and for a long time cannot understand. This point we think very important. It is the firm and unanimous conviction of the members of the Dakota mission, that if you would teach an Indian boy English, the easiest way is to teach him his own language first. He will not then be groping so entirely in the dark. He will have some idea of the value of the thing and of the way in which it is to be accomplished. Add to this the discipline and the culture thus secured, and it will readily appear that teaching in a vernacular tongue is, in the beginning, the most profitable teaching.

4. It follows from these experiences that the boarding school, in which young children are taken and cared for and taught in and through the English language alone, is not the quickest and most economical way of reaching the desired end. It does result

in imparting to a limited extent a knowledge of the English tongue, with much that is very useful and important, but only to a small number of a tribe. But the great mass of the people are not reached by it. And so it often happens that by a large expenditure of money and time a few are raised above their people in culture and knowledge, only to be dragged down again, in many cases, to nearly the same level.

5. Above all, as a means of evangelization, education should be in the vernacular. Men's hearts are reached through their understanding. But it is found that a language imperfectly understood is a poor medium for conveying religious instruction and making religious impressions. The language of childhood and home is the language that stirs the religious sensibilities, and wakes echoes in the soul; it is the language that God uses in reaching and moulding anew the spiritual nature.

6. We come, then, to the conclusion that, most easily and successfully to accomplish these great ends of education, all the members of a tribe, as far as possible, should be reached by some system of common schools; and so all, or a large portion, will be elevated together, through their own language first, and then up through the English tongue, thus finally bringing the Indian, as well as the African, up to the high place of knowledge and progress occupied by the white man.

The plan of educating Indians heretofore employed by the government has accomplished very little. This is partly because, in too many instances, it has been in the hands of men who cared only for the money; but more, I think, because they have been unwilling to adopt any extended ideas of education. Valuable as a knowledge of English is, and necessary too, we may say, for the future growth and prosperity of any people on this North American continent, it is very manifest that one may talk English and yet have no education worthy the name.

There is something in every human being deeper than language, which must be reached by the communication of thoughts and principles. And even more radical still is the power of thinking itself, which cannot be easily educated except through a familiar language. Ideas must be communicated which will beget in them a new life. In an Indian as well as a white man, a right purpose needs to be formed. So long a time will be required to do this, if only the English language is employed, that the opportunity for doing it will have passed away.

What the government ought to do is to organize a system of common schools, which shall, as soon as possible, reach the whole people. First reach them in and through their own tongues; and then as soon as practicable raise them up to be an English speaking people So far as the Dakotas are concerned, if the government will adopt some such plan, they can easily avail themselves of the books which have been prepared by our mission, and also of the natives who are already educated. Almost immediately two hundred Dakota teachers might be put into the field.

The experience of the last third of a century should not be ignored. The present situation of the Indian tribes calls very loudly on our nation for wiser counsels in dealing with them, and the application of some more effective plan of education.

As a means for the further successful prosecution of this work among the Dakota people, the books already prepared by the mission deserve some particular notice. In writing the language, the English characters were used, with the addition of a few marked letters, which represent sounds foreign to us. School-books have been prepared at various times in the progress of the work. *Bunyan's Pilgrim's Progress* and *Precept upon Precept* have been translated and printed by the Tract Societies of New York and Boston. A Catechism has been prepared and circulated among those who are readers. A Dakota hymn-book, containing more than one hundred hymns, has been in the hands of the people for many years, and is highly valued.

In 1851, a Dictionary and Grammar of the Dakota Language was printed under the direction, and chiefly at the expense, of the Smithsonian Institution. This was distributed to the various colleges and seminaries of learning in this country and in

Europe. The Dictionary contains about fifteen thousand words. The book is not now in the market. Prof. Henry of the Smithsonian Institution, recently expressed the regret that it had not been stereotyped, since, as he said, there was more demand for that than for any of the other volumes published by the Institution. It is a missionary contribution to science, and possibly may be the means of perpetuating the remembrance of the Dakotas, beyond the time when, as a distinct people, they shall have disappeared from the continent.

As soon after the commencement of the mission as it was possible to do so, portions of the word of God were prepared and printed for the Dakotas. This work of translation has been continued from year to year, until now they have the entire New Testament and several books of the Old Testament electrotyped and printed by the American Bible Society. Among a heathen people the Bible rightly takes its place in the fore-front of the efforts to civilize and educate.

CHAPTER XXV.

1863–1869.

EVANGELIZATION.

Release of Davenport prisoners. — Taken to Niobrara. — Meeting their friends. — Visit of Dr. Williamson and Mr. Riggs. — Re-organization of the church. — John B. Renville licensed and ordained. — Incident at Mankato. — Artemas and Titus licensed. — Their ordination. — Others licensed — Simon, Peter, Robert Hopkins, and Solomon. — Louis at Fort Wadsworth. — Kettle Lakes church organized, and Louis licensed. — Camp-meeting at Dry Wood Lake. — Daniel Renville licensed. — Churches of Ascension, Dry Wood Lake, and Long Hollow. — Gathering at Buffalo Lake. — Solomon ordained. — Missionary tour among the wild bands of Dakotas. — What means this preparation but the nation's evangelization?

"But unto you that fear my name shall the Sun of Righteousness arise with healing in his wings."

WHEN President Lincoln was killed, and the nation was thrown into mourning, the Indian prisoners at Davenport also mourned. They had a personal reason for their sorrow, for his death put off the day of their deliverance. While he was yet alive, their release had been determined on, and only needed to pass through the requisite forms. But when Mr. Johnson came in, the work had all to be done over again, and they were not released until 1866. In April of that year they were taken to join their families on the Missouri. More than one hundred had died in the three years they were kept at Davenport, but as some thirty men with their families had been added after their first coming there, and a few children had been born, about two hundred and forty souls made their exodus from this house of their bondage.

They were landed in the northeast corner of Nebraska, at a place called Niobrara, immediately south of the stream of that name. Niobrara, in the Ponca language, means "swift running water," as Nebraska, in the Omaha, means the Platte or *flat water*.

It was expected that the families and other friends of these men, who had been kept at

Crow Creek for three years, where they had failed to raise any corn, would meet them on their arrival at this new place, which had been selected for their future home. But there was an unaccountable delay in bringing them down. The Davenport people had arranged to meet their friends with a religious ceremony. They were to go forth in a body, and on approaching them were to kneel down and have a prayer, after which were to come the greetings of the long-separated ones. But this plan could not be carried out. They were so long in starting from Crow Creek, and then so long on the road, as they came by land, that young men slipped off in the night to meet them. In this way the majority had joined their friends before they reached the neighborhood of the Niobrara. As described by themselves, the meeting was both a sad and a glad one. Many wives looked in vain for their former husbands; they had gone to the spirit land. So there was wailing. Some men returned to find their women the wives of other men. But to the greater part, on both sides, there were causes of rejoicing. Many met for the first time as Christian men and Christian women, and, as soon as practicable thereafter, they had this relation solemnized in a Christian way. During the next few months, Mr. J. P. Williamson joined in marriage about fifty couples.

In the July following, Dr. Williamson and myself, having visited the Dakotas at the head of the Coteau near Fort Wadsworth, passed over to the Missouri, and came to the new settlement at Niobrara. While we remained there, two of the elders who had shown themselves apt to teach, were selected and licensed to preach the gospel to their own people. As the church at Crow Creek and the one in the prison had met, a re-organization and re-adjustment of the classes became necessary. Would they constitute one church or two? Their choice was to be consolidated into one, which then numbered nearly four hundred members. This church, from its numerous removals, has been properly named *Ohne'hday*, or *the Pilgrim Church*.

When the gospels of Mark and John were being translated from the French by Mr. Joseph Renville of Lacquiparle, more than a quarter of a century ago, there was a little boy who often played in the room where we wrote. He was the youngest of Mr. Renville's eight children. His name was John Baptiste. The old man called him *Koda' mita'wa*, "my friend." This little boy, as he grew up, acquired a pretty good Dakota and English education, and, coming to man's estate, he married Miss Mary A. Butler of Galesburg, Ill. After being employed as a teacher, both by the government and the mission, he was licensed to preach the gospel by the Dakota Presbytery in the spring of 1865, and ordained as an evangelist in the autumn following. Mr. Renville, as a preacher, is "eloquent and mighty in the scriptures," and has had a general supervision of the work near Fort Wadsworth.

An incident occured in connection with the licensure of Mr. J. B. Renville, which is significant of the temper of the times, another phase of the opposition to be stemmed by the mission. It took place at Mankato. The meeting of the Presbytery had been appointed for that time and place, eight months before. But so it was, that on that very day a party of hostile Dakotas, coming down from the British settlements, had made a "strike" but a few miles out of town. It devolved on Dr. Williamson, the last Moderator of the Presbytery, to open the present session with a sermon. In that sermon he enforced the necessity laid upon this great Christian nation to deal justly with the inferior races, — the African and the Indian. That evening one John Campbell, a half-breed Dakota, was brought into town. The Jewett family had been murdered, and there was abundant evidence that Campbell had participated in the murders. The popular excitement was of course very great. The next day Campbell, without a trial, was taken by the mob and hung on a tree. The unreasonable populace said this Indian raid and massacre had taken place because Dr. Williamson had come to their town; that on a certain previous time he had passed through, and immediately thereafter, in the neighborhood, white people had been killed by Indians. Dr. Williamson should not stay in the town of Mankato. So they sent a committee of the principal men of the place, to demand his immediate departure. This committee came to the Presbyterian church, where the Presbytery was in session, engaged in the examination and licensure of John B. Renville. Some members of the Presbytery were disposed to resent the visit of that committee on such an errand. But Dr. Williamson yielded to the unreasonable demand of the excited people and left.

In the summer of 1867, the Dakota Presbytery met for the second time with the Pilgrim Church, which was then at Bazil Creek, a few miles below the Niobrara. At this time the church was counselled to choose pastors of their own. It was a step forward which we desired them to take, as necessary to a progressive and permanent work of evangelization among them. Accordingly, a meeting was held at which the members, both male and female, voted for their spiritual guides. The election resulted in the choice of *Artemas E'hua-ma-ne* and *Titus Mah-pe'-ya-wa-kan'*, our licentiates of the year previous.

In their low log building, with earthen floor and dirt roof, at an assembly of the church, we set apart these native men to the work of preaching the gospel and administering its ordinances among their own people, and especially to this church. They have already obtained a good report as apt to teach, and earnest, faithful shepherds of Christ's flock. The church to which they minister has undertaken to contribute for their support at the rate of fifty cents a quarter for each male, and twenty-five cents a quarter for each female member.

On the Coteau des Prairies there was need of more laborers, and of men especially set apart to the work. Accordingly, in the summer of 1866, *Simon Ana'-wang-ma-ne* and *Peter Big-Fire* were licensed to preach the gospel. They both had been, for several years, acting as ruling elders and class-leaders. Both have been honorably spoken of before in this history.

In the year following, two more were licensed; namely, Robert Hopkins, who was the leader of the religious meetings in prison, and Solomon Toon-kan′-sha-e′-che-ya, a comparatively young man, whose religious teachings have been both acceptable and profitable. Besides these, there are many, both men and women, who are aiding in the work of evangelization as leaders of classes and religious meetings, and as teachers of schools.

In the early part of the winter of 1867, one of the elders in the Pilgrim Church went over to Fort Wadsworth and commenced holding religious meetings. There he found about twenty young Dakota men who had enlisted as soldiers. Some of them had families, who, with other Indians living near by, and the frequent visitors of the place, helped to make a good Dakota congregation. Among these people *Louis Ma'-za-wa-kin'-yan-na* commenced a good work. When the missionaries went thither in August, 1868, they received a request from the people that a church might be organized, and Louis licensed to preach the gospel to them, they promising to provide for his support. This request was granted, and the church of Kettle Lakes was organized with twenty-eight members. The chaplain of the port, Rev. G. D. Crocker, has taken quite an interest in Louis and his work, and helped both him and it.

For several years past, it has been the practice of the missionaries, at their annual visit to this part of the field, to hold an old-fashioned "four-days meeting," which is a real camp meeting. After spending some time in visiting and preaching to them at their various localities or planting places, a central point is selected and the time appointed. It might answer somewhat to the feast of Tabernacles. A booth is constructed of forks and poles, and covered with willows and grass, under which to hold public meetings. From various distances, even twenty-five or thirty miles, the people come with their tents, their families, and their provisions, and camp there.

In August of the past summer such a gathering took place at Dry Wood Lake. On that occasion there was something more than a common religious interest. The number received to those mountain churches during that time and the few weeks before was about sixty; and as they stood up on that sabbath to be baptized, they and their children, they formed three very long rows!

The week that followed this scene at Dry

Wood Lake, was witness to a significant gathering at Buffalo Lake. As the families were becoming more and more settled, and local churches could be arranged, it seemed good to the members of the mission to re-organize them. Accordingly, besides the Kettle Lakes church already mentioned, three others were organized on the mountain, and one within the borders of the State of Minnesota.

The Ascension church, or church of the south mountain, had chosen Daniel Renville, a young man of much promise, to be their preacher, and we had licensed him. The church at Dry Wood Lake was ministered to by Simon and Peter; and the Long Hollow church, or the church of the north mountain, had elected Solomon to be their pastor. The gathering at Buffalo Lake was for his ordination. It took place in a large, circular summer house; for it was a raw day outside, and the bright fire that blazed in the centre was very comfortable. Our friends, Rev. G. D. Crocker and wife, and Doctor Comfort, surgeon of Fort Wadsworth, were present. It was quite an impressive scene. After a sermon by Dr. Williamson, and other necessary parts of the service, we proceeded to lay hands on the fourth native Dakota pastor, and to charge him, in the name of the Lord, to be a faithful worker in Christ's vineyard. Mr. Crocker, through an interpreter, gave the charge to the people.

Several weeks were spent last summer in visiting wild bands of the Dakotas. Accompanied by one of the native pastors, and an elder of the Pilgrim church and Rev. John P. Williamson, the writer passed up the Missouri River, on a missionary tour among the Yanktons, the Brulés, the Two Kettles, and the Hoonkpatees. Everywhere we were kindly received, and found some to listen to the proclamation of the way of life through Jesus. This part of the field is open. There are also other bands of Dakotas to the westward of the Missouri, who have not yet heard of Christ — the Sansarcs, the Minnekonjoos, the Cut-heads, the Hoonkpapas, and the Black Feet.

Voices have come to us also from places north of Fort Wadsworth, — from Fort Ransom, at the Bear's Den on the Cheyenne, from Abercrombie, on the Red River of the north, and from Fort Totten, at Devil's Lake. They are asking for books and teachers. Indeed, the Dakota nation is opening to the gospel of salvation. The work of their civilization, education, and evangelization is being pressed upon us. We ask ourselves if God means their redemption. Why those four ordained ministers of the gospel? Why those other five licentiates? What means the large number of ruling elders and class-leaders raised up in those six native churches? What is the meaning of that army of more than half a thousand professors of the religion of Jesus among the Dakotas? What mean those books in their language? yea, those words of Christ and his Apostles, and of Moses and David? What does all this mean, under God, but the evangelization of the Dakotas?

So will there be a lasting glory in this work, — in the elevation of the degraded and in the purification of the impure; in the salvation of the lost, through faith in Jesus Christ our Lord.

APPENDIX.

I. DAKOTA MEDICINE.

II. DAKOTA SONGS AND MUSIC.

III. LABORS OF OTHER SOCIETIES.

DAKOTA MEDICINE.

BY REV. T. S. WILLIAMSON.

Spirits the cause of diseases. — Conjurers first find out what spirit causes the sickness. — Casting out spirits. — Use of the rattlesnake's rattles. — Character of the conjurers. — Many of them partly idiotic. — Some give medicines alone. — Kind of medicines used. — Methods of nursing. — Bloodletting. — Vomiting and purging. — The use of a species of euphorbium, and its effects. — How to promote appetite. — The process of sweating. — Anæsthesia and anæsthetics. — Their practice of surgery and treatment of wounds.— Treatment of swellings and burns.

AMONG the Dakotas, as among other heathen races, the office of physician and priest were, for the most part, united in the same person. This being the case, it is not strange that their pathology should be shaped by their ideas of the spiritual world. Supposing every object, artificial as well as natural, to be the habitation of a spirit capable of hurting or helping them. and that all diseases were caused by some one or more of these spirits taking possession of a part or the whole of the body of the patient, to determine the name and nature of the spirit causing the trouble was regarded as the first business of the physician or *conjurer*, as we usually call the medicine man of the aborigines of our country. This he attempted, not only by observing the symptoms, but by incantations addressed to the spirit or spirits which were the special objects of his worship, and expected on that account to befriend him.

The second business of the medicine man was to drive out the intruding spirit. This was attempted by all kinds of horrid noises and gestures, not omitting to call upon his god or gods for assistance. He also, in most cases, applied his mouth to the skin of the patient near the diseased part, and, after sucking for some time with all his might, would put his mouth in water kept in a vessel usually made of bark for that purpose, and blow into the water phlegm, mucus, or blood, which he pretended to have drawn from the seat of the disease through the skin; but in most cases they doubtless came from his own mouth or throat. In many cases he would also introduce through his mouth into the water a small pebble or shell, which he would show as evidence that he had extracted the offending cause of the disease through the skin. As in this work, by shrieking, screaming, groaning, shaking his rattle, stamping and other threatening motions, the conjurer exerted all his strength, it was customary, even in cold weather, to divest himself of all clothing except his breechcloth, moccasins, and leggins; and the latter, instead of being bound about his legs, hung trailing from his ankles.

When medicines are administered, their

efficacy is attributed to the god or spirit residing in the plant, rather than to any mechanical, chemical, or other power inherent in the medicine itself.

The number of practitioners is large, in some villages not less than one man in ten and one woman in thirty. Among them are to be found some of the shrewdest, strongest intellects, and a very large proportion of those who are only one step above idiots. A proper idiot I have never met with among Indians, probably because such are left to perish in infancy; but the proportion of those who make an approach to idiocy is much greater among savages than among civilized people; and a large part of these are applied to in cases of sickness. Many of the conjurers are known as such by that peculiar cast of countenance which belongs to the spiritist of civilized nations; others have countenances strongly indicative of cunning and deceit. I have met with two or three men among them of good, plain, common sense, and open, honest countenances. The most eminent of these, when on a certain occasion he came to me for medicine for a disease brought on by over-exertion and exposure in the practice of their orgies, on being charged with deceiving his people, acknowledged the charge, and excused himself on the ground of his poverty and his need of the promised reward, and the number and urgency of those who applied to him to shew them by his incantations how and when they might find and destroy their enemies.

There are a few individuals who give medicines without conjuring or invoking the aid of spirits. I have known one such who attained a deservedly high reputation among his own people and was sometimes called to practise among the whites. With intellectual and perceptive faculties strongly developed, and such knowledge of the powers of roots as is attainable among his people, naturally polite, and very observant of all those little things which contribute to the comfort of a patient, I have often thought he might have acquired fame and money among civilized men, if he had not justly preferred to live among his own people and do what he could for them.

The medicines used by the Dakotas were mostly roots, and hence their name for a physician, Pay-zhe-hoo-ta we-chashta, Herb-root-man. They, however, used not only other parts of plants, but sometimes animal and mineral substances. In general their medicines were all secret, the knowledge of them concealed as far as possible from each other, except in cases where large fees were paid by such as were not likely to become rivals in the same community, or where an individual not expecting to practise his profession much longer, owing to age or infirmity, might communicate to some descendant or other near relative the knowledge which he possessed. This disposition to conceal their knowledge, so prevalent among quacks, not less than the want of books, prevented the transmission and accumulation of knowledge; so that if any important discoveries were made, they were liable to perish with the discoverer.

With such false pathology and such hindrances to the transmission of knowledge, we could not expect that the sick would be much benefited by the medicine men. So far as I have had an opportunity of observing their practice in cases of fever and some other diseases, with very few exceptions, they did more harm than good. But I know of no way of accounting for the high value set on their services without supposing that, in many cases, they gave relief. My observation inclines me to think that this occurs especially in wounds and pains from local inflammation more frequently than we should expect from what has been said above.

The perceptive faculties among the Dakotas are far more acute than among civilized men. The successful medicine man, like the successful warrior, attains to the highest honor, and is more sure of getting property largely, than either the warrior or hunter; and thus his faculties are stimulated to the highest degree of activity; and having usually only one patient at a time he can observe more closely the effect of the medicine he uses. Some of this class are excellent nurses of the sick, and most attentive to all those thousand little things so conducive to the comfort of their patients. The family is removed from the tent, or the patient and tent from them; and the ground which constitutes the floor of the tent is carpeted, in summer, with ferns or other soft herbage, and scented with aromatic herbs, and, in seasons of the year when these cannot be obtained, with the best substitutes for them accessible. Some of the medicine men watch their patients very thoroughly, and to prevent noise exclude children, and in many cases women too, unless the nearest relatives.

They practise blood-letting, which with them is an operation generally performed with a sharp flint which serves very well for scarifying. When a vein is to be cut, the flint is made fast in a stick, which serves as a handle, and, like a fleam used in bleeding horses, it is driven in with a stroke. As this is a difficult operation, few attempt it; but local blood-letting is very common, the operator usually drawing the blood directly into his own mouth. Some, however, use a horn, or a part of one, applying the large end to the surface whence the blood is to be drawn, and taking the smaller end, which is perforated, into the mouth.

They attribute many of their diseases to bile, or "yellow water," as they call it, and for its removal use emetics, purgatives, and clysters. Most of them, however, freely acknowledge that none of the native remedies for certainty and safety equal those used for purging and puking by civilized men, since to secure vomiting the Dakota doctor is commonly obliged to tickle the throat with a feather.

For purging, the Dakotas who lived near the Mississippi, in common with their eastern neighbors, the Ojibwas, relied chiefly on the root of a tall and very handsome species of euphorbium which abounds on the prairies between Saint Paul and Red Wing. Coarsely powdered it is administered in small quantities, and it operates quickly and often severely. They say it is safe if used dry and the patient abstains entirely from drink until the operation is over, but very dangerous if the patient drinks freely soon after taking it. The Ojibwa chief Firm Earth, the predecessor and older brother of the first Hole-in-the-Day, who died near Fort Snelling in 1843, was said by his companions to have come to his end by drinking freely after taking a dose of this root. He died in a few minutes after walking about, and apparently from the effects of acrid poison. The plant is not found on the Upper Minnesota or farther west, and consequently I have had but few opportunities of witnessing its effects. The Indians who have not access to it, use various other plants, none of which appear to have much efficacy. The same may be said of those used as diuretics.

To promote appetite, especially after fevers, they used cranberries, preferring for this purpose the fruit of the tree cranberry, and sometimes substituted bitter aromatic roots.

Sweating in a small tent, over heated stones, was a frequent and perhaps their most efficacious remedy for the removal of disease. It was resorted to not only in cases of pain and sickness, but as an antidote or purifier by those who had killed any person, or otherwise contracted ceremonial uncleanness. The process is described elsewhere.

Contrary to what might be expected, many of them use anæsthetics. I have frequently heard of persons reviving after being apparently dead, and seen several such who appeared very much as is common with those who are recovering from the effects of an excessive dose of opium, who nevertheless, I have good reason to believe, had not taken it. In consequence of the conjurers interfering with some of my own patients, I had an opportunity of observing one or two in the state of anæsthesia. It is caused by making the person inhale the fumes of calamus roots, and some other substances, burnt on coals. Whether the effect is produced by the calamus or some of the other ingredients, or by the combination, I am unable to say. This state is sometimes produced for the purpose of allaying that extreme restlessness which attends some diseases, but chiefly, I suppose, that the practitioner may have the credit of restoring a dead person to life.

The Dakotas were far more successful in the practice of surgery than medicine. Their constant practice in cutting up animals slain in the chase, made many of them well acquainted with comparative anatomy. Yet their ignorance about the circulation of the blood caused them to lose patients, who might have been saved by a judicious use of bandages, or the entire removal of them. They use tents to keep open deep wounds or abscesses, and prepare good ones for the purpose from the inner bark of the slippery elm. They sometimes apply wet dressings to wounds or sores, and cover them with green leaves, either fresh or boiled; but not possessing the materials for making poultices, plasters, or cerates, they generally endeavor to dry up and scab over wounds and running sores. Sometimes they cover the raw surface with a paste made by chewing certain roots, bark, or leaves. At other times the medicine is reduced to a powder and dusted over the sore. A variety of substances are used for this purpose, among which none is more highly esteemed than the root of the Asclepias tuberosa, a species of milk-weed. This is also sometimes given internally.

To reduce swellings, especially those arising from sprains or bruises, they apply various stimulating vegetables, including tobacco. Among these they most value what they call *blue root*, a species of Pyrethrum very common in the prairies of Minnesota and Dakota.

A few of them are skilful in the treatment of burns, but this is not generally the case. Commonly they apply oil or grease of some kind, when it is to be obtained, and carefully conceal the knowledge of the other remedies they use. I once saw an excellent effect produced on a very extensive and severe burn, by covering the entire raw surface with the inner bark of the yellow, or, as it is called in Minnesota, the Norway pine. The bark had been shaved thin and made soft by beating it, and the inner mucilaginous surface applied, which allayed the pain and inflammation. I do not think any of the medicines of the shops could have a better effect.

When suffering from disease they will, with few exceptions, gladly avail themselves of the services and medicines of regularly educated physicians, and the conjurers not less willingly than others; although they endeavor to prevent others from doing so, claiming that their medicines are superior to the white man's.

DAKOTA SONGS AND MUSIC.

BY REV. A. L. RIGGS.

A people's songs the key to their life. — War songs. — Love songs. — Giving the ring. — Songs of medicine and magic. — Songs of sacred mysteries. — Song of "Sounding Cloud." — Its interpretation. — Song of Oon-ktay′-he. — Social songs. — Dakota poetry. — The sacred language. — Dakota music. — The minor key the favorite. — Two Dakota melodies. — Musical instruments. — The drum. — The rattle. — The Cho′-tan-ka. — How made. — Power of savage song. — Christian hymns. — Dakotas love to sing. — The Dakota hymn-book.

THE songs of a people furnish an entrance to their inner life, which, if we would understand them, we cannot neglect. This is especially true of a barbarous people, whose outward life is rough and forbidding. It is not enough for us to note their uncouth dress and rude ways. Such curiosity-shop knowledge is neither complete nor just, because it is not sympathetic; being content with observing the life of habit, it does not reach the real life, the life of feeling. Taking the truer method, we find the Dakotas to be men and women of like passions with ourselves. And they in like manner find in music and song their greatest means of emotional expression; either in the stirring songs of the chase or of war, or the plaintive melodies of love, or the weird chants of their sacred mysteries.

The first class from which we will draw examples is that of their

WAR SONGS.

I.

I have cast in here a soul,
I have cast in here a soul,
I have cast in here a buffalo soul;
I have cast in here a soul.

One characteristic of Dakota poetry must be mentioned here by way of explanation. It is, never to call things by their common names, if it can be avoided. Thus, "buffalo" is here the poetic term for man. This is a song of the "circle dance," and is a war incantation. It is sung by the officiating priest, as he concocts his war magic in a hole in the earth, while the chorus dances in circle around him.

II.

I make my way with my face covered,
I make my way with my face covered;
The people are buffaloes;
I make my way with my face covered.

This, like the preceding one, is a song of preparation for war. It is a vision of the night. The four black spirits have come to the aspiring war-leader, and he dreams. He sees the enemy an easy prey, like herded buffaloes, while he, with "covered face," goes disguised and protected. This and the next two are called "armor songs."

III.

Night now passes along,
Night now passes along;
It passes along with a thunder bird;
Night now passes along.

Another vision of the war-leader, by which he attests his divine commission to lead on the war-path. To us it means but little; but to the Dakota it presents a terrible vision. The four black spirits have come up, and black Night appears with a thunder bird in her mouth.

IV.

Whose sacred road lies plainly,
Whose sacred road lies plainly;
The sacred road of day lies plainly.

The war-leader has another revelation, and sees the mysterious or wakan′ war-path as plain as day before him; and, with such credentials, he goes forth to gather recruits. The war-drum goes day and night, and the dancers go circling round, while the young braves are brought to the enlisting point by such recruiting songs as these, which, if not very excellent, are as good as our own, and answer their purpose as well.

V.

Ojibwa, hurry along!
Ojibwa, get out of the way!
We're coming there again.

VI.

Ojibwa, hallo!
Tell your older brother
You're too slow.

The line, "Tell your older brother," conveys something of the same idea as the phrase, "Does your mother know you're out?"

In the next song, we may suppose the warrior prepared for his campaign, and, as it were, mustering and parading his forces, physical and spiritual.

VII.

Terrifying all I journey,
Terrifying all I journey;
By the *Toon-kan'* at the North,
Terrifying all I journey.

He goes forth invested with supernatural power from the great lingam, or stone god of the North.

Now the war party returns, having been successful; and this is the warrior's song:—

VIII.

Something I've killed, and I lift up my voice,
Something I've killed, and I lift up my voice;
The northern buffalo I've killed, and I lift up my voice;
Something I've killed, and I lift up my voice.

Here we have a double metaphor; for the "northern buffalo" means a black bear, but "black bear" means a man. The "lifting up the voice" is a mourning for the slain enemy; for the successful warriors must paint themselves black, and go dressed as though they had lost their best friend. Another version of this song, in place of "the northern buffalo," etc., has the line,

An *Eastern two-legged one* I've killed, etc.

In all these songs, the words form but a small part of the song, as it is sung. By the use of meaningless syllables, such as *hay, hay, hay, hay, he, he, he, he, ah, ah, ah, ah*, any couplet may occupy an indefinite time. The same is true of their religious chants; while, on the contrary, their love songs have little of this, and are quite regular.

LOVE SONGS.

I.

Cling fast to me, and you'll ever have a plenty;
Cling fast to me, and you'll ever have a plenty;
Cling fast to me.

We may imagine that the suitor, in this case, has little to recommend him, in the way of worldly wealth, except his good right arm and bow or gun. The plenty he promises is a plenty to eat, which, in a hunter life, is the highest good that can be named. If all goes well, we may suppose the maiden saying, —

II.

Whenever we choose,
Together we'll dwell;

Mother so says.
This finger ring
Put on and wear.

She is supposed to say this, but really does not. Her young brave sings to her what he believes or hopes she would say. And so it is in most of these songs. The reference to the ring may seem to contradict this; but the ring is generally given by the woman, and is put on the right little finger of the man; though the women also receive rings, and wear them, as we shall see.

III.

Wear this, I say;
Wear this, I say;
Wear this, I say;
This little finger ring,
Wear this, I say.

IV.

Stealthily, secretly see me,
Stealthily, secretly see me,
Stealthily, secretly see me.
Lo, thee I tenderly regard;
Stealthily, secretly see me.

By which we may judge that the course of true love is not sure to run smooth, even on the prairies. All difficulties, however, may seem to be overcome, and love is triumphant. The hunter goes off with light heart to the chase; but time drags heavily with the heart left behind. And here the feelings of the lonely maiden find expression: —

V.

I cried, but now —
I cried, but now —
I cried, but now —
My little cousin, a prairie fire appears!
And I cried, but now —

She is disconsolate until a smoke rises in the distance, which she hopes is the sign of the hunter's returning. "My little cousin" is the younger brother of her betrothed. Or, it may be, she sings, —

VI.

Come again, come again, come again, come again,
Come again, come again, come again;

I look upon my finger ring, and my heart is sad.
  Come again, come again, come again.

In this case, the woman has received a ring as well as the man. There may, however, be rivals in the field. Mercenary relations may be favoring another suitor; and while her chosen brave is absent, his absence is held up as the sign of waning affection. But the still faithful maid replies, —

VII.

Stay there, I say!
Stay there, I say!
  Come he will;
He'll come; he said so.
  Scarlet Eagle, he will come,
He'll come; he said so.

Or perhaps the passion of the rejected suitor is held in terror over her head, and she makes light of it.

VIII.

Who would of such an one be afraid!
  Be afraid, indeed!
Who would of such an one be afraid!
  Be afraid, indeed!

It may, however, to tell the whole truth, be the supposed utterance of one already wedded, and whose unfaithfulness would lawfully entitle her husband to clip off her nose with his scalping knife. But, on the ground of the cowardice of her lawful lord, she willingly takes all such risks.

Now we come to one more like a dirge than a love song; and it is fittingly set to most plaintive music.

IX.

Lo, greatly I am distressed;
Lo, greatly I am distressed.
My child's father!
My child's father!
My child's father!
My child's father!
Lo, greatly I am distressed.

This song is appropriate to the courtship of a widow. Her heart is besieged through sympathy with her grief, while the meaning is, that the place of so good a father to her child ought to be filled by another.

The case may be more desperate yet; for there is that which is harder to endure than bereavement or death. Two may be unhappily mated, and the wife, enduring it no longer, resolves to risk all and elope with another. This is her song: —

X.

Sorely I am distressed;
Sorely I am distressed;
Sorely I am distressed.
The earth alone continues long;
I speak as one not expecting to live.
Sorely I am distressed;
The earth alone continues long.

Does not the last line reveal a depth of heart-weariness and desperation which cannot be told in words?

SONGS OF MEDICINE AND MAGIC.

I.

This mysterious medicine take!
This mysterious medicine take!
May this man mysteriously recover.

The physician sings this, as he concocts a

medicine for the sick, to give it efficacy. It should be borne in mind, that the Dakota word *wakan′* and it its derivations, here and elsewhere translated *mystery*, *mysterious*, *mysteriously*, carries with it an idea of the supernatural, and hence of the sacred and divine. It is sometimes appropriately rendered magic. Here some potion is the medium of the wakan′ power; but in the next the physician or conjurer acts directly by his own indwelling power, without the aid of any material medium.

II.

Something have I in my breast;
Something have I in my breast!
A snake have I in my breast;
Something have I in my breast.

With the consciousness of great power in his own snake, he approaches his patient to cast out the snake in him which has caused his sickness. In other cases it may be some other animal or spirit.

III.

He whose face I admire;
He whose face I admire;
In his face may I shoot him.

Another version of which runs thus: —

The two-legged one whose face I admire;
The two-legged one whose face I admire;
In his face may I shoot him.

The "two-legged one" is a man. And this is the song of the old wizard or conjurer who is raising enchantments for a war-party against their enemy. By his enchantment, he is supposed to be able to bring death to one whose goodly countenance shows him to be a man of rank and authority among his people.

SONGS OF THE SACRED MYSTERIES.

The whole ritual of their worship is chanted, whether engaged in by the single devotee or the sacred assembly. Thus, the seeker after a divine inspiration, having hung up in his tepee something embodying wakan′ or mysterious power, utters his prayer in this song:—

I.

In the home of mysterious life I lie;
In the home of mysterious life I lie;
In the home of mystery, may I grow into mystery;
In the home of mysterious life I lie.

Or he goes forth in the fields with a prayer to *Tah′-koo-skan-skan′*, the *motion god*, whom he calls father.

II.

Shooting an arrow, I come;
Shooting an arrow, I come;
In the east my father sings for me:—I come,
Shooting an arrow, I come.

This is a morning song; but if it is evening, he sings instead:—

In the *west* my father sings for me, etc.,

and it is an evening song.

The next is a song of the sun-dance. Whoever dances to the sun is expected to make a song which embodies the god-communication to him. This is the song of Sounding Cloud.

III.

1. Having those, may I come;
Having those four souls, may I make my camp-fires.

2. The day that is determined for me;
May it come earthward.

3. I have four souls;
Holy boy! I give them to thee.

4. Sun-gazer (a bird), where have you gone?
Behold your friend!

5. The day to see thee;
May it come.

6. Encrowned with glory,
I come forth resplendent.

7. Sounding Cloud, my friend!
Do you want water?

The dance to the sun begins with the day.* The dancer fixes his eyes on the sun, and follows it with unaverted gaze

---

* For fuller particulars, see Chapter VI, on "Dakota Worship."

while above the horizon, and then turns to the moon, now usually at the full, which shares the divine honors of the sun. He dances continuously, with but short intervals of rest, through the day, and through the night, and on in the next day, as long as flesh and will can endure. All this time, he goes without food or drink, and is further tortured with great weights hanging by thongs fastened into his living flesh. A chorus of singers attends, with the drum and deer-hoof rattle, encouraging the dancer, accompanying his song, or at times responding to it.

Of this song, verses 1 and 2 are his prayer to his god. He prays (verse 1) that he may take four scalps, and return safely; and (verse 2) that the appointed day may soon be revealed to him. The sun-god now looks down in favor upon his suppliant, and rewards his devotion. He promises (verse 3) to give four of the enemy into his hand, and recognizes him as now wakan′, (Holy boy!) and as henceforth belonging to the mystic circle of the gods. With this assurance of divine acceptance, the devotee claims (verse 4) relationship with the sun-bird himself. Like him, he is henceforth the companion of his god. He, too, has looked upon his face, and lives. Now the night comes on, and its weary, painful hours wear by. Hardly can the dancer, fevered and faint, keep time with the hollow-sounding drum and shrill rattles. But dawn begins to break, and the chorus utter, as their prayer in his behalf, verse 5,—that the god may again look upon him in favor. The sun hears the prayer of the watchers, and now (verse 6) bursts forth, crowned with mysterious splendors, re-animating the flagging powers of his servant. However, as the midday beams again beat down upon the wretched dancer, his sufferings are inexpressible. But now the chorus, instead of cheering him up, in order to make the final test of his fortitude, calls out to him, faint with fasting and dancing, and all on fire with a burning thirst and his torturing wounds, —

Sounding Cloud, my friend!
Do you want water?

Following the rounds of their Pantheon, we come now to the liturgy of *Wah-kin′-yan*, or the thunder-god. Here are two specimens: —

IV.

I sing to a Spirit;
This is the Thunder.

This is properly a war song. The warrior has commenced with the thunder, and the four black spirits of the night have told him that he will kill an enemy. For this he sings this song of praise.

V.

Lo! a cloud is let down from above!
Father! shall I fly upon it?

In this it would seem that, as the god rolls his cloud-chariot across the sky, almost touching the earth, the enthusiast deems it a messenger of the Deity to himself, and perhaps sent to bear him into the high realm of mystery.

The next four songs belong to the ritual of the society of the sacred dance, of which order *Oon-ktay'-he*, god of water and earth, is the patron god. The god sings thus: —

VI.

Across the lake mysteriously I lie;
Across the lake mysteriously I lie;
That, decoying some soul, I may eat him alive.
So may it be.

Again he sings out of the whirlwind and thunder storm:

VII.

This wakan' I whirled,
This wakan' I whirled,
This house I levelled.

This wakan′ I whirled,
This house I levelled,
This wakan′ I whirled.

In praise of their "mystery sack," improperly called "medicine sack," the members of the order sing: —

VIII.

Grandfather made me mysterious medicine;
That is true.
Being of mystery, grown in the water,
He gave it me.
To grandfather's face wave the imploring hand;
Holding a quadruped, wave the imploring hand.

The god is addressed as grandfather. "Wave the imploring hand" is not the literal rendering of the Dakota words here used, which are "Stroke the face of my grandfather;" but, used with reference to the Deity, it signifies a stroking motion of the hand towards the face of the god, expressive of adoration and entreaty. The "quadruped" is the wakan′ or mystery "sack," often made of the skin of some four-footed animal, with the head and claws retained. In its praise, they sing again: —

IX.

In red down he made it for me;
In red down he made it for me;
He of the water, he of mysterious countenance,
Gave it to me,
Grandfather!

Swan's-down, dyed red, is a sacred article, and used continually in their worship as an offering to the gods, and as an ornament of consecrated articles, such as the weapons and feathers of the warrior. It is much delighted in by the gods, who are said to wear it largely. It may be because of this that it is employed in the "mystery sack," to embody the supposed spiritual presence.

SOCIAL SONGS.

The Dakotas have many societies for social intercourse, which are called "friendship leagues," and bear such names as "the buffaloes," "little foxes," "northmen," and "owl feather caps." There are separate societies for men and women. There are also dancing companies, including both sexes, under such appropriate names as "leg-shakers," "grasshoppers," etc. These all have their songs, of which, however, no specimens are at hand.

DAKOTA POETRY.

Some idea of the character of their poetry may be had even from the foregoing versions. A prominent feature in its structure is the repetition of some line, usually the first, of the stanza, one, two, and even four times. Alliteration is much employed. The rythmical flow is even and pleasant. Rhymes are used; but this is too easy to be noteworthy. In connection with the more regular rythmical forms, such as have been given, the recitative is introduced in their dances, for narrative and description.

The language of their poetry, like that of their oratory, is highly figurative. In addition to the common figures of speech, a sacred language is often employed, in which common words are used in a sense totally different from that which they ordinarily bear. This makes the true interpretation of their poetry very difficult, and, indeed, impossible to one who has not the key.

DAKOTA MUSIC.

Their native music is of the simplest kind. It has only a melody, with rude vocal and instrumental accompaniments. These accompaniments are more for marking time than for harmonic effect. In their dances, the chant or melody is sung by the men, while the chorus of women utter a single shrill falsetto note, — an "ai," "ai," "ai," — given with an explosive shriek, and keeping time with the drums. The appreciation of harmony is said to be an acquired taste, born of civilized society. This is, at least, the case among the Dakotas. When a melodeon was first introduced into the mission chapel, Eagle Helper, an old Indian, said: "It sings well at one end; but why do you have it grumble away at the other, like so many bull-frogs?"

The minor key is the favorite one. It is universally used in their love songs, and generally in other songs. The major key is, however, recognizable in some of their war songs and in the songs of the "friendship leagues."

Here are two love-song melodies. The first of them belongs to No. VII, and the second to No. VIII, of the foregoing selections. In reading the Dakota words, give the European sounds to the vowels, and pronounce *c* as *ch* soft, and final *n* as a nasal.

NO. I.

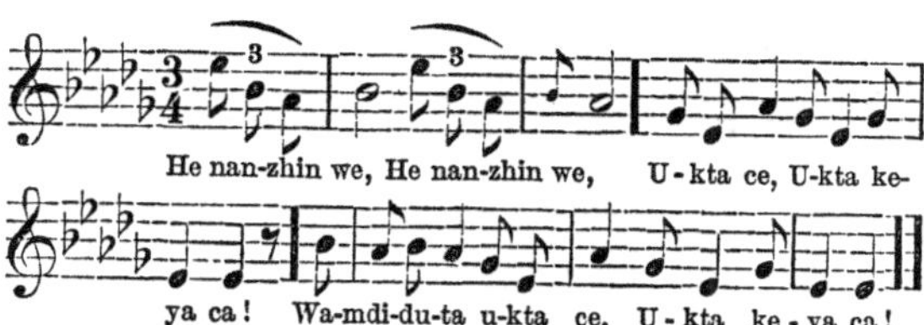

NO. II.

MUSICAL INSTRUMENTS.

Their musical instruments are the drum, the rattle, and the pipe or flute. The *drum* is called *chan′-chay-ga*, or "wood-kettle." The hoop of the drum is usually from a foot to eighteen inches in diameter, and three or four inches deep. Sometimes it is as much as ten inches deep. The skin covering is stretched over only one side of the hoop, making a drum with one end. A single drumstick is used.

The rattle is made by hanging the hard segments of deer-hoofs to a wooden rod a foot long, and three fourths of an inch in diameter at the handle end, tapering to a point at the other. The part to which the rattles are hung is first covered with a sheath of skin, and into this the short strings which suspend them are fastened. The clashing of these hard, horny bits makes a sharp, shrill sound, somewhat like that of a string of sleigh-bells at a distance. The Dakota name, *tah-shah'-kay*, means literally, "deer-hoofs." The conjurers sometimes use, in their incantations over the sick, a rattle made in another way. A gourd-shell is emptied of its contents through a small hole; smooth pebbles or plum-stones are put in, and the opening plugged up. This gives a more hollow sound.

The pipe or flute is called *cho'-tan-ka*, which means literally, "big-pith." It has two varieties; one made of wood, and the other of bone. The first is the most common, and much resembles the flageolet. It is made by taking of the sumac — a wood which has the requisite "big-pith" — a straight piece nineteen or twenty inches long, and, when barked and smoothed down, an inch and a quarter in diameter. This is split open in the middle, and the pith and inner wood carefully hollowed out to make a bore of five eighths of an inch diameter, extending through the whole length, except that it grows smaller at the mouth-piece, and, at a point four inches below that, it is interrupted entirely by a partition three eighths of an inch thick, which is left to form the whistle. The halves are glued together. Finger-holes, one quarter of an inch in diameter, and usually six in number, are burnt along the upper face. On the same face the whistle is made by cutting a hole three eighths of an inch square each side of the partition. Then, over these, and connecting them, is laid a thin plate of lead, with a slit cut in it, a little more than an inch long and three eighths of an inch wide. On top of this is a block of wood, two inches long and three fourths of an inch wide, flat on the bottom, and carved above into the rough likeness of a horse; and a deer-skin string binds the whole down tight. A brass thimble for a mouth-piece, some ribbon streamers, a few lines of grotesque carving, and a little red and yellow paint, and the instrument is complete.

The pitch of the particular pipe to which this description mainly refers, seems to have been originally A prime, and changed to G prime by boring a seventh hole. One formerly in my possession was pitched on E♭ prime; and from it the airs which are here given were taken down.

The second variety of the *cho′-tan-ka* is made of the long bone of the wing or thigh of the swan and crane. To distinguish the first from the second, they call the first the *murmuring* (literally "bubbling") *cho′-tan-ka*, from the tremulous note it gives when blown with all the holes stopped.

POWER OF SAVAGE SONG.

The power of Dakota music is not to be measured by its rudeness or undeveloped character, judged according to our standards. But, if rightly considered, it will be found that just here lies the secret of its power. Its wild and plaintive tones being in perfect harmony with the savage wilderness and the more savage life inhabiting it, they wake deeper chords than more artistic notes could do, or than they themselves can give. That it has great power over the Dakota himself, no one can doubt who sees the dancers keep their monotonous round for hours, while the wild chant moves on. Of course, it is the emotion within, which thus finds expression; that is the ultimate motive power; but the music is not its unfit embodiment, whether it be the revenge of the breathless ambush or the shrieking onset, pantomimed in the scalp-dance, or, again, tender love thoughts droned out by the flute of some wandering serenader.

And would the white stranger realize its power for himself, it will not be by curiously inspecting the lifeless specimens here given, or by humming over these poor melodies, but by placing himself in the midst of savage life, where, under misty moonbeams, the night air bears the wavering chant of the fierce dancers, now high and clear, then a low murmur, with the incessant hollow drum beat and the heartless clash of the rattles rising and falling on the breeze. As the note of the whip-poor-will at noonday would stir no heart, yet in the edge of night thrills the hearer with its now touching note, so these wild notes of savage life, to be felt in their power, must be heard on the border, where scalps are fresh, and one's life is at the mercy of the foe each bush may cover. In such an atmosphere, palpitating with possible war-whoops, the sound of chant and rattle and drum have a depth of meaning elsewhere inexpressible.

CHRISTIAN HYMNS.

However, for all that part of the Dakota nation known as the Mississippi and Minnesota Sioux, all this belongs to the past. Christian hymns have taken the place of the heathen mystic chants. Jehovah is praised instead of *Oon-ktay'-he*. The young braves now hold the axe and hoe with their own hands, and cannot strut in greasy ribbons through the cornfields which the maidens are tending, nor bewitch them with the love melodies of the light-fingered flute. But a purer love rears homes of virtue and of peace, and, when it needs them, will bring forth songs better than these. The war-songs, also, live only in the echoes of the past; while the once famous warriors go forth on a better war-path, armed with psalms and gospel for the conquest of their still savage brothers of the western plains.

The Dakotas love to sing, as the song-worship of their Christian assemblies will prove. All voices uniting on the melody of some world-known tune like Silver Street, Ortonville, Martyn, Olivet, or again on one of their own irregular but impressive native airs, they raise a song which, in heartiness, power, and worshipfulness, one may go far to parallel.

Among the earliest labors of the missionaries, on gaining some knowledge of the language, was the translation of a few hymns, which even now could hardly be improved — a fact which seems a special providence, or as though there had been a gift of inspiration. The number of these hymns has been continually increased by new compositions and versions of English hymns, until they have reached one hundred and fifty or over. Some of the best of these are from the pens of native Christians. During this while, four different hymn-books have been published, each passing through several editions. Thus "the song of the redeemed" has been gathering power among the Dakotas. May its notes soon ring forth from the united voices of their whole nation!

LABORS OF OTHER MISSIONARY SOCIETIES.

1. The Swiss mission. — 2. The Methodist mission. — 3. The Roman Catholic mission. — 4. The Episcopal mission.

In this Dakota field there have been laborers of other denominations, for a longer or shorter period of time, of whom a brief notice here is proper.

THE SWISS MISSION.

In the year 1836, the Evangelical Missionary Society of Lausanne, Switzerland, sent to this country two young men, Rev. Francis Denton and Rev. Daniel Gavan. They appear to have approached the Dakota country by the way of Canada. Reaching the mission of the American Board at Mackinaw, Mr. Denton tarried awhile, and was there married to Miss Persis Skinner, who had been for several years a teacher in that school.

They reached the Mississippi in February, 1837, Mr. and Mrs. Denton locating with the Indians at the village of Red Wing; and Mr. Gavan commencing a station with Wabashaw's band at Mont Trempaleau. The winter of 1838–9 Mr. Gavan spent at the Lacquiparle mission, as there were greater facilities there for learning the language than elsewhere. During his stay at Lacquiparle the translation of the Gospel of John was commenced. In the spring of 1839, Mr. Gavan returned to the Mississippi country, and that summer he was married to Miss Lucy Cornelia Stevens, teacher at Lake Harriet. Not long after this, Mr. Gavan left the Dakotas, and went to labor among the French in Canada West, where he died some years ago.

Mr. and Mrs. Denton remained at Red

Wing about ten years; when they also retired from the Dakota field, and for a while resided at Red Rock in Minnesota, and afterwards removed to southern Illinois. Mr. Denton had been long afflicted with disease of the heart, and died suddenly several years ago, when on a visit to Saint Louis. Mrs. Denton and four sons are still living.

THE METHODIST MISSION.

The Pittsburgh Methodist Conference, in 1835, appointed Elder Brunson superintendent of missions on the Upper Mississippi. Mr. Brunson removed to Prairie du Chien. But it was not until the spring of 1837, that he was able to establish any missions. In May of that year he ascended the Mississippi with a small company, and put up some buildings at Kaposia, or Little Crow's Village, a few miles below the city of Saint Paul. This mission was occupied by Mr.

Holton's family. One of the daughters soon learned the language, so as to be able to act as interpeter in religious meetings. Rev. Mr. King, who joined the mission soon after its commencement, made good proficiency in the language, and remained there until the suspension of the mission.

In 1839, Elder Brunson's health failed, and Elder Kavanaugh was appointed superintendent in his stead. But the Dakota Indians of this village seem to have been very imperative, and often required the missionaries to do unreasonable things. Finally, in the spring of 1841, Little Crow, the father of the one who was engaged in the Sioux outbreak of 1862, ordered the school to be stopped. This was the closing of the Methodist mission. It had not been conducted without some good results. The Indians of the village, a few years after, sent a request to the agent for missionary teachers.

THE ROMAN CATHOLIC MISSION.

In this same year of 1837, Father Ravaux, a Romish priest, who has been now for many years stationed at Saint Paul, came to the Dakota country, and built a house at the trading post of Oliver Ferribault, near the Little Rapids. Here he remained several years teaching French half-breeds and Indians to say "pater nosters" and "aves," etc. It was no part of his work to give the Dakotas the Bible, or to teach them to read it. Mr. Ravaux visited Lacquiparle and spent some time in the family of Mr. Renville. And he made such progress in acquiring the Dakota language, that he was able to give the teachings of his church to any Dakota, who, condemned to die, desired such instruction. Mr. Ravaux has limited his offices among the Dakotas to such cases, and given his life work to the French Catholic population of Minnesota.

THE EPISCOPAL MISSION.

In the summer of 1860, Bishop H. B. Whipple visited the Lower Sioux Agency, and invited the Indian men to come together. When they assembled, he held service, it is said, reading the Lord's Prayer and portions of Scripture which had been translated by the missionaries of the American Board, and singing their hymns. This was claimed to be the first Christian service performed among the Dakotas. The Bishop proposed to establish a mission among them; which was commenced in the autumn of that year, and placed in charge of Rev. S. D. Hinman. Mr. and Mrs. Hinman were accompanied by Miss West as teacher. They have usually had, for several years past, some Dakota youth at their school in Ferribault, Minn. At the time of the outbreak they were engaged in erecting a stone chapel.

During the next winter, Mr. Hinman spent much of his time in the camp at Fort Snelling. He visited the prison at Mankato and at Davenport also, but did not stop long with the prisoners. He also visited those who were taken to Crow Creek Agency, and re-established his station at Niobrara, when the prisoners and their families were again united. Quite a considerable number of these Indians are now counted as belonging to the Episcopal church. Mr. Hinman has translated and printed the Episcopal Prayer Book. He has erected on Breckenridge Bottom, where the Santee Agency is at present located, quite an expensive and commodious mission-house, in which he has a chapel and accommodations for his own family and others.

www.ingramcontent.com/pod-product-compliance
Lightning Source LLC
LaVergne TN
LVHW021303110826
845150LV00003B/460

* 9 7 8 1 4 2 5 5 5 9 6 6 3 *